ROUTLEDGE
INTENSIVE
GERMAN COURSE

ROUTLEDGE INTENSIVE LANGUAGE COURSES

Other books in the series:

Routledge Intensive Italian Course
by Anna Proudfoot, Tania Batelli-Kneale, Anna Di Stefano and Daniela Treveri Gennari
ISBN 0-415-24080-8

Routledge Intensive Italian Workbook
ISBN 0-415-24079-4

Routledge Intensive Italian CDs
ISBN 0-415-24081-6

Routledge Intensive Dutch Course
By Gerdi Quist, Christine Sas and Denis Strik
ISBN 0-415-26192-9

Routledge Intensive Dutch CDs
ISBN 0-415-26191-9

Coming soon:

Routledge Intensive Russian Course
By Robin Aizlewood
ISBN 0-415-22300-8

Routledge Intensive Russian CDs
ISBN 0-415-22301-6

ROUTLEDGE
INTENSIVE
GERMAN COURSE

Paul Hartley

Routledge
Taylor & Francis Group

LONDON AND NEW YORK

First published 2006 by Routledge
2 Park Square, Milton Park, Abingdon, Oxon OX14 4RN

Simultaneously published in the USA and Canada
by Routledge

270 Madison Ave, New York, NY 10016

Routledge is an imprint of the Taylor & Francis Group, an informa business

© 2006 Paul Hartley

Typeset in DIN and Rotis by
Fakenham Photosetting Limited, Fakenham, Norfolk
Printed and bound in Great Britain by Scotprint, Haddington

British Library Cataloguing in Publication Data
A catalogue record for this book is available from the British Library

Library of Congress Cataloging in Publication Data
Hartley, Paul.
      The Routledge Intensive German course / Paul Hartley.
         p. cm. – (Routledge intensive language courses)
      1. German language—Textbooks for foreign speakers—English.
      2. German language—Self-instruction.   I. Title.   II. Series.
      PF3112.5.H37 2006
      438.2´421—dc22

2005029933

ISBN10: 0-415-25346-2 (coursebook)
ISBN10: 0-415-25347-0 (CDs)

ISBN13: 9-78-0-415-25346-8 (coursebook)
ISBN13: 9-78-0-415-25347-5 (CDs)

CONTENTS ROUTLEDGE INTENSIVE GERMAN COURSE

Topics
Greeting people
Giving a simple description of yourself
Understanding others talking about themselves
Handling simple numbers
German regions and cities
Some countries and nationalities

Grammar
Verbs (**ich**, **Sie**, **er/sie/es** forms)
Questions
Introduction to noun genders
Simple numbers

Topics
Simple shopping and transactions
Use of the telephone
Asking and giving the time
Days and dates

Grammar
Verbs (**wir** form + **du** form)
Use of **nicht**
Möchte
More numbers

Test your knowledge

Topics
Asking for and giving directions
Making travel arrangements

Grammar
Accusative case

INTRODUCTION: FOR THE TEACHER

The aims of this course

This German language course is intended primarily for those students with no prior knowledge of the language. It is also suitable for those who have studied German to a basic level in the past, but whose knowledge is 'rusty'. It is not a self-study course but requires teacher support.

The course comprises 10 units, and contains enough material for at least one year's work, assuming a total student *study* time of about five hours per week over 25 weeks. This would assume two hours per week class contact, and a further three hours per week private study.

The course is ideally suited to those students following a German language programme either as a specialist route, or as part of an institution-wide language programme designed for non-specialists.

Course structure

Each unit follows a standard sequence of dialogues and texts with exploitation exercises, a 'Grammar' section (with exposition of grammatical structures) and a 'Language in use' section (which has exercises to test knowledge of the structures covered in 'Grammar'). The first page of each unit gives brief details of the topics and grammatical structures to be covered.

Most of the dialogues and texts are also recorded for use as aural comprehension exercises, and these and additional recorded materials are available on the two separate cds. The texts used are topical and intended to give an insight into various aspects of German life.

Key vocabulary is given after many of the texts and dialogues, but these vocabulary lists are not exhaustive. The students should be encouraged to make use of a good quality dictionary to aid understanding of the material. Similarly, several of the texts in each unit are quite deliberately challenging, both to accelerate understanding of structures and vocabulary, and to demonstrate to the student that even with a rudimentary knowledge of the language, and with the aid of a dictionary, some quite complex vocabulary and structures can be understood.

There are occasional 'Test your knowledge' sections, which contain a series of exercises designed to test comprehension of the vocabulary and structures covered to that point of the course.

This uniform structure throughout the book will facilitate familiarisation with the material, and acquisition of the key grammatical structures of the German language. The course thus provides a very solid basis for further study.

As the course progresses so does the number of texts designed to reinforce understanding of the written language. Some of these are quite complex, and are not intended to be understood fully, but to encourage gist reading. The course is quite fast moving, but there is a sufficient variety of material in each of the chapters to meet the needs of learners moving at different speeds.

The tenth unit comprises texts designed to allow students to test their comprehension of the spoken and written language, and to reinforce their knowledge of language structures. The texts in this unit could be attempted at any time after completion of unit 6. The texts are graded according to level of difficulty, and some of them are quite taxing, but it is not necessary for students to be able to understand all of the structures and expressions – they are intended to reinforce vocabulary and to build confidence in handling the language.

Reference sections

The book contains the following reference sections:

- Glossary of grammatical terms
- German grammar
- German–English vocabulary
- English–German vocabulary

There is also on the supporting website (www.routledge.com/textbooks/0415253462) a key to many of the exercises. There is no key to the 'test your knowledge' sections, to facilitate their use as class tests if you so wish.

Students are advised to read through the glossary of grammatical terms if they are not already familiar with the terminology: this will facilitate understanding of the German grammar sections of the course.

Additional material

Additional texts and exercises, and suggestions for exploitation, are available on the website which supports this course. Teachers and students should log onto www.routledge.com/textbooks/0415253462 to access this additional material.

The material used in this course uses the revised German spellings.

INTRODUCTION: FOR THE STUDENT

This German language course is aimed at those of you who have no knowledge of German, and also those who might have studied in the past but have forgotten much of what you learnt. It is suitable for students on institution-wide language programmes as well as those following an *ab initio* German course as a main language.

You will find that each unit follows the same pattern of texts and dialogues, many of which are recorded. Each unit also has notes on language use, some background information, and a 'Grammar' section which gives more detailed information on aspects of grammar and usage. The 'Language in use' section at the end of each unit tests the language structures you have encountered in that unit. There are also (after every two units) 'Test your knowledge' exercises to revise the language structures and usage you have met so far in the course.

At the end of the book there are a number of reference sections to help you:

- Glossary of grammatical terms
- German grammar reference
- English–German vocabulary list
- German–English vocabulary list

The vocabulary lists are not exhaustive, and you should ensure that you are equipped with a good bilingual dictionary. Your tutor can advise on this. Similarly, the grammar reference section gives basic information on the structures you will meet in this course, but for more detailed explanations you should consult a more comprehensive grammar guide. Once again, your tutor can advise on this.

Learning a new language is an exciting and dynamic process, and you will be surprised at the rapid progress you can make, particularly if you invest the time to prepare the material, and to revise what you have covered, as you proceed through the course.

The course has a clear and consistent structure to help you find your way through it, with periodic test sections to allow you to check your knowledge. The following hints will help you get the most out of your language learning:

- Use a good quality dictionary and, with guidance from your teacher, make sure you are familiar with how it works.
- Do read the Glossary of grammatical terms if you are unsure of some of the terminology.
- Do not try to understand every word in a new text or dialogue straight away. Language learning is a gradual, accumulative process, and it does take time for new structures to 'bed in'. In many cases you will be able to guess the meaning of a word from its context, and you will see that you are frequently urged to get the gist of a text rather than the full meaning.

- Remember that many German words are very similar to English (**Bier, Milch, Katze, Wein, Tee** to name but a few). You will recognise lots of familiar words even from an early stage.
- Last, but not least: don't be afraid to make mistakes – we all do, all of the time – even in our own language. It can be part of the fun of learning a new language!

GLOSSARY OF GRAMMATICAL TERMS

Adjectives
Adjectives are words which describe a noun:

the *new* car
the *long* book
the *lazy* cat

There are also words called *demonstrative adjectives*, which indicate or point out nouns:

this car
that factory
these computers
those books

Adverbs
Adverbs describe verbs:

She runs *quickly*
He reads *slowly*
He drives *hesitantly*

(adverbs often, but not always, end in –ly: look at the following examples)

She works *well*
He works *hard*
He runs *fast*
We called *yesterday*
He will arrive *tomorrow*
He is reading *now*

Adverbs can also be used to 'describe' or to 'modify' an adjective:

This book is *really* (adverb) good (adjective)

That car is *strikingly* (adverb) beautiful (adjective)

Auxiliary (= auxiliary verb)
This is a verb which is used together with a past participle (see below) to form a compound tense:

I *have* driven ('have' = auxiliary; 'driven' = past participle)

She *has* eaten ('has' = auxiliary, 'eaten' = past participle)

They *have* left ('have' = auxiliary, 'left' = past participle)

Comparative
A form of the adjective which indicates degree of comparison:

a *bigger* car
a *smaller* table
a *brighter* lamp
a *healthier* lifestyle

Some comparatives are 'irregular':

His condition grew *worse*

Compound tense
A tense formed with more than one verb:

I *have eaten*
They *have arrived*
She *had finished*

See also **auxiliary**, and **past participle**

Conjunctions
Conjunctions are words which *join* the various parts of a sentence:

They drove into town *and* found a parking space *because* the play started early *and* they wanted to make sure *that* they arrived on time.

Conjugate / conjugation
Putting a verb into its various forms (other than the infinitive)

For example:

(to) go = infinitive form
I go, she goes, they go – are all 'conjugated'
   forms

Definite article
The word 'the'.

Direct object
The word to which the action of a verb is done:

She buys a *book* (*book* is the *direct object* of the
   verb 'buys')
He drives the *car* (*car* is the *direct object* of the
   verb 'drive')

Gender
In many languages nouns have genders. In
English (and in German), there are three:

Masculine
Feminine
Neuter

In German, gender is extremely important, and
it has an impact on the 'behaviour' of nouns,
pronouns and adjectives in the sentence.

Note also that grammatical gender is not linked to
biological gender. For example, the German word
for 'girl' is 'das Mädchen', which is a neuter noun.

Imperative
The form of the verb used to give a command:

Sit down!
Shut up!
Heel!
Eat up your lunch!
Forget that!

Indefinite article
The word 'a', 'an'.

Indirect object
A further object in a sentence, but one which is
not the 'direct' recipient of the action of the verb:

He gave the *dog* a bone ('dog' is the indirect
   object here, since 'bone' is the direct object
   of the verb 'gave')
She wrote *him* a long letter ('him' is the indirect
   object)

*Note: a reliable 'test' for the indirect object is if 'to'
can be inserted before it:*

She wrote him a long letter (= to him)
He gave the dog a bone (= to the dog)
He read her a story (= to her)

Infinitive
The verb in its most basic form:

to drive
to run
to laugh
to cry
to dig
to buy

Noun
The word denoting an object or a person:

the *man*
the *cat*
the *woman*
the *lamp*

'Collective nouns' refer to a group of people or
things:

flock
army
police

**If a noun refers to an *idea* rather than a concrete
object or a person, it is called an *abstract noun*:**

fear
anger
hunger
thirst
suspense
tension
sadness

Past participle
This is the part of the verb which combines with the 'auxiliary' (see above) to form the perfect or the pluperfect tense:

I have *finished* (perfect)
She has *written* (perfect)

They had *arrived* (pluperfect)
He had *swum* (pluperfect)

Possessive (= possessive adjective)
Indicates 'ownership' of a noun:

your house
my garden
his dog
her credit card

Preposition
Is used to qualify a noun or pronoun

under the table
on the roof
in the fridge
by the wall
at the bank
with me
without her
towards them
against him

Pronoun
A word which substitutes for a noun:

Nouns = Mr Rogers saw Mrs Dickinson yesterday

Pronouns = *He* saw *her* yesterday

Nouns = The policemen arrested the burglars

Pronouns = *They* arrested *them*

Subject
The person or thing which does/carries out the action of a verb:

The *man* sees the dog
The *girl* buys the computer
He is reading
The *boy* reads the paper
The *table* falls over
The *lamp* burns brightly
Where is my *book*?

Tense
The tense of a verb indicates when the action of the verb 'happens':

The table below indicates some of the main tenses in English

Tense	Examples
Present	I run; she goes; he buys; they eat
Continuous present	I am running; she is eating; they are reading
Future	I shall go; they will arrive; he will eat
Imperfect/preterite/ Simple past	I bought; she carried; he swam
Perfect	I have bought; she has swum; he has read
Pluperfect	I had listened; she had played; he had eaten

Verb
A verb is a word which states *action*:

I *buy*
I *run*
We *eat*
She *reads*
He *sleeps*

There are various types of verb:

Transitive verbs can take an *object*:

He *reads* the book (the book is the *object* of the verb *read*)
She *mows* the lawn (the lawn is the *object* of the verb *mow*)

Intransitive verbs **cannot** take an object:

She *sleeps* (for example, we cannot say 'she sleeps the book')
He *snores* (we could not say 'he snores the garden')

Some verbs can be either transitive or intransitive:

Run:

He runs into town (intransitive)
He runs a bath (transitive)

Verbs can be ***regular*** – i.e. they have a standard pattern when forming their various tenses:

I type	I typed	I have typed
I bake	I baked	I have baked
I cough	I coughed	I have coughed

or ***irregular*** – i.e. not having such a standard pattern:

I catch	I caught	I have caught
I write	I wrote	I have written
I speak	I spoke	I have spoken

When young children are learning English, they frequently impose a standard pattern onto an irregular verb: we have all heard (or used!) expressions such as:

'I catched it'
'I bringed it'

Unit 1
Ich heiße ...

TOPICS	
	• Greeting people
	• Giving a simple description of yourself
	• Understanding others talking about themselves
	• Handling simple numbers
	• German regions and cities
	• Some countries and nationalities

GRAMMAR	
	• Verbs (**ich**, **Sie**, **er/sie/es** forms)
	• Questions
	• Introduction to noun genders
	• Simple numbers

 Dialogue 1

Ursula: Guten Tag!
Ilse: Tag, Ursula!
Ursula: Wie geht's?
Ilse: Gut, danke.

Dialogue 2

Dieter: Guten Abend, Otto!
Otto: Guten Abend, Dieter – wie geht's?
Dieter: Ach, nicht schlecht.

Vocabulary

guten Abend	good evening
guten Tag	hello (literally: good day)
Wie geht's?/(abbreviation of: **wie geht** es)	how are you?
nicht schlecht	not bad

Dialogue 3

Doris and Wolfgang introduce themselves:

Doris: Guten Tag! Wie heißen Sie, bitte?
Wolfgang: Ich heiße Wolfgang Kruser. Und Sie?
Doris: Mein Name ist Doris Ketterer. Woher kommen Sie?
Wolfgang: Ich komme aus Freiburg. Und Sie?
Doris: Ich komme aus Regensburg.

Vocabulary

ich heiße	I am called
ich komme aus	I come from

Language note

Wie heißen Sie 'What's your name'
Note that the verb used with **Sie** (polite form of 'you') ends in **-en**.

Ich heiße   I am called
The verb ending after **ich** (I) with most verbs in the present tense is **-e**.

Dialogue 4

Marlene welcomes Oliver to a social function:

Marlene: Guten Abend, und herzlich willkommen! Wie ist Ihr Name?
Oliver: Guten Abend. Ich heiße Oliver Bauer. Und Sie sind?
Marlene: Ich heiße Marlene Kruser.
Oliver: Wohnen Sie hier in Essen?
Marlene: Ja, ich wohne hier.
Oliver: Kommen Sie aus Essen?
Marlene: Nein, ich komme aus Freiburg. Und Sie?
Oliver: Ich komme aus Hamburg, aber ich wohne und arbeite jetzt in Essen.

Vocabulary

herzlich willkommen!	a warm welcome!
arbeiten	to work
wohnen	to live
aber	but

🎧 ✍ Übung 1

Listen to these four people introducing themselves, and write down where they live and where they come from.

Dialogue 5

	Comes from	Lives in
Dietmar	*Frankfurt*	*Berlin*
Lisa	*Bonn*	*Hamb*
Clara	*Essen*	*London*
Theo	*Berlin*	*Paris*

🎧 📚 Dialogue 6

Herr Kramer is being greeted at a formal gathering:

Frau Fellbach: Guten Tag – wie heißen Sie?
Herr Kramer: Kramer – mein Name ist Kramer.
Frau Fellbach: Wohnen Sie hier in Stuttgart, Herr Kramer?
Herr Kramer: Ja, ich wohne hier, aber ich komme aus München. Und Sie – sind
                 Sie aus Stuttgart?
Frau Fellbach: Nein, ich bin Berlinerin – aber ich wohne seit 4 Jahren hier.

Language note

Ich wohne seit 4 Jahren hier = I have lived here for 4 years
seit 4 Jahren ≠ (literally) since 4 years.

English uses the past tense, but German uses the present in this context.

In German, as in English, you can take the name of a city, and add **-er** or **-erin** to give the name of the inhabitant:

Frankfurt	**Frankfurter** (male)	**Frankfurterin** (female)
Hamburg	**Hamburger** (male)	**Hamburgerin** (female)
Berlin	**Berliner** (male)	**Berlinerin** (female)

(**Berliner** is also the German name for a jam-filled doughnut!)

🎤 ✍ Übung 2

How do you say in German?

1   What's your name?   *Wie heissen sie?*
2   My name is Fritz   *Mein namer ist .*
3   I live in Heidelberg   *Ich wohne in Heidelberg*
4   I work in Hamburg   *Ich arbeite in H.*
5   I come from London   *Ich komme aus Ldon.*

🎤 Übung 3

With a partner in class, introduce yourselves to each other using the following outlines:

You will also find this good practice in pronouncing some German cities!

Name	Comes from	Lives in	Works in
Max	Köln	Essen	Oberhausen
Doris	Hamburg	Düsseldorf	Wuppertal
Beate	München	Regensburg	Regensburg
Astrid	Saarbrücken	Saarbrücken	Neunkirchen

🎧 📚 Dialogue 7

Oliver meets a Bavarian guest:

Oliver: Guten Tag!
Michael: Grüß Gott!
Oliver: Sie kommen aus Bayern?
Michael: Ja, aus Augsburg – aber ich arbeite und wohne jetzt hier in Hamburg.
Oliver: Fahren Sie oft nach Bayern?
Michael: Nein, leider nicht.

Language note

In the South of Germany, particularly in Bavaria, but also in parts of Baden-Württemberg, the standard greeting is **grüß Gott** rather than **guten Tag**. It is not reserved for greeting friends, but is also commonly used when entering shops, or greeting people on the street.

The German you will hear on the recordings is largely 'standard' German pronunciation, but there are lots of dialects and accent varieties – it can be difficult for someone from the north of Germany to understand someone from Bavaria, and vice versa.

'Standard' German is known as **Hochdeutsch** (high German). Some of the northern dialects are referred to as **Platt** ('flat' or 'low German').

 Text 1

Two students describe themselves:

Guten Tag. Mein Name ist Doris Ketterer. Ich bin 24 Jahre alt, und ich komme aus Regensburg. Ich studiere in Freiburg. Ich studiere Englisch und Geschichte.

Guten Tag. Ich heiße Otto Liedtke, und ich bin 23. Ich komme aus Essen und ich studiere auch dort. Ich studiere Mathematik. Ich wohne in Recklinghausen. Ich habe eine Wohnung dort. Ich habe ein Auto, und ich fahre jeden Tag nach Essen.

Vocabulary

die Geschichte   history
die Wohnung   flat

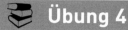 **Übung 4**

Are the following statements true or false?

1   Doris is a student in Regensburg
2   Doris studies English and history.
3   Otto is a geography student.
4   He lives in Recklinghausen.
5   He has a car.

Language note

German numbers are very logical and easy to learn:
Look at the following numbers, and listen to them on the recording:

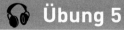 **Text 2**

1	eins	11	elf	21	einundzwanzig
2	zwei	12	zwölf	22	zweiundzwanzig
3	drei	13	dreizehn	30	dreißig
4	vier	14	vierzehn	35	fünfunddreißig
5	fünf	15	fünfzehn	40	vierzig
6	sechs	16	sechzehn		
7	sieben	17	siebzehn		
8	acht	18	achtzehn		
9	neun	19	neunzehn		
10	zehn	20	zwanzig		

For more numbers see the **Grammar** section at the end of the unit.

Übung 5

Listen carefully to the numbers spoken, and tick the ones you hear:

Text 3

1 ✓	2	3 ✓	4	5 ✓	6
7	8 ✓	9	10	11	12 ✓
13	14	15 ✓	16	17	18 ✓
19	20 ✓	21	22	23	24 ✓
25	26	27	28	29 ✓	30
31	32	33	34	35	36

  ## Text 4

An office worker:

> *married*
>
> Ich heiße Walther Fleming. Ich bin 36 Jahre alt, und ich bin <u>verheiratet.</u> Ich komme aus München, aber ich arbeite jetzt in Frankfurt. Ich arbeite bei einer großen Bank. Meine Frau ist Verkäuferin.

Language note

In order to give your age in German, simply say **ich bin X**, or **ich bin X Jahre alt** ('I am X years old').

Übung 6

Listen to these two people introducing themselves, and fill in the gaps in the sentences:

Text 5

Ich *heiße* Gabi Rossler. Ich bin *20* Jahre alt, und ich wohne in *Berlin.* Ich *studiere* Deutsch.

Mein Name ist Theo Kahn. Ich *arbeite* in Dortmund, aber ich *wohne* in *Essen.*

  ## Übung 7

Respond to the following questions about yourself:

1   Wie heißen Sie?
2   Wo wohnen Sie?
3   Studieren Sie?
4   Wo arbeiten Sie?
5   Woher kommen Sie?

 Übung 8

Work in pairs and introduce yourselves, giving information about:

*   Names
*   Places of study or work
*   Where you come from
*   Your age

 Übung 9

Now 'interview' other members of the group, and note down their details.

 Übung 10

Write a brief self-description of the following person (using **ich**):

*   Name = Marcus Felling
*   28 years old
*   Student
*   Studying History in Munich
*   Comes from Hamburg
*   Has a flat in Munich

 Dialogue 8

Ulrike works as a sales assistant:

Interviewer:	Guten Abend. Wie ist Ihr Name, bitte?
Ulrike:	Ich heiße Ulrike Fleming.
Interviewer:	Woher kommen Sie?
Ulrike:	Ich komme aus München.
Interviewer:	Arbeiten Sie dort?

sales assistant

Ulrike:	Nein, ich arbeite hier in Frankfurt. Ich wohne auch hier.
Interviewer:	Und was machen Sie?
Ulrike:	Ich bin Verkäuferin. Ich arbeite bei Dietmann – Dietmann ist ein großes Kaufhaus hier in Frankfurt.
Interviewer:	Wie lange arbeiten Sie jeden Tag?
Ulrike:	Ich arbeite jeden Tag von 8 Uhr bis 17 Uhr.
Interviewer:	Und sind Sie verheiratet?
Ulrike:	Ja – mein Mann arbeitet auch in Frankfurt. Wir haben zwei Kinder.

Vocabulary

das Kaufhaus	department store
Wie lange?	how long?
jeden Tag	each day

 ## Übung 11

Without reading the following text first, listen to this description of someone and note down as much information as you can:

Give the information about the person whom you have just heard described:

- Name
- Age
- Where is he from?
- Where does he live?
- What job does he do?
- Where does he work?
- What does his wife do?
- Do they have any children?

Now read the text and check your answers.

Text 6

Guten Tag. Meine Name ist Erich Hartmann. Ich bin 30 Jahre alt, und ich wohne in Stuttgart. Ich komme aus Dortmund, aber ich arbeite jetzt in Stuttgart. Ich bin Mechaniker. Ich bin verheiratet. Meine Frau ist Lehrerin, und wir haben drei Kinder. Wir haben eine kleine Wohnung. *flat*

MORE NUMBERS!

In the **Grammar** section, check the numbers 50 to 100. You will see they follow a very logical pattern once more.

 ## Übung 12

Now read out the following numbers in German. You can also do this exercise in pairs, to see if your class partner notes down the correct numbers!

2	19	67
4	20	34
8	31	43
7	33	56
13	44	58
16	25	90

  ## Text 7

HERR UND FRAU FLEMING

Using your dictionary to help you with new words, read the following passage. There will be structures which are new to you at this stage, but do not dwell on those. Try to get the key meaning of the text.

Walther und Ulrike Fleming kommen beide aus München, aber sie wohnen jetzt in Frankfurt. Herr Fleming arbeitet bei einer Bank in der Stadtmitte, und Frau Fleming ist Verkäuferin in einem großen Kaufhaus. Sie arbeitet auch in Frankfurt. Sie haben eine nette Dreizimmerwohnung etwa 10 Kilometer von der Stadtmitte, und sie fahren beide mit der Straßenbahn zur Arbeit. Frau Fleming arbeitet bis 17 Uhr, und sie ist jeden Tag gegen 18 Uhr wieder zu Hause. Am Wochenende besuchen sie ihre Eltern oder ihre Freunde.

wie *they. visit.* *city centre*

Vocabulary

beide	both
die Stadtmitte	city centre
die Straßenbahn	tram

Language note

sie arbeitet – the verb after **er** ('he'), **sie** ('she'), **es** ('it') ends in the present tense in **-e**, or **-et**.

Dreizimmerwohnung – German is a language in which it is possible to form nouns (compound nouns) by adding words together. Other examples =

Hotelzimmer	hotel room
Rheindampfer	Rhine steamer
Stadtmitte	city centre
Wochenende	weekend
Straßenbahn	tram

 Übung 13

Richtig oder falsch?

1 Frau Fleming arbeitet bei einer Bank.
2 Herr Fleming kommt aus Frankfurt.
3 Sie fahren mit der Straßenbahn zur Arbeit.
4 Frau Fleming ist um 18 Uhr wieder zu Hause.
5 Die Wohnung hat vier Zimmer.
6 Am Wochenende besuchen sie Freunde.

Übung 14

You are Frau Fleming. Respond to the following questions:

1 Woher kommen Sie? *Where r u from?*
2 Wo wohnen Sie jetzt? *Where do you currently work?*
3 Sind Sie verheiratet? *Are you married?*
4 Wo arbeiten Sie? *Where do you work?*
5 Wie fahren Sie zur Arbeit? *How do you get to work?*
6 Was machen Sie am Wochenende? *What do you do at whnds?*

 Übung 15

Using your dictionaries, check the German equivalent of the following jobs/professions (including the feminine version if this is different):

Manager *Leiter*   Doctor *Ärztin*   Engineer   Lawyer *Anwalt*
Bus driver   Teacher *Lehrin*   Student   Vet

Übung 16

Using the nouns you have checked, make up 8 sentences about each one, using the names you have already met. (E.g. **Theo ist Student, er wohnt in** …)

Übung 17

Match up the halves of the following sentences:

Herr und Frau Fleming	Mathematik an der Universität.
Otto studiert	hier?
Sie haben	mit der Straßenbahn zur Arbeit.
Frau Fleming	wohnen in Frankfurt.
Sie fahren	drei Kinder.
Arbeiten Sie	ist Verkäuferin.

Übung 18

Working in pairs 'interview' your partner and note down any information you get about him/her. Write this down using the **sie/er** form of the verb: **X wohnt in …** etc. Then exchange notes with other pairs and create a further set of sentences.

Dialogue 9

Marcus talks to Herr Oswald, who is from the former East Germany.

Marcus:	Wo kommen Sie her?
Herr Oswald:	Ich komme aus Dresden, aber ich wohne jetzt in Hamburg.
Marcus:	Und wo liegt Dresden?
Herr Oswald:	Dresden ist im Osten.
Marcus:	Wie weit ist es von hier?
Herr Oswald:	Von Hamburg, etwa drei Stunden im Zug.
Marcus:	Haben Sie noch Familie in Dresden?
Herr Oswald:	Ja, meine Großmutter wohnt noch da.
Marcus:	Und Ihr Großvater?
Herr Oswald:	Mein Großvater ist leider vor 4 Jahren gestorben.
Marcus:	Haben Sie andere Verwandte in Dresden?
Herr Oswald:	Nein, nicht in Dresden, aber ich habe zwei Onkel und eine Tante in Berlin. Ach, und auch zwei Vettern.
Marcus:	Was macht Ihre Großmutter?
Herr Oswald:	Sie ist Rentnerin.

Vocabulary

wo liegt?	where is?
im Osten	in the East
wie weit?	how far?
die Stunde	hour
der Großvater	grandfather
ist ... gestorben	has died
Verwandte	relatives
die Großmutter	grandmother
der Onkel	uncle
die Tante	aunt
Vettern	cousins
der Rentner/die Rentnerin	pensioner (male/female)

Language note

Wo kommen Sie her? – alternative to **woher kommen Sie?** ('where do you come from?')

Mein Großvater ist ... gestorben – 'my grandfather died' (this is the perfect tense, which you will meet later in the course)

✍ Übung 19

Write a simple description of Herr Oswald (**Er kommt aus Dresden**, etc.).

✍ Übung 20

Re-read the dialogue above, and complete the grid of relatives below. Use your dictionary to complete any which you have not yet met:

German	English	German	English
die Frau,	wife	der Vater	father
der Mann	husband	die Mutter	mother
der Großvater	grandfather	die Tante	aunt
die Großmutter	grandmother	der Onkel	uncle
der Brüder	brother	die Schwester	sister

Germany is a federal republic (**die Bundesrepublik Deutschland**) divided into various **Länder** or **Bundesländer** (literally: states). The German **Länder** have local control over education, for example, and each has its own governing body (the **Landesregierung**).

⚲ GERMANY: DIE DEUTSCHEN BUNDESLÄNDER

German	English	Hauptstadt/Capital
Baden-Württemberg	Baden-Württemberg	**Stuttgart**
Bayern	Bavaria	**München**
Berlin	Berlin	**Berlin**
Brandenburg*	Brandenburg	**Potsdam**
Bremen	Bremen	**Bremen**
Hamburg	Hamburg	**Hamburg**
Hessen	Hesse	**Wiesbaden**
Mecklenburg-Vorpommern*	Mecklenburg-West Pomerania	**Schwerin**
Niedersachsen	Lower Saxony	**Hannover**
Nordrhein-Westfalen	North Rhine-Westphalia	**Düsseldorf**
Rheinland-Pfalz	Rhineland-Palatinate	**Mainz**
Saarland	Saarland	**Saarbrücken**
Sachsen*	Saxony	**Dresden**
Sachsen-Anhalt*	Saxony-Anhalt	**Magdeburg**
Schleswig-Holstein	Schleswig-Holstein	**Kiel**
Thüringen*	Thuringia	**Erfurt**

* These are the Länder which were in the former East Germany. They are referred to as **die neuen Bundesländer** (the new federal states).

Germany was divided after the Second World War into two halves, the German Democratic Republic (die deutsche demokratische Republik) which was part of the Eastern bloc, and the German Federal Republic (die Bundesrepublik Deutschland), which was part of the western alliance. The infamous Berlin Wall was built in 1961, and was a symbol of the division of East and West. Following mass demonstrations in 1989 the wall finally came down, and the two Germanies were officially reunited in October 1990.

Use a suitable internet search engine to collect more facts and figures about Germany before and after reunification.

Übung 21

Using an appropriate website, check the populations of the German Länder, and the total population of Germany.

AND OTHER COUNTRIES …

Country		Adjective	Inhabitant
German	English		
Großbritannien	Great Britain	**britisch**	**Brite/Britin**
Deutschland	Germany	**deutsch**	**Deutsche/r**
Amerika	America	**amerikanisch**	**Amerikaner/in**
Frankreich	France	**französisch**	**Franzose/Französin**
Spanien	Spain	**spanisch**	**Spanier/in**
Griechenland	Greece	**griechisch**	**Grieche / Griechin**
Australien	Australia	**australisch**	**Australier/in**
Italien	Italy	**italienisch**	**Italiener/in**
die Schweiz	Switzerland	**schweizerisch**	**Schweizer/in**
die Türkei	Turkey	**türkisch**	**Türke/Türkin**
Belgien	Belgium	**belgisch**	**Belgier/in**

Language note

NATIONALITIES

To form the adjective of nationality from a country, German usually adds **-isch**:

Japan   japanisch
Italien   italienisch

(note that the adjective takes a *small* letter, not a capital)

To say someone is of a particular nationality, you can say:

Er ist Spanier ('he is Spanish'), **Sie ist Französin** ('she is French')

✍ Übung 22

Complete the sentences by giving the nationality of these people (you may need to refer to a dictionary to help you with some of these):

1   Pierre kommt aus Bordeaux. Er ist *französisch*.
2   Thor kommt aus Oslo. Er ist _____.
3   Adele kommt aus Perth. Sie ist *australisch*.
4   Carla kommt aus Rom. Sie ist *italienisch*.
5   Tina kommt aus Barcelona. Sie ist *spanisch*.

AND, GOODBYE FOR NOW ...

Petra: Auf Wiedersehen!
Ursula: Bis morgen!

Otto: Bis später.
Dieter: Tschüs!

Language note

There are many ways of saying goodbye. You don't have to say **Auf Wiedersehen**, for example, just **Wiedersehen** will do.

The other expressions mean:

bis morgen   till tomorrow
bis später   till later
tschüs   bye ('cheers')

Grammar

1. Verbs

The infinitive form of all German verbs ends in **-n** or **-en**.

Examples:

arbeiten	to work
fahren	to go, travel
heißen	to be called
verheiraten	to marry
wohnen	to live
sammeln	to collect
studieren	to study
pendeln	to commute

The first person singular (**ich** = 'I') form of regular verbs ends in **-e**

ich habe	I have
ich heiße	I am called
ich trinke	I drink
ich wohne	I live
ich esse	I eat

The 'polite' form (**Sie** = 'You') ends in **-n** or **-en** (like the infinitive):

Sie wohnen
Sie haben
Sie pendeln
Sie fahren

The third person singular (**er** = 'he'; **sie** = 'she'; **es** = 'it') ends in **-t** or **-et**:

er heißt
sie arbeitet   *er/sie/es*
sie wohnt
er fragt

The main exception to the above forms is the verb **sein** (= 'to be'). This is highly irregular in German:

ich bin	I am
Sie sind	You are
er/sie/es ist	He/she/it is

Note also that the verb **haben** (= 'to have') is also irregular:

ich habe	I have
Sie haben	You have
er/sie/es hat	He/she/it has

2. Asking questions

In order to ask a question in German, you simply invert the subject and the verb:

Sie haben ein Auto	You have a car
Haben Sie ein Auto?	Do you have a car?
Er wohnt in Frankfurt.	He lives in Frankfurt
Wohnt er in Frankfurt?	Does he live in Frankfurt?

3. Genders of nouns

Nouns in German can have one of three genders:

- Masculine
- Feminine
- Neuter

Gender in the grammatical sense is not linked with biological gender. For example, the German for 'girl' is **das Mädchen**, which is neuter, and the German for 'sentry' is **die Wache**, which is feminine.

The definite article ('the') and the indefinite article ('a') differ in German according to the gender of the noun in question:

Masculine	**der Lehrer**	**ein Lehrer**
Feminine	**die Studentin**	**eine Studentin**
Neuter	**das Haus**	**ein Haus**

4. Origin

In German we can either say where we are from, using **aus**:

ich komme aus München
ich bin aus Hamburg

Or we can use a noun, by adding **-er** (or in the case of females **-erin**) to the city in question:

Ich komme aus Berlin   Ich bin Berliner/in
Ich komme aus München   Ich bin Münchner/in
Ich komme aus Wien   Ich bin Wiener/in

5. Cities

German has its own version of many cities, particularly in Europe. Here are a few of the common ones:

Nizza	Nice
Neapel	Naples
Athen	Athens
Lüttich	Liège
Moskau	Moscow
Warschau	Warsaw
Brüssel	Brussels
Dünkirchen	Dunkirk
Rom	Rome

6. Numbers

German numbers are highly logical in their structure:

eins	1	sieben	7	dreizehn	13	neunzehn	19
zwei	2	acht	8	vierzehn	14	zwanzig	20
drei	3	neun	9	fünfzehn	15		
vier	4	zehn	10	sechzehn	16		
fünf	5	elf	11	siebzehn	17		
sechs	6	zwölf	12	achtzehn	18		

einundzwanzig	21
zweiundzwanzig	22
dreiundzwanzig	23

and so on.

dreißig	30
vierzig	40
fünfzig	50
sechzig	60
siebzig	70
achtzig	80
neunzig	90
hundert	100

zweiunddreißig   32
vierundsechzig   64

Language in use

✍ 📚 Übung 23

Read out the following numbers in German, and then write them out in full:

22   25   74   83   47   10   98
52   44   48   56   16   29   33

📚 Übung 24

Check the gender and the meaning of the following nouns in the dictionary, and then add the appropriate definite and indefinite article:

Example:
Kellner   der Kellner   ein Kellner

der / das = ein
die (f)

Bank   *das* Haus   *eine Haus*
Universität   *der* Wagen   *ein Wagen*
das Auto   *die* Tochter   *eine tochter*
der Manager   *das* Büro   *eine Büro*
die Lehrer(in) *die* Haltestelle   *eine ..*
Student   *der* Tisch
Straßenbahn   *der* Computer
Anwalt   *die* Maus
die Lampe   *das* Buch
die Zeitung   Magazin
(newspaper)

🎙 Übung 25

Respond to the following questions positively. When you have responded orally, write down your responses.

Example:
Wohnen Sie in Stuttgart? Ja, ich wohne in Stuttgart

1   Heißen Sie Wolfgang?
2   Arbeiten Sie in Dortmund?
3   Wohnen Sie in Dortmund?

4   Wohnen Sie allein?
5   Fahren Sie mit der Straßenbahn zur Arbeit?

✍ Übung 26

Insert the correct form of the verb in each sentence:

1   Herr Imping _arbeitet_ in Recklinghausen (arbeiten)
2   _Wohnen_ Sie hier? (wohnen)
3   Sie (she) _verdient_ 800 Euro pro Monat (verdienen)
4   Wir _fahren_ in die Stadtmitte (fahren)
5   Er _kauft_ ein neues Auto (kaufen)
6   Der Hund _heißt_ Maxi (heißen)
7   Der Computer _kostet_ 3000 Euro. (kosten)
8   _Lesen_ Sie diese Zeitung? (lesen)

✍ Übung 27

The following are verbs which are all 'regular' in their present tense.

(to make)	write	to go	laugh	to open	to close	to put/place	to lay/put
machen	**schreiben**	**gehen**	**lachen**	**öffnen**	**schließen**	**stellen**	**legen**
drink	come from	to put/place	to clean		reserve	to order	
trinken	**kommen**	**stecken**	**putzen**	**lächeln**	**reservieren**	**bestellen**	
to run	to lie	to climb		to call			
rennen	**liegen**	**steigen**	**ziehen**	**rufen**			

1   Use your dictionary to check the meanings.
2   In each case, give the **ich** form and the **er/sie/es** form of the present tense.

✍ Übung 28

Insert an appropriate verb from the above list into each of the following sentences:

1   Ich _schreibe_ einen Brief an meine Mutter.
2   Herr Bauer _trinkt_ ein Bier.
3   Ich _stelle_ das Buch in meine Tasche.
4   Frau Fleming _öffnet_ die Tür.
5   Er _kommt_ heute in die Stadt.
6   Marcus _____ das Fahrrad – es ist sehr schmutzig.
7   Ich _lege_ den Computer auf den Tisch.
8   Doris _putzt_ einen Tisch im Restaurant.
9   Herr Fleming findet das sehr komisch – er _lacht_. (laughs).
    funny

Kennen → to know

✍ Übung 29

Make the following statements into questions:

1   Herr Brenner arbeitet in Dortmund.   *Arbeitet er in Dortmund?*
2   Frau Brenner hat ein neues Auto.   *Sei hat ein neues Auto?*
3   Markus kennt Ulrich.   *Er kennt Ulrich?*
4   Sie lesen die Zeitung.   *Lesen Sie die Zeitung?*
5   Sie wohnen hier.   *Wohnen Sie hier?*
6   Doris studiert in Hamburg.   *Wo studiert sie in Hamburg?*
7   Herr Brenner bereitet das Abendessen.   *Er bereitet das Abendessen?*
8   Sie bleiben heute Abend hier.   *Bleiben sie heute Abend hier?*
9   Er geht bald.   *soon.*
      geht er bald?

bereiten – to prepare

bleiben – to stay

Unit 2
Ich möchte bitte . . .

TOPICS
- Simple shopping and transactions
- Use of the telephone
- Asking and giving the time
- Days and dates

GRAMMAR
- Verbs (**wir** form + **du** form)
- Use of **nicht**
- **Möchte**
- More numbers

TEST YOUR KNOWLEDGE

Dialogue 1

IN THE DEPARTMENT STORE (IM KAUFHAUS)

Verkäuferin:	Guten Tag! Bitte schön?
Wolfgang:	Was kostet die Tischlampe, bitte?
Verkäuferin:	Moment mal ... Die hier? Sie kostet 70 Euro.
Wolfgang:	Gut, ich nehme sie.
Verkäuferin:	So, bitte schön.
Wolfgang:	Vielen Dank – auf Wiedersehen.
Verkäuferin:	Wiedersehen.

Vocabulary

bitte schön?	can I help you?
bitte schön.	(here) there you are
nehmen	to take

Dialogue 2

IM KAUFHAUS

Doris is trying to find the restaurant in the department store.

Verkäufer:	Bitte schön?
Doris:	Ich suche das Restaurant.
Verkäufer:	Das Restaurant finden Sie in der dritten Etage.
Doris:	Danke sehr.
Verkäufer:	Bitte sehr.

Vocabulary

suchen	to look for
in der dritten Etage	on the third floor
Bitte sehr	you're welcome, don't mention it

  Dialogue 3

AT THE SUPERMARKET CHECKOUT (AN DER KASSE)

Verkäufer:	Also, das macht 45 Euro.
Wolfgang:	Ach – ich möchte auch diese Rasierklingen, bitte.
Verkäufer:	Dann noch zwei Euro – 47 Euro, bitte.
(Wolfgang gives him a 50 Euro note.)	
Verkäufer:	Und drei Euro zurück, danke.
Wolfgang:	Vielen Dank. Wiedersehen.
Verkäufer:	Auf Wiederschauen.

Vocabulary

das macht	that comes to
Rasierklingen	razor blades
zurück	literally: back, here = change.
auf Wiederschauen	alternative to **auf Wiedersehen** ('goodbye')

Language note

45 Euro – note that Euro is not used in the plural here. Similarly **35 Pfund** ('35 pounds').

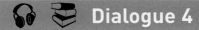 **Dialogue 4**

IM KAUFHAUS

Marlene is buying a blouse.

Marlene:	Was kostet diese Bluse, bitte?
Verkäuferin:	Die blaue Bluse?
Marlene:	Ja.
Verkäuferin:	Sie kostet 84 Euro.
Marlene:	Sie ist aus Baumwolle?
Verkäuferin:	Aus reiner Baumwolle, ja.
Marlene:	Dann nehme ich sie.
Verkäuferin:	So – Sie zahlen bitte an der Kasse dort.
Marlene:	Danke.

Vocabulary

die Bluse	blouse
die Baumwolle	cotton
aus Baumwolle	(made from) cotton
rein	pure
zahlen	to pay
nehmen	to take
die Kasse	payment point, desk

Language note

aus Baumwolle = made out of cotton
Similarly, **aus Leder** = made of leather
ist diese Jacke aus Leder? = is this jacket leather?

 Übung 1

Here are pictures of various items together with their prices. Working with a partner, ask/give the price of each item.

Vocabulary to assist you

die Tischlampe
der Pullover
die Jacke

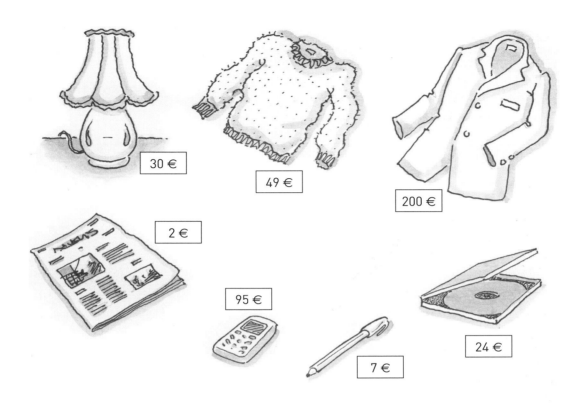

die Zeitung
das Handy
der Kugelschreiber
die CD

 **Übung 2**

Using your dictionary to help, find words for another five items you might buy. As before, ask and give the price of each.

🎧  **Dialogue 5**

At the market.

Otto: Was kosten die Nektarinen?
Verkäufer: Die kosten 2 Euro pro Kilo.
Otto: Zwei Kilo, bitte.

Verkäufer:	So … Und sonst noch was?
Otto:	Und vier Bananen bitte.
Verkäufer:	Gerne. Also, macht zusammen 7 Euro.
Otto:	Danke sehr.
Verkäufer:	Vielen Dank. Wiedersehen.
Otto:	Auf Wiedersehen.

Vocabulary

| **sonst noch was?** | anything else? |
| **zusammen** | together |

Language note

Sonst noch was is regularly used. Also commonly heard is the slightly more formal:
sonst noch einen Wunsch (lit: 'do you have another wish?')

🎧 ✍ Übung 3

Dialogue 6

Listen to the following dialogue, and fill in the gaps based on the information you hear:

Martin ist im _____ Er kauft eine Uhr.

Verkäufer:	Bitte schön?
Martin:	Was _____ diese Uhr, bitte?
Verkäufer:	Sie kostet _____ Euro.
Martin:	Das ist etwas zu _____.
Verkäufer:	Und diese? Sie kostet nur _____ Euro.
Martin:	Gut! Ich _____ sie.
Verkäufer:	Sonst noch _____?
Martin:	Nein, danke.

Using your dictionaries, read this advertisement carefully.

Paul's Fliesenmarkt

Bahnhofstrasse 25   Neunkirchen

Riesenauswahl!   Fliesen in allen Farben

Beste Preise! Erstklassiger Service

Professionelle und freundliche Fachberatung

Geöffnet: Sa. 9–16 Uhr
Mo., Di., Mi., Fr. 8.00–19.00 Uhr
donnerstags 8.00–20 Uhr

Jeden Sonntag Schau-Tag 14–18 Uhr (leider kein Verkauf)

📚 ✍ Übung 4

1   What does the supermarket sell?
2   In what colours are they available?
3   On what day can you shop until 8p.m.?
4   What service is there on Sundays?
5   If you are new to Neunkirchen, where are you likely to find this store?

Language note

Days of the week

Sonntag	Sunday
Montag	Monday
Dienstag	Tuesday
Mittwoch	Wednesday
Donnerstag	Thursday
Freitag	Friday
Samstag	Saturday
Sonnabend	Saturday (alternative version)
am Samstag	on Saturday
samstags	on Saturdays

 Übung 5

Working with a partner from the class, compose your own advertisement using a similar structure:

Decide on the location
Decide what you want to sell, and the days and times of opening

 Übung 6

Working in pairs, act out the following role-plays:

(You will need to check vocabulary first)

1   Ask the price of apples – buy 1 kilo of these, and four oranges.
2   You are buying a jacket. Cost = 250 Euros. You are directed to the cash desk to pay.
3   Check the price of a lamp. Cost = 45 Euros. Pay for it, and receive 5 Euros change.
4   Ask the cost of a shirt. At 100 Euros, it is too expensive (= zu teuer). You buy a different one at 42 Euros.

Language note

Numbers from 101 to 1 million – easy!

101	hunderteins	300	dreihundert
102	hundertzwei	1000	tausend
110	hundertzehn	1001	tausendeins
120	hundertzwanzig	2000	zweitausend
130	hundertdreißig	1000000	eine Million
200	zweihundert		

  Dialogue 7

Ursula bumps into Ilse during the lunch hour.

Ursula:	Hallo Ilse! Was machst du hier?
Ilse:	Ich warte auf eine Kollegin.
Ursula:	Du hast also jetzt Mittagspause?
Ilse:	Ja, bis ein Uhr.
Ursula:	Was machst du heute Abend?
Ilse:	Ich habe nichts vor.
Ursula:	Dann treffe ich dich später?

Ilse:	Ja, gerne. Um wieviel Uhr?
Ursula:	Sagen wir, um 7 – hier?
Ilse:	OK – um 7 Uhr also – bis später.
Ursula:	Tschüs!

Vocabulary

warten (auf)	to wait (for)
die Mittagspause	lunch break
ich habe nichts vor	I don't have any plans
nichts	nothing
tschüs!	bye!

Language note

Um 7 = at 7
(um 7 Uhr)

Telling the time in German is very similar to English:

8.50 = **acht Uhr fünfzig** (**Uhr** means 'clock')
6.30 = **sechs Uhr dreißig**

8.15 = **Viertel nach acht** (quarter past eight)
9.45 = **Viertel vor zehn** (literally 'quarter before ten')

But note:

halb sieben = six thirty (half way to seven)

See the **Grammar** section for more detail.

USE OF **DU**

Note that after **du** (the word for 'you' which is used when speaking to friends and young children), the ending in the present tense of regular verbs is **-st** or **-est**:

du machst	you do
du kommst	you come
du fragst	you ask

Übung 7

Working in pairs, ask your colleague to note down ten different times of the day, and to read them out to you in German. You write down the English version, and then compare notes.

If you are still having any difficulty with this, check the section in **Grammar** again.

MEDIA-MARKT

Oldenburger Strasse 36   **Bremen**

Video   TV   HiFi   Computer

Foto   CD   Telekommunikation   Elektro

Ihr Fachgeschäft in der Stadtmitte!

Geöffnet: Mo. bis Fr. 08.00–20.00

samstags 09.00–16.00

Vom 04.07 bis 08.07 – Computer-Woche

Ausstellung   Beratung   Sonderpreise

 ## Übung 8

1   Where in Bremen is this shop located?
2   What does it sell?
3   What are the opening times on Saturdays?
4   What is of particular interest to customers in July?

Dialogue 8

AM TELEFON

Marlene:	Kruser, guten Tag.
Otto:	Tag, Marlene. Otto hier. Ich möchte bitte mit Wolfgang sprechen.
Marlene:	Guten Tag Otto. Wolfgang ist leider nicht da. Er kommt um 6 Uhr nach Hause.
Otto:	Gut, ich rufe dann später noch mal an. Wiederhören.
Marlene:	Auf Wiederhören.

Vocabulary

ich möchte	I would like
leider nicht	unfortunately not
nach Hause	(to) home
ich rufe später noch mal an	I'll ring again later
auf Wiederhören	goodbye (on phone)

Language note

The standard practice in Germany is to give your surname when answering the phone, as Marlene does here.

ich möchte bitte mit Wolfgang sprechen – the infinitive goes to the end of the sentence after **ich möchte** ('I would like')

Auf Wiederhören ('until I *hear* you again') – quite logical. **Auf Wiedersehen** is not used on the phone.

Dialogue 9

AM TELEFON

Sekretärin:	Dietmann, guten Tag.
Walther:	Guten Tag – ich möchte bitte mit Frau Fleming sprechen.
Sekretärin:	Moment bitte, ich verbinde Sie gleich.

Vocabulary

Dietmann	the name of the company
verbinden	to connect
gleich	straight away

Übung 9

Complete the gaps with suitable words

A: _____ Tag. Ich _____ mit Frau Kruser _____.
B: _____ Tag. Frau Kruser ist _____ da.
A: Dann _____ ich später _____.
B: Auf _____.
A: _____.

Übung 10

Before reading the written version, listen to the telephone conversation and answer the questions:

1   What type of business is the call made to?
2   To whom does the caller wish to speak?
3   What is the caller told?
4   What is the caller's surname?

Now read the printed version below and check your answers.

 Dialogue 10

Empfangsdame:	Hotel Adler, guten Tag.
Wolfgang:	Guten Tag. Ich möchte bitte mit Herr Kahn sprechen.
Empfangsdame:	Moment bitte ... Leider ist Herr Kahn nicht da. Können Sie bitte heute Abend anrufen?
Wolfgang:	Ja, kein Problem.
Empfangsdame:	Und Ihr Name bitte? *your (possessive)*
Wolfgang:	Mein Name ist Kruser.
Empfangsdame:	Danke. Auf Wiederhören, Herr Kruser.
Wolfgang:	Auf Wiederhören.

 Übung 11

Once again, before reading the text, listen to the conversation and answer the questions:

1   What are the names of the two gentlemen involved in the conversation?
2   When must they meet?
3   What is the problem with the first day suggested?
4   What day is agreed on?
5   What time is suggested?

Now read the text and check your answers.

 Dialogue 11

Otto and Norbert try to set up a meeting.

Otto:	Bauer, guten Tag.
Norbert:	Guten Tag Herr Bauer! Norbert Schrader hier. Wie geht's?
Otto:	Sehr gut, danke. Und Ihnen?
Norbert:	Nicht schlecht. Herr Bauer, ich muss Sie diese Woche treffen.
Otto:	Ja, sicher.
Norbert:	Sind Sie morgen da?
Otto:	Morgen leider nicht – ich bin in Hamburg. Mittwoch ist aber möglich.
Norbert:	Moment mal – ja, das geht – sagen wir also Mittwoch. Um wieviel Uhr?
Otto:	Um 10 Uhr?
Norbert:	Prima – dann komme ich zu Ihnen.
Otto:	So, bis Mittwoch – auf Wiederhören.
Norbert:	Wiederhören, Herr Bauer.

Vocabulary

muss (müssen)	must, have to
möglich	possible
prima	great, excellent

Language note

Ich muss Sie diese Woche treffen – the infinitive (**treffen**) goes to the end of the sentence.

Müssen is a 'modal verb' – and is often used together with another verb:

ich muss gehen
wir müssen hier bleiben
er muss arbeiten

You will meet this and other modal verbs in more detail later in the course.

✍️ Übung 12

Give the German for:

1 I'd like to speak to Doris.
2 I'll connect you now.
3 She isn't there.
4 I'll ring later.
5 Bye. (*on the phone*)

Grammar

1. Use of **nicht**

In order to make a verb negative, all that is required is to insert **nicht** after it:

Ich gehe	I am going
Ich gehe nicht	I am not going
Er ist hier	He is here
Er ist nicht hier	He is not here
Wir essen	We are eating
Wir essen nicht	We are not eating
Trinken Sie nicht?	Aren't you drinking?
Arbeitet sie nicht?	Isn't she working?

2. **Möchte**

Möchte (in grammatical terms a modal verb in German) is very useful either alone or in combination with another verb:

ich möchte	I would like
du möchtest	you would like
er/sie/es möchte	He/she/it would like
Sie möchten	You would like
Ich möchte hier bleiben	I should like to stay here
Möchten Sie essen?	Would you like to eat?
Ich möchte ein Bier	I would like a beer.
Möchtest du ein Eis?	Would you like an ice cream?
Wir möchten dort essen.	We should like to eat there.

Note that the infinitive form of this verb is **mögen**.

3. The time

Once you have mastered numbers, telling the time in German is very easy.

Wieviel Uhr ist es?	What time is it?
Wie spät ist es?	What time is it?
Es ist 2 Uhr	It is 2 o'clock
Um wieviel Uhr?	At what time?
Um ein Uhr	At one o'clock
Um zwei Uhr	At two o'clock, etc.

morgens (morning)
nachmittags (afternoon)
abends (evening)

can be added to aid clarity:

um 4 Uhr morgens	at 4 a.m.
um 4 Uhr nachmittags	at 4 p.m.
um 7 Uhr abends	at 7 p.m.

There is a tendency to use the 24-hour clock far more than we do in spoken English:

um 18 Uhr	at 6p.m.
um 23 Uhr	at 11p.m.

A very easy way to give the time in German is simply to add the minutes to the hours as in English ('eleven fifty', 'twelve thirty', etc.):

elf Uhr fünfzig	11.50
zwölf Uhr dreißig	12.30
fünfzehn Uhr acht	15.08
drei Uhr zwanzig	3.20

There are also other possibilities:

zehn nach elf	11.10 (literally: 'ten after eleven')
fünfzehn nach drei	3.15 (fifteen after three)
zehn vor elf	10.50 (ten before eleven)
fünf vor zehn	9.55 (literally: 'five before ten')
zehn vor neun	8.50 (ten before nine)

Note the following alternative ways of telling the time:

halb fünf	4.30 ('half the way round to five')
viertel fünf	4.15 ('quarter of the way round to five')
dreiviertel fünf	4.45 ('three quarters of the way round to five')

(English 'half five' means five thirty, which could lead to confusion!)

Finally:

um Mitternacht	at midnight
am Mittag	at midday
am Vormittag	in the morning
am Nachmittag	in the afternoon

4. Verb forms: present tense, first person plural (**wir**)

The **wir** form of verbs in German is in almost all cases the same as the infinitive form:

gehen	wir gehen
lesen	wir lesen
kaufen	wir kaufen

Note an important exception = **wir sind** ('we are')

5. Days of the week and months of the year

Sonntag	Sunday
Montag	Monday
Dienstag	Tuesday
Mittwoch	Wednesday
Donnerstag	Thursday
Freitag	Friday
Samstag	Saturday

(sometimes **Sonnabend** is used instead of 'Samstag')

Note:

on Friday	**am Freitag**
on Tuesday	**am Dienstag**

| **dienstags** | on Tuesdays |
| **samstags** | on Saturdays |

(without a capital letter because these are adverbs of time)

Januar	January
Februar	February
März	March
April	April
Mai	May
Juni	June
Juli	Juli
August	August
September	September
Oktober	October
November	November
Dezember	December

| **im Januar** | in January |
| **im Juli** | in July |

Ende Januar	at the end of January
Mitte Januar	in the middle of January
Anfang Januar	at the beginning of January

6. More numbers

hunderteins	101
hundertzwanzig	120
hundertdreißig	130
hundertvierunddreißig	134
zweihundert	200
zweihundertvierundfünfzig	254
dreihundert	300
dreihundertzweiunddreißig	332
tausend	1000
tausendeins	1001
zweitausend	2000
viertausend	4000
eine Million	1000000

Language in use

1. Verbs

✍ ÜBUNG 13

Insert the correct form of the verb in each of these sentences:

1 Ich _fahre_ morgen nach Hamburg. (fahren)
2 Wir _kaufen_ heute ein Auto. (kaufen)   *kaufen - to buy*
3 _Haben_ Sie ein Wörterbuch? (haben)
4 _Kommt_ du mit (uns) nach München? (kommen)   *us.*
5 _Rufen_ Sie Frau Kramer später an? (rufen)
6 Ja, ich _rufe_ Sie um 7 Uhr. (rufen)
7 Wir _bleiben_ nur bis 8 Uhr. (bleiben)
8 _Trinken_ Sie ein Bier? (trinken)
9 _Kennst_ du meinen Bruder? (kennen)
10 Wir _gehen_ gleich nach Hause. (gehen) *immediately*

2. Negative

✍ ÜBUNG 14

Make the following sentences negative by inserting **nicht** in the appropriate place:

1 Wir bleiben, die ganze Woche hier.   *Wir bleiben nicht die ganze Woche hier*
2 Er arbeitet in Hamburg.   *Er arbeitet nicht in Hamburg*
3 Ich kenne Frau Lessing.   *Ich kenne nicht F.L.*
4 Der Bus kommt um 7 Uhr.   *Der Bus kommt nicht um 7 Uhr*
5 Wolfgang studiert in Berlin.   *W. Studiert nicht in Berlin*
6 Doris wohnt in Potsdam.   *Doris wohnt nicht in Potsdam*
7 Ich spiele jeden Tag Fußball.   *Ich spiele nicht jeden Tag Fußball*
8 Meine Frau möchte heute ausgehen.
9 Ich kaufe es!   *Ich kaufe nicht es! I don't buy it!*
10 Ich rufe heute an.

🎙 ✍ ÜBUNG 15

Respond negatively to the following questions:

Example: Fahren Sie nach Hamburg? Nein, ich fahre nicht nach Hamburg.

1   Bleibst du hier?
2   Arbeitest du bis 8 Uhr?
3   Möchtest du essen?
4   Kommst du?
5   Wohnen Sie hier?
6   Studieren Sie Französisch?

3. Möchte/möchten

✎ ÜBUNG 16

Insert the appropriate form of möchte/n:

1   Ich ___möchte___ ein Eis bitte.
2   Was ___möchten___ Sie?
3   ___Möchtest___ du ein Bier?
4   Ich ___möchte___ hier bleiben.
5   Er ___möchte___ in Essen studieren.
6   Doris ___möchte___ in München wohnen
7   Herr und Frau Lessing ___möchten___ dort essen.
8   ___Möchtest___ du ein Buch kaufen?
9   Was ___möchtest___ du jetzt tun?
10 Wie ___möchten___ Sie bezahlen?
                               to pay -

✎ ÜBUNG 17

Compose as many sentences as you can making use of **möchte/n** and the verbs and nouns listed below:

Nouns   *Verbs*
Zimmer   essen
Lampe   reservieren
Zeitung   trinken
Eis   kaufen
Ei
Kotelett

4. Times and Dates

🎤 ✎ ÜBUNG 18

What time is it?

1   Halb drei
2   Viertel vor eins
3   Acht Uhr zehn
4   Neun Uhr dreiundzwanzig
5   Achtzehn Uhr vierundvierzig
6   Dreiviertel sechs
7   Viertel neun
8   Halb zehn
9   Zehn vor elf
10 Viertel nach neun

🎧 ÜBUNG 19

Listen to these recorded times (Text 1) and note them down.

8·20   3·30   10·50   4·30   6·30   9·35   15·23.

🎧 ÜBUNG 20

Listen to the following dates (Text 2) and note them down.

11 Dez./ 1 März/ 17 Juli/ 19 Juni/ 23 Oktober/ ·

✎ 🎤 ÜBUNG 21

Write out (or speak) the following times in German, in as many ways as you can:

10.40	11.30	12.10	17.34	18.00	6.00
12.00	00.03	15.20	03.45	04.15	05.45
13.56	15.36	20.20	21.20	20.21	19.59

🎤 ✎ ÜBUNG 22

Speak or write out in full the following dates:

1   December 14
2   January 12
3   March 15
4   July 21
5   February 13
6   September 5
7   August 11
8   April 29
9   June 22
10 November 5

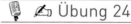 **ÜBUNG 23**

Working in pairs, each note down twenty numbers between 1 and 1000. Read them out to your partner in German, and when s/he has noted them down, check their version against your original. Then repeat the task, reversing the roles.

Test your knowledge

✍ Übung 24

Give responses to the following questions:

1   Wie heißen Sie?   *Ich heiße Zoe*
2   Woher kommen Sie?   *Ich komme aus UK.*
3   Wo wohnen Sie?   *Ich wohne in Cornwall.*
4   Seit wann wohnen Sie dort?
5   Wie alt sind Sie?   *Ich bin 34 Jahre alt.*
6   Sind Sie verheiratet?   *Nein*
7   Sind Sie Student?   *Nein.*
8   Was studieren Sie?
9   Wie fahren Sie zur Universität?

✍ Übung 25

Match up the words and their meanings:

city   **die Großmutter**
city centre   **das Auto**
department store   **arbeiten**
car   **die Wohnung**
grandmother   **jeden Tag**
every day   **die Stadt**
to work   **das Kaufhaus**
married   **einfach**
to stay   **die Stadtmitte**
simple   **bleiben**
flat   **verheiratet**

✍ Übung 27

Give the German for:

1   Spain   *Spanien*
2   France   *Frankreich*
3   Italy
4   Turkey
5   Belgium
6   Australia
7   Germany
8   Liège
9   Bavaria
10 Brussels
11 Moscow
12 Munich

✍ Übung 28

Rewrite the following sentences replacing **ich** with **er**, and changing the form of the verb if needed:

1   Ich wohne in Hamburg.
2   Ich heiße Dieter.
3   Ich studiere Mathematik.
4   Ich komme aus Hannover.
5   Ich trinke gern Kaffee.
6   Ich habe ein Auto.
7   Ich bin nicht verheiratet.

🎧 Übung 29

TEXT 1

Listen to the recording and write down the numbers you hear.
5 / 12 /

🎤 ✍ Übung 30

What questions would you ask to get the following responses?

1   Das Radio kostet 50 Euro.
2   Das Restaurant ist in der zweiten Etage.
3   Ich habe nichts vor.
4   Es ist halb sieben.
5   Sehr gut, danke.

Übung 31

Read out the following times in German, in as many ways as you can:

6.10	7.30	7.45	8.12	8.36	12.51
9.40	15.32	16.58	11.30	10.45	9.50

Übung 32

Give the German equivalent of:

1   Can I help you? *Bitte schön?*
2   Would you like anything else? *Und sonst noch was?*
3   I'll take them. *Ich nehme sie*
4   I'd like to speak with Dieter. *Ich möchte bitte mit Frau sprechen*
5   He's not here at the moment. *Er ist nicht da ..*

Übung 33

Complete the gaps in this vocabulary list:

floor (of a building)	
	die Zeitung
cotton	
	der Kugelschreiber
cash point	
	die Uhr
to buy *kaufen*	
	Freitag
Wednesday	

Übung 34

Rewrite the following sentences replacing **ich** with **wir** and changing the verb form:

1   Ich fahre gleich.
2   Ich kaufe die Uhr.
3   Ich nehme es.
4   Ich suche das Restaurant.

5   Ich lese die Zeitung.
6   Ich rufe später an.
7   Ich treffe Sie um 8 Uhr.
8   Ich kann das nicht lesen.
9   Ich möchte einen Weißwein.
10 Ich studiere Geschichte.

Unit 3
Wie komme ich zum ...?

TOPICS	• Asking for and giving directions
	• Making travel arrangements
GRAMMAR	• Accusative case
	• Present tense of strong/irregular verbs
	• Separable verbs
	• Comparative adjectives
	• Introduction to modal verbs

Dialogue 1

Dieter is asking the way.

Dieter: Entschuldigen Sie bitte, wie komme ich zum Bahnhof?
Ulrike: Gehen Sie hier geradeaus, und dann nach rechts.
Dieter: Danke schön.
Ulrike: Gerne.

Vocabulary

Entschuldigen Sie	excuse me
der Bahnhof	station
zum Bahnhof	to the station
geradeaus	straight on
nach rechts	to the right

Language note

Entschuldigen Sie is a common way of saying 'excuse me'. It is also possible to use the noun **Entschuldigung**.

Dialogue 2

Dieter gets directions to the hotel.

Dieter: Entschuldigen Sie bitte, wo ist das Hotel Adler?
Walther: Moment bitte – ja, das Hotel Adler ist hier geradeaus, dann die zweite Straße links.
Dieter: Ist es weit von hier?
Walther: Nein, nur zwei Minuten zu Fuss.
Dieter: Danke.

Vocabulary

links	left
weit	far
zu Fuss	on foot

Language note

Die zweite Straße	the second street

German forms the ordinal numbers (first, second, third, etc.) by adding **-t** to the end of the number, plus an adjective ending which varies depending on the gender and case of the noun which the ordinal number refers to. (You will deal with the adjective endings in more detail later in the course.)

Examples:

vier	**die vierte Straße**	the fourth street
fünf	**die fünfte Straße**	the fifth street
zehn	**die zehnte Straße**	the tenth street

Note the following irregular examples:

erst	first	**die erste Straße**
dritt	third	**die dritte Straße**

  Dialogue 3

Dieter asks the way to the theatre.

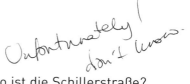

Unfortunately I don't know.

Dieter: Entschuldigen Sie bitte, wo ist die Schillerstraße?
Ulrike: Ach, die Schillerstraße kenne ich leider nicht. Was suchen Sie?
Dieter: Ich suche das Theater.
Ulrike: Das Stadttheater? – also, Sie gehen hier hoch, und dann nach links.
Dieter: Danke sehr.

Vocabulary

kennen	to know
suchen	to look for
hier hoch	up here

Language note

die Schillerstraße kenne ich ... nicht – 'I don't know the Schillerstraße'

Literally: 'The Schillerstraße know I not.' German does not necessarily follow the same word order pattern as English, and it is possible in German for the object of a verb to precede the subject, as it does here. This is sometimes used for emphasis. The important thing is that the verb is, in a normal sentence, the second 'idea' (not necessarily the second word) in the sentence. Look at these examples:

Ich kenne das Theater in Hamburg nicht.
Das Theater in Hamburg kenne ich nicht.

In the first sentence the subject (**ich**) comes before the verb; in the second it comes after. In both sentences the verb (**kenne**) is the second 'idea' – but in the second sentence the verb is the *fifth* word ('the theatre in Hamburg' is one 'idea' or 'concept').

 Dialogue 4

Dieter is looking for the post office.

Dieter: Entschuldigen Sie, wie komme ich zur Post?
Ulrike: Tut mir leid. Ich weiß nicht. Ich bin hier fremd.

Vocabulary

die Post	post office
tut mir leid	I'm sorry
ich weiß nicht	I don't know
fremd	strange, a stranger

Dialogue 5

Horst is asking directions to Hölderlinplatz.

Horst: Entschuldigen Sie bitte, wie komme ich zum Hölderlinplatz?
Klara: Tut mir leid – den Hölderlinplatz kenne ich nicht – ich bin hier fremd!

 Übung 1

Using expressions from the above dialogues, give suitable responses to the questions:

1   **Wie komme ich zum Postamt?** (straight on) *geradeaus.*
2   **Ist es weit von hier?** (no, just three or four minutes' walk) *3/4 minuten zu Fuss*
3   **Wo ist hier eine Bank?** (second street on the right) *Zweite Strasse zu rechts*
4   **Kennen Sie bitte die Viktoriastraße?** (yes – first on the left) *ja, erste strasse zu links*
5   **Wie komme ich zum Stadttheater** (don't know!) *Ich weiße nicht.*
6   **Ist die Post weit von hier?** (no, third street on the left)

 Übung 2

Using the map, and from your location, give directions to the following places:

1   Hotel Adler
2   Post office
3   Car park
4   Bank
5   Supermarket
6   Dietrichallee

 Übung 3

If you follow the directions, where do you get to?

1   Zweite Straße rechts, auf der linken Seite
2   Erste Straße links, auf der rechten Seite
3   Geradeaus, auf der rechten Seite
4   Zweite Straße rechts, auf der rechten Seite
5   Immer geradeaus

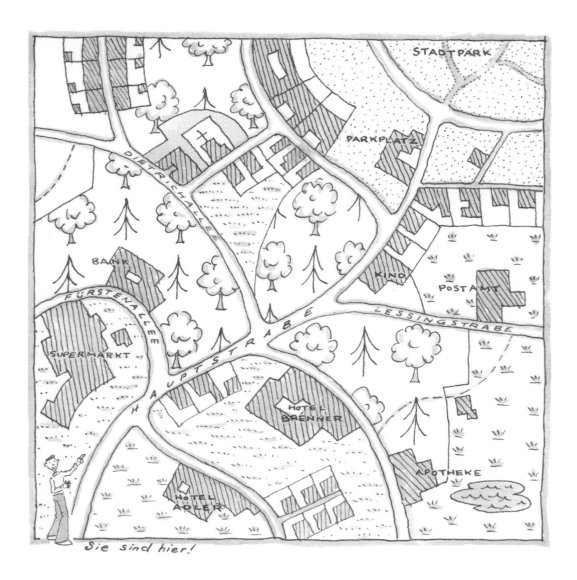

Sie sind hier!

📖 Übung 4

Look at the map again. Are the following statements true or false?

1　Der Parkplatz ist nicht weit vom Stadtpark.
2　Das Postamt ist in der Viktoriastraße
3　Das Kino ist in der Hauptstraße, auf der rechten Seite.
4　Der Supermarkt ist in der Fürstenallee, auf der rechten Seite.
5　Die Bank ist nicht weit vom Supermarkt.

Dialogue 6

AM BAHNHOF – AT THE STATION

Beamter:	Bitte schön?
Marlene:	Berlin einfach, bitte.
Beamter:	So, 40 Euro bitte.
Marlene:	Danke.
Beamter:	Bitte schön.

Dialogue 7

Marlene is buying a train ticket to Hamburg.

Schalterbeamter:	Bitte schön?
Marlene:	Nach Hamburg, bitte.
Schalterbeamter:	Einfach, oder hin und zurück?
Marlene:	Hin und zurück.
Schalterbeamter:	Also, eine Rückfahrkarte nach Hamburg. Erster oder zweiter Klasse?
Marlene:	Zweiter Klasse.
Schalterbeamter:	125 Euro bitte.

Vocabulary

einfach	single
hin und zurück	return (lit: there and back)
die Rückfahrkarte	return ticket

Language note

1 **nach Hamburg** – **nach** is used to express direction to a named country or city (**nach Frankfurt**, **nach Deutschland**, **nach England**).
   Note that if the country in question is feminine (e.g. **die Schweiz** = 'Switzerland'), then we use **in die** + the name of the country:

In die Schweiz	to Switzerland
In die Türkei	to Turkey

2 **zweiter Klasse** – this is actually in the genitive case, hence the ending of the number. You will meet the genitive case in more detail later in the course.

Note there are two ways here of saying 'return'. **Hin und zurück** is more colloquial, but is very widely used. **Eine Rückfahrkarte** is the formal term.

 **Dialogue 8**

Otto wants to know the time of the next train to Munich.

Schalterbeamtin:	Bitte schön?
Otto:	Wann ist der nächste Zug nach München?
Schalterbeamtin:	Moment mal. Also, der nächste Zug fährt um 9.35 Uhr.
Otto:	Und wann kommt er an?
Schalterbeamtin:	Um 11.45 Uhr.
Otto:	Danke sehr.
Schalterbeamtin:	Gerne.

Language note

1   **Der nächste Zug fährt** ... – Some verbs add an umlaut in the **du** and **er/sie/es** forms of the singular:

ich fahre	I go, travel
du fährst	you go, travel
er/sie/es fährt	he/she/it goes, travels

2   **Wann kommt er an**? – this is an example of a *separable* verb. **ankommen** = 'to arrive', but when it is conjugated the **an** (which is the 'separable prefix') separates and goes to the end of the clause:

ich komme um 8 Uhr an	I'll arrive at 8 o'clock
wir kommen am Samstag an	We are arriving on Saturday

   Other examples:

   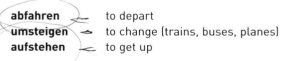

abfahren	to depart
umsteigen	to change (trains, buses, planes)
aufstehen	to get up

 **Dialogue 9**

Klaus is booking a ticket to Bremen.

Schalterbeamtin:	Ja bitte?
Klaus:	Wann fährt der nächste Zug nach Bremen?

Schalterbeamtin:	Sie haben einen Zug um 10.50 Uhr – er kommt um 14.25 Uhr an.
Klaus:	Kann ich die Fahrkarte hier kaufen?
Schalterbeamtin:	Ja, gerne. Möchten Sie auch einen Platz reservieren?
Klaus:	Ja, bitte.
Schalterbeamtin:	Raucher oder Nichtraucher?
Klaus:	Nichtraucher.
Schalterbeamtin:	So, das macht dann 158 Euro, bitte.
Klaus:	Danke sehr.

Vocabulary

der Zug	train
ankommen	to arrive
der Platz	seat, place
der Raucher	smoker
der Nichtraucher	non-smoker

Language note

Sie haben *einen* Zug um 10.50 – This is an example of the accusative case – used here because **Zug** is the *object* of the verb.

The definite (**der**, **die**, **das**) and the indefinite article (**ein**, **eine**) change in accordance with their case. This is explained fully in the **Grammar** section at the end of this unit.

Dialogue 10

Wolfgang is buying a ticket to Kiel, but finds he has to change trains on the way.

Schalterbeamtin:	Bitte schön?
Wolfgang:	Der nächste Zug nach Kiel, bitte?
Schalterbeamtin:	Der fährt um 11.00 Uhr ab – von Gleis 15 – aber Sie müssen in Bremen umsteigen.
Wolfgang:	Und wann komme ich an?
Schalterbeamtin:	Um 14.23 Uhr.
Wolfgang:	Danke.
Schalterbeamtin:	Bitte sehr.

Vocabulary

abfahren	to depart
das Gleis	platform (lit: track)
umsteigen	to change

Language note

ab Gleis 15 – 'from platform 15'. Strictly speaking, **Gleis** means 'rail' or 'track', but in Germany it is the standard term to indicate the platform of departure/arrival of trains. The 'platform' in the sense of the area on which the passengers stand is **der Bahnsteig**.

Rail travellers in Germany enjoy much better standards of service, both on trains and on stations, than their British counterparts. At the ticket office/information desk you can not only get details of arrival and departure times, but a computer printout of connecting times, and even of which platform your train arrives at and departs from. Even the smaller stations will often have a good quality food outlet, and flower shops are also a common sight on many German stations.

Übung 5

With a partner from the class, alternate in taking the role of speaker B in this and the following dialogue:

A: Ja, bitte?
B: (*single to Munich*) *Einfach nach München*
A: Erster oder zweiter Klasse?
B: (*second class – check the price*) *zweiter classe*
A: 15 Euro bitte.
B: (*thanks*)

 Übung 6

A: Bitte schön?
B: (*next train to Hamburg?*) *der nächste Zug nach Hamburg*
A: Um 18.40 Uhr.
B: (*is the train direct?*)
A: Nein, Sie müssen in Frankfurt umsteigen.
B: (*cost – second class?*) *Zweiter classe*
A: Einfach, oder hin und zurück?
B: (*single*) *Einfach*
A: 56 Euro bitte.
B: Danke schön.
A: Bitte.

 Übung 7

With a partner from the class, act out the following role-plays in pairs:

A:	B:
Return to Munich	Class?
First	Give price
Check next train time	Give time, and platform
When does it arrive?	Give arrival time

A:	B:
Single to Augsburg	Give price
Check time of next train	Train in ten minutes, but not direct – change in Ulm
Next direct train?	Give time (11.45)
Arrival time?	14.55
Reserve seat – smoker	

✍ Übung 8

Complete sentences based on the following grid:

Example:

Ich fahre von Hamburg nach Bremen. Ich komme um 18.30 an.

(When you have done this, read out the times in each sentence.)

von	nach	Ankunft (= arrival)
Hamburg	Bremen	18.30
Berlin	Rostock	09.15
Bamberg	Freiburg	14.30
München	Regensburg	2.20
Saarbrücken	Kaiserslautern	12.35
Heidelberg	Heilbronn	08.10

🎧 Übung 9

Listen to the following railway station announcements and answer the questions. You will not understand every word at this stage, but you will be able to grasp the key points of information. When you have listened to the announcements and attempted the questions, then read through the transcript printed below and check your answers.

The vocabulary below will help you:

Vorsicht	caution, be careful
planmäßig	scheduled
der Abschnitt	sector (of platform)
der Wagen	carriage
die Verspätung	delay
voraussichtlich	expected, probably
dringend	urgent

ANNOUNCEMENT 1

1   What is the announcement for passengers on platform 3?

ANNOUNCEMENT 2

1   What are we told about the position of the first class carriages?
2   Where is the train restaurant?

ANNOUNCEMENT 3

1   What is the important announcement for passengers on platform 4?
2   What is the scheduled departure time of the Intercity for Berlin?

ANNOUNCEMENT 4

1   What time is the train from Cologne to Amsterdam?
2   What is the number of this train?
3   At what time does the Intercity for Koblenz and Stuttgart leave?
4   From which platform?

ANNOUNCEMENT 5

1   What is Herr Siegen asked to do?

ANNOUNCEMENT 6

1   What platform alteration is mentioned?

Text 1

1 Achtung Gleis 3! Der Intercity nach Stuttgart fährt sofort ab. Bitte Vorsicht bei der Abfahrt.

2 Achtung Gleis 8! Der Eurocity Franz Liszt fährt gleich ein: planmäßige Ankunft 14.32 Uhr, planmäßige Abfahrt 14.35 Uhr. Wagen der ersten Klasse befinden sich in den Abschnitten A und B, Wagen der zwoten Klasse in den Abschnitten C, D und E. Das Bordrestaurant befindet sich in der Mitte des Zuges, im Wagen 15.

3 Achtung Gleis 4! Der Intercity nach Berlin, planmäßige Ankunft 15.27, hat voraussichtlich 20 Minuten – ich wiederhole – 20 Minuten Verspätung.

4 Hier Köln Hauptbahnhof, Köln Hauptbahnhof. Sie haben direkten Anschluss an Eurocity 437 nach Amsterdam um 14.25 Uhr von Gleis 16. Sowie an Intercity 523 nach Bonn, Koblenz und Stuttgart, planmäßige Abfahrt 14.50 Uhr von Gleis 7.

5 Achtung, eine Durchsage an Herrn Norbert Siegen, ich wiederhole, an Herrn Norbert Siegen. Herr Siegen wird dringend an den Informationsschalter neben Gleis 1 gebeten.

6 Achtung Gleis 5! Der Intercity 638 nach Hamburg, Abfahrt 14.57 Uhr fährt jetzt von Gleis 8 ab.

 Übung 10

Listen to the following announcements (this time you do not have a transcript to assist you), and take notes of the details. Once again, the vocabulary list should help you.

Vocabulary

der Anschluss	connection
Wien	Vienna
planmäßig	scheduled
der Interregio	'regional' train (covers quite long distances)
Vorsicht!	careful!
die Verspätung	delay

 Übung 11

1 On what station are the announcements being made? (*General*)
2 What is the number of the train going to Vienna? (*Announcement 1*)
3 What time should the Vienna train leave, and from which platform? (*Announcement 1*)

4   Which train is arriving at platform 14? (*Announcement 2*)
5   What time is this train due to leave? (*Announcement 2*)
6   Which train is late, and how late is it? (*Announcement 3*)
7   Which train is leaving platform 8? (*Announcement 4*)

ON-LINE TRAIN TIMETABLES

German railways have a very useful on-line timetable and booking system. Using a suitable search engine, try to locate the relevant website, and to check times of trains between pairs of German cities (e.g. Hamburg and Stuttgart, Munich and Cologne). If you enter the names of some smaller towns and cities (check these on a map), you will see how the system gives you various connection times.

  Text 3

DIE LANGE REISE

Wolfgang has a long day!

Wolfgang fährt heute von Heidelberg zu einer Messe in Köln, und er muss deshalb sehr früh aufstehen. Er fährt im Taxi zum Bahnhof, aber er kommt zu spät am Bahnhof an und verpasst den Zug. Der nächste Zug nach Köln fährt erst in anderthalb Stunden ab, und er hat deshalb Zeit, eine Zeitung zu kaufen und einen Kaffee zu trinken. Dieser Zug fährt leider nicht direkt nach Köln – Wolfgang muss in Frankfurt umsteigen. Er kommt also zwei Stunden später in Köln an, als erwartet. Zum Glück ist die Rückfahrt viel leichter – er kann direkt von Köln nach Heidelberg fahren, und er ist um 23.00 Uhr wieder zu Hause. Glücklicherweise ist es heute Freitag – er kann morgen ausschlafen.

Vocabulary

die Messe	exhibition, trade fair
aufstehen	to get up
verpassen	to miss
anderthalb	one and a half
zum Glück	fortunately
ausschlafen	have a lie in

Language note

1 **er muss sehr früh aufstehen** – 'he has to get up very early'
   muss (infinitive = müssen) is a *modal* verb. It is frequently used with another
   verb, as here:

er muss aufstehen	he must get up
ich muss arbeiten	I must work
wir müssen nach Hamburg fahren	we have to go to Hamburg

2 **er kann direkt von Köln nach Heidelberg fahren**. Another *modal* verb (**können**).
   Note that the other verb (**fahren**) goes to the *end* of the clause.

Other examples:

ich kann heute nach Frankfurt fahren
wir können morgen nach Amerika fliegen

🎙 ✍ Übung 12

1 Where is Wolfgang going?
2 Why?
3 When is his next train?
4 What does he do to pass the time?
5 When does he arrive at his destination?
6 Why is the journey home easier?

✍ Übung 13

Match up the halves of the sentences:

Wolfgang muss heute	nicht direkt nach Köln
Der Zug fährt	ist nicht so schwierig
Morgen muss Wolfgang	den Zug
Die Fahrt von Köln nach Heidelberg	mit dem Zug nach Köln fahren
Er verpasst	am Bahnhof an *– W: arrives late at station*
Wolfgang kommt spät	nicht arbeiten

ankommen

Übung 14

You are Wolfgang. Answer the questions put to you.

1 Wohin fahren Sie heute?
2 Warum?
3 Wie kommen Sie zum Bahnhof?
4 Wann fährt der nächste Zug?
5 Ist der Zug direkt?
6 Wann sind Sie wieder zu Hause?

 ## Übung 15

Now write in German in the **ich** form an account of your day (as Wolfgang).

 ## Übung 16

Here is a brief diary of another 'typical' day for Wolfgang. Describe to a partner in class what he does.

09.00	Taxi Bahnhof (nach Bonn)
12.30	Mittagessen (Frau Bauer)
14.30	Bahnhof (nach Köln)
19.00	Theater (Herr und Frau Lessing)

  ## Text 4

ZUVIEL GEPÄCK? KEIN PROBLEM!

Wenn Sie mit der Bahn fahren, müssen Sie nicht Ihr Gepäck mitnehmen. Mit dem Kurier-Gepäck- und Post-Gepäck-Service reist das Gepäck ohne Sie – hin und zurück! Der Kurier-Gepäck-Service holt Ihr Gepäck bei Ihnen zu Hause ab und stellt es an der Zieladresse zu. Oder Sie geben das Gepäck an Postfilialen und Postagenturen auf.

✍ Übung 17

Use your dictionaries to check any new words, and then summarise the main points of the service offered here.

  ## Dialogue 11

AM FLUGHAFEN

Sabine works at the airport, and is checking in two passengers.

Sabine:	Guten Tag.
Herr Bauer:	Guten Tag.
Sabine:	Ihre Flugscheine und Reisepässe bitte.
Herr Bauer:	Bitte schön.
Sabine:	Danke. Also zwei Passagiere nach Singapur? Wieviele Gepäckstücke möchten Sie einchecken?

Herr Bauer:	Nur die zwei Koffer.
Sabine:	Setzen Sie sie bitte auf das Band ... Danke. Möchten Sie einen Fensterplatz?
Herr Bauer:	Wenn möglich bitte.
Sabine:	Moment – ja, kein Problem. So, das sind Ihre Pässe, und Ihre Bordkarten. Flugsteig D36.
Herr Bauer:	Danke sehr.

Vocabulary

der Flugschein	ticket (airline)
der Reisepass	passport
der Koffer	suitcase
das Band	belt
der Fensterplatz	window seat
die Bordkarte	boarding card
der Flugsteig	gate

Language note

1 **Ihre Flugscheine, Ihre Bordkarten – Ihr** means 'your' (it is the possessive form of **Sie**). Note that it has a capital letter.

Some other possessive pronouns are:

mein	my
dein	your
sein	his/its
ihr	her
unser	our
ihr	their

2 <u>einen</u> **Fensterplatz** – another example of the accusative.
3 **Fensterplatz** is also a compound noun (i.e. a noun made of two nouns, **Fenster** and **Platz**).
4 German compound nouns take the gender of the last noun in the series – since **Platz** is masculine (**der Platz**), **Fensterplatz** is also masculine (**der Fensterplatz**).

Further examples:

die Zimmertür	room door
der Schullehrer	school teacher
der Zimmerschlüssel	room key

Übung 18

Herr und Frau Dietrich fliegen heute nach Singapur … (continue to write this in the third person, based on the above dialogue).

Übung 19

Dialogue 12

Sabine is now checking in Frau Dietrich. Listen carefully to the dialogue, and complete the gaps:

Sabine:	Guten _Abend_ (a) Bitte schön?
Frau Dietrich:	Guten Abend.
Sabine:	Ihren _Reisepass_ (b) bitte – und auch Ihren _Flugschein_ (c).
Frau Dietrich:	So, bitte schön.
Sabine:	Wohin _fliegen_ (d) Sie heute?
Frau Dietrich:	Heute nach Amsterdam, und dann _morgen_ (e) von Amsterdam nach Chicago.
Sabine:	Ja. Moment bitte. Leider hat der _Flug_ (f) nach Amsterdam Verspätung.
Frau Dietrich:	Wie lange?
Sabine:	Etwa _30_ (g) Minuten.

Grammar

1. The accusative case

Since German is an inflected language, the case of a noun or pronoun is indicated by its form: this can mean a different ending on an adjective or a noun, or a different form of the indefinite or definite article.

In English there are very few visible examples of the accusative in use:

We see *her*.	'her' is the object of the verb 'see', and is therefore in the accusative case
We see *the car*	'the car' is also in the accusative case, but here the form is the same as the nominative

In German the definite article changes to indicate the case of the noun:

Der **Wagen ist hier**.	The car is here. (**der Wagen** is the subject of the verb 'to be' and is therefore in the nominative case.)
Wir sehen *den* **Wagen**	We see the car. (**car** is the object of the verb, and so is in the accusative case, indicated by the change of **der** to **den**.)

The changes of the *definite* article are shown in the table below:

	Masculine	Feminine	Neuter
Nominative	**der Wagen**	**die Lampe**	**das Haus**
Accusative	**den Wagen**	**die Lampe**	**das Haus**

Note that there is no difference between feminine nominative and accusative, or neuter nominative and accusative.

The indefinite article changes as follows:

	Masculine	Feminine	Neuter
Nominative	**ein Wagen**	**eine Lampe**	**ein Haus**
Accusative	**einen Wagen**	**eine Lampe**	**ein Haus**

The third person singular pronouns in German changes as follows:

	Masculine	Feminine	Neuter
Nominative	**er** (he)	**sie** (she)	**es** (it)
Accusative	**ihn** (him)	**sie** (her)	**es** (it)

The pronouns **ich**, **wir**, and **Sie** follow the pattern below:

Nominative	**ich** (I)	**wir** (we)	**Sie** (you)
Accusative	**mich** (me)	**uns** (us)	**Sie** (you)

euch. (Ihr 'you' plural)

2. Strong/irregular verbs

Some verbs, commonly known as strong or irregular verbs, have a number of vowel changes in the various forms of the present tense.

Common examples are:

fahren	to go	**lassen**	to let, leave
ich fahre	I go	**ich lasse**	I let, leave

but	*but*
du fährst	**du lässt**
er/sie/es fährt	**er lässt**
wir fahren	**wir lassen**
ihr fahrt	**ihr lasst**
sie fahren	**sie lassen**
Sie fahren	**Sie lassen**

Two of the most irregular verbs are **haben** ('to have') and **sein** ('to be').
Note their formation:

haben

ich habe	I have
du hast	you have
er/sie/es hat	he/she/it has
wir haben	we have
ihr habt	you have
sie haben	they have
Sie haben	you have

sein

ich bin	I am
du bist	you are
er/sie/es ist	he/she/it is
wir sind	we are
ihr seid	you are
sie sind	they are
Sie sind	you are

3. Separable verbs

Some verbs in German have a prefix (known as the separable prefix) which is separated from the verb in main clauses, and is placed at the end of the clause:

ausgehen	to go out
wir gehen um 8 Uhr aus	we are going out at 8
ankommen	to arrive
sie kommt um 9 Uhr an	she arrives at 9

4. Comparative of adjectives

The comparative form of adjectives ('bigger', 'smaller') is formed in German in the same way as in English: by adding **-er** to the adjective. If the adjective has only one syllable, and this is comprised of the vowel a, o, or u, then an Umlaut is added to the vowel to form the comparative:

klein	**kleiner**
billig	**billiger**

groß   **größer**
arm   **ärmer**

Note:

gut   good
besser   better

---

5. Modal verbs

German has a series of verbs (*modal* verbs) which are used with the infinitive form of
another verb (called the dependent infinitive).

The modal verbs are:

wollen   to want
können   to be able
dürfen   to be permitted
mögen   to like
lassen   to let, allow
müssen   to have to
sollen   to be supposed to

`leave` *(handwritten annotation beside lassen)*

Examples of use:

können	**wir könnnen hier bleiben**	we can stay here
müssen	**Sie müssen jetzt gehen**	you have to go now
dürfen	**sie dürfen hier essen**	they may eat here
wollen	**wir wollen das Auto kaufen**	we want to buy the car

Note that these verbs have an irregular singular form:

können	**müssen**	**dürfen**
ich kann	ich muss	ich darf
du kannst	du musst	du darfst
er/sie/es kann	er/sie/es muss	er/sie/es darf
wir können	wir müssen	wir dürfen
ihr könnt	ihr müsst	ihr dürft
sie können	sie müssen	sie dürfen
Sie können	Sie müssen	Sie dürfen

mögen	**lassen**	**wollen**
ich mag	ich lasse	ich will
du magst	du lässt	du willst
er/sie/es mag	er/sie/es lässt	er/sie/es will

(handwritten annotation: learn)

(handwritten annotation: Ich mag lieber)

wir mögen	wir lassen	wir wollen
ihr mögt	ihr lasst	ihr wollt
sie mögen	sie lassen	sie wollen
Sie mögen	Sie lassen	Sie wollen

(handwritten note:) ich solle / du sollst / er/sie solle / wir sollen

Note that **mögen** is very frequently used in a particular form (called the 'imperfect subjunctive') in order to express politeness (compare with English: 'I should like', as opposed to 'I want'.

ich möchte	I should like
wir möchten	we should like

Language in use

✏ Übung 20

ACCUSATIVE CASE

In the following sentences insert the appropriate form of the definite article in the gap. The nominative form of the noun is given in brackets to help you.

1 Wir lesen _____ Zeitung. (die Zeitung)
2 Sie schreibt _____ Brief an ihre Mutter. (der Brief)
3 Wir kaufen _den_ Wagen morgen. (der Wagen)
4 Er trinkt _____ Bier. (das Bier)
5 Sie trinkt _____ Wein. (der Wein)
6 Herr Dietrich verpasst _den_ Zug. (der Zug)
7 Sie kann _das_ Ei nicht essen. Es ist zu weich. (das Ei) *(handwritten: undercooked)*
8 Frau Lessing mag _____ Zimmer nicht. (das Zimmer)

✏ Übung 21

SEPARABLE VERBS

Form sentences from the components given, ensuring that you use the separable verb correctly in each case:

Example
Der Zug fährt um 10 Uhr ab.

1 der Zug; um 10 Uhr   abfahren
2 der Bus; um 7 Uhr   ankommen

3   Herr und Frau Dietrich; am Samstag   ausgehen
4   Walter; in Essen   umsteigen
5   Wir; nach 11 Uhr heute   anrufen   over
6   Ulrike; in 5 Minuten   vorbeikommen
7   ich; das Gepäck; hier   abstellen

✍ Übung 22

MODAL VERBS

Rewrite the sentences making use of the appropriate form of the modal verb:

Example:
Sie trinkt Wein. (mögen)   Sie möchte Wein trinken.

1   Ich gehe heute nach 9 Uhr. (mögen) ✗
2   Frau Lessing findet die Wohnung nicht. (können)
3   Wir gehen gleich! (müssen)
4   Er bleibt nicht länger hier. (dürfen)
5   Wann reserviert er das Zimmer? (können)
6   Was essen Sie? (wollen)   *Was wollen sie essen or was*
7   Wie lange sitzen wir hier? (dürfen)   *möchten sie*
8   Was kauft sie jetzt? (müssen)   *essen*
    Was muss sie jetzt kaufen

✍ Übung 23

COMPARATIVE ADJECTIVES

Insert the comparative form of the following adjectives:

1   Das Hemd ist weiß. Die Bluse ist noch _weißer_ .   *(polite)   (rude)*
2   Der Chef ist nicht sehr höflich. Die Verkäuferin ist viel _höflicher_. *unhöflich*
outside 3   Draußen ist es nicht sehr warm. Hier ist es viel _wärmer_.
4   Der Wein ist kalt, aber das Bier ist _kälter_.
5   Der Koffer ist viel _schwerer_ (schwer) `heavy'.   *leicht (light)*
6   Die Arbeit ist heute _schwieriger_ (schwierig)
    einfach (easy)   or easy

✍ Übung 24

PRONOUNS

Replace the underlined noun(s) with an appropriate pronoun:

Example:
Ich lese das Buch jetzt. Ich lese es jetzt.

1   Wir kaufen das Auto morgen.   *Wir kaufen es morgen*
2   Er verkauft den Wagen jetzt.   *Er v. ihn jetzt*
3   Ich kenne Herrn Wolf.   *Ich kenne ihn*
4   Wir kennen Frau Kramer nicht.
5   Er sieht das Haus nicht.   *Er sieht es nicht*
6   Wir lesen die Zeitung gleich.   *Wir lesen sie nicht*
7   Der Computer funktioniert nicht.
(Sehen) 8   Frau Kramer sieht Herrn Walter.   *Sie sieht ihn*
9   Herr Walter sieht Frau Kramer nicht.   *Er sieht sie nicht –*
10   Wir lassen das Buch hier.

He doesn't see her.

Wir lassen es hier

(savoir) Kennen – to know person
(connaître) wissen – to know a fact

Unit 4
Freizeit und Urlaub

TOPICS
- Leisure pursuits
- Holidays

GRAMMAR
- Perfect tense of weak verbs
- **dass** and word order
- Adjective endings after the definite article
- Plurals of nouns

TEST YOUR KNOWLEDGE

🎧 📚 Dialogue 1

Dieter and Otto discuss their plans for the evening.

Dieter: Was machst du heute abend?   *Very like*
Otto   Ich weiß noch nicht. Ich gehe wahrscheinlich ins Kino. Ulli ruft mich später an.
Dieter: Du kommst dann nicht ins Eiscafe?
Otto   Vielleicht nachher. Ich treffe Steffi um 7 Uhr. Sie möchte den neuen Film
          maybe later (sehen) sehen. Was machst du?   *that*   *maybe*
Dieter: Ich weiß, dass Ulli und Andrea ins Eiscafe gehen – gegen 8.30 Uhr. Ich treffe
          sie dort. Wolfgang kommt auch mit.   *mitkommen*
Otto   Schön. Also nach dem Film kommt ihr ins Eiscafe? Wir sehen euch gegen
          9 Uhr dort.
Dieter: OK. Ich rufe dich später an.   *anrufen*   *Sie? Ihr (dative)*
          Ruft er später an?

Vocabulary

anrufen	to telephone
(das) Eiscafe	ice-cream parlour
treffen	to meet
gegen	about, approximately

Language notes

1 **ins Eiscafe – ins = in das** ('into').
2 **wir sehen euch gegen 9 Uhr dort** – the expression of *time* (**9 Uhr**) precedes the
   expression of *place* (**dort**).
3 **euch** – accusative form of **ihr** (plural of the **du** form).
4 **dass ... ins Eiscafe gehen** – after **dass** the verb goes to the end of the clause.

🎧 📚 Dialogue 2

Andrea and Marlene are in the garden.   *yesterday*

Andrea: Was hast du gestern gemacht?
Marlene: Nicht viel. Ich habe bis 6 Uhr im Supermarkt gearbeitet. Und dann war ich
           den ganzen Abend zu Hause.
Andrea: Im Supermarkt? Has du einen neuen Job?
Marlene: Ja, ich arbeite seit Samstag da.   *since*   *wichtig = important*
Andrea: Und?
Marlene: Die Leute sind sehr nett, aber ich war sehr müde. Ich habe aber etwas
           Geld für meinen Urlaub verdient. Und was hast du gestern gemacht?
           holidays   *earned*

verdienen –
to earn

(handwritten: Ihre)

Andrea: Ich? Ich war im Eiscafe mit Ulli. Seine Freunde waren auch da. Wir gehen
           alle später aus, vielleicht ins Lokal. Kommst du mit?
Marlene: Ich weiß noch nicht – ich rufe dich später an.

(handwritten: I don't know yet)

Vocabulary

gestern	yesterday
(der) Supermarkt	supermarket
den ganzen Abend	for the whole evening
verdienen	to earn
der Urlaub	holiday
mitkommen	to come along

(handwritten: Lokal   pub/restaurant)

Language note

1   **im Supermarkt** – **in dem Supermarkt** (**dem** is the dative singular of **der**).

See the **Grammar** section for more information.

2   **ich habe gearbeitet** – 'I worked' – this is the *perfect tense*, formed by using ***haben***
    ('to have'), with the past participle (in this case ***gearbeitet***).

See the **Grammar** section for more information.

3   **den *ganzen* Abend** – 'the whole evening'. Note the ending on the adjective
    – German adds different adjective endings according to the *gender* and the *case* of
    the noun, and the endings are also dependent on whether the noun is preceded
    by the definite article (**der**, etc.), the indefinite article (**ein**, etc.), or stands alone.
4   **ich arbeite seit Samstag da** – 'I have been working there since Saturday'.
    Literally: 'I work there since Saturday'. **Seit** is used with the present tense in
    German whereas 'since' is used with the perfect in English.

✎ Übung 1

(handwritten in margin: reichten / neffen)

Insert suitable verbs from the box into the gaps:

Heute ___ist___ Marlene sehr müde. Sie ___arbeitet___ bis 6 Uhr im Supermarkt,
denn sie ___hat___ einen neuen Job. Sie ___verdient___ Geld für ihren Urlaub. Andrea
___sitzt___ im Cafe mit Otto und seinen Freunden. Heute ___gehen___ sie aus. Marlene
___weiß___ nicht, ob sie mitkommt.

---

ist   sitzt   arbeitet   gehen   hat   verdient   weiß

(handwritten: wie die fixe gute-nacht sagen)

Freitag – 'bank holiday'

Osten – easter
Weinachten – christmas

Übung 2

 Dialogue 3

Before reading it, listen to this interview with Ursula, then answer the questions below.

Before ich her kann

You might find this list of key vocabulary helpful:

leider	unfortunately
(die) Prüfung	test, examination
(das) Blumengeschäft	flower shop
an der Uni studieren	to study at university
fernsehen	to watch television

1 Ursula hat ziemlich viel Freizeit	Richtig?	Falsch?
2 Wo arbeitet Ursula?		
3 Wann arbeitet sie dort?		
4 Sie spielt Klavier	Richtig?	Falsch?
5 Ursula macht ihre Prüfung im Mai	Richtig?	Falsch?
6 Wo studiert Ursula?		

Now read through the dialogue and check your answers:

Interviewer: Ursula, was machst du gerne in deiner Freizeit?
Ursula: Ich habe leider nicht viel Freizeit. Im Juni habe ich meine Prüfungen.
              Ich studiere an der Uni in Lübeck, und ich habe auch einen Job am
              Wochenende. Ich arbeite in dem Blumengeschäft.
Interviewer: Ja, aber wenn du nicht arbeitest?
Ursula: So, dann gehe ich gern ins Theater und ins Kino. Und im Sommer
              spiele ich Tennis.   *to be at home*
Interviewer: Und wenn du zu Hause bleibst?
Ursula: Dann sehe ich fern, oder ich lese. Ich spiele auch manchmal Klavier,
              aber nicht so oft! *tele*
                        nach Hause gehen

Übung 3

1   Using your dictionary, find the German noun or verb for *six* hobbies or leisure
    pursuits. You should then:
2   Compose ten simple sentences using the expressions you have found. Vary these
    between the use of **ich er/sie** and **wir**.

tun allem (everything).

Übung 4

With a partner in class, interview each other about your hobbies and leisure pursuits. Note down the responses, and then try to write them down using complete sentences.

Übung 5

Dialogue 4

Listen to the details of Paul's day, then answer the questions below.

This vocabulary will help you:

besuchen   to visit
beide   both
die Prüfung   test, exam
der Nachmittag   afternoon

1 Where did Paul work in the morning?   Zu hause
2 Until what time?   zwei hr.
3 What did he do at 2 o'clock?   arrive.
4 What does Fritz study?   English
5 What is happening next week?   test.

Dialogue 5

Ursula asks Marcus about his holidays.   der Sommer (plural)

Ursula: Marcus, was machst du in den Sommerferien?
Marcus: Normalerweise fahre ich mit meinen Freunden in Urlaub.
Ursula: Wohin?
Marcus: Gewöhnlich nach Spanien oder Griechenland. Dieses Jahr aber in die Schweiz.

Regularly

Ursula: Und was machst du gerne im Urlaub?   beach
Marcus: Ich faulenze. Ich schlafe viel, oder ich sitze am Strand und lese ein Buch.

lazy

Ursula: Treibst du auch Sport?
Marcus: Ab und zu. Ich spiele Tennis mit meiner Schwester, und ich surfe gern.

Ich mag leibe unternehmen.

Vocabulary

in Urlaub	on holiday
die Schweiz	Switzerland
faulenzen	to laze around
Sport treiben	to do sport(s)
ab und zu	now and then

Language notes

nach Spanien, in die Schweiz

You have already met this earlier in the course.

Remember:

Most countries in German are neuter (e.g. **Deutschland**, **England**, **Frankreich**, **Spanien**, **Italien**) but a few are feminine (e.g. **die Schweiz**, **die Türkei**).

With neuter countries, travel to the country is expressed using the preposition **nach** – **ich fahre nach Deutschland**; **wir fahren nach England**.

With feminine countries, the definite article is used, together with the preposition **in** (plus the accusative case):

in die Türkei   to Turkey
in die Schweiz   to Switzerland

Present tense

  ## Übung 6

Re-read the dialogue, and then replace the gaps in the text below with suitable verbs:

Marcus ___fahrt___ normalerweise mit seinen Freunden in Urlaub. Er ___lest___ (?) gerne Bücher, und er ___faulenst___ (?) am Strand. Er ___triebst___ nicht viel Sport, aber er ___spielt___ Tennis und ___surf___ gerne.

 ## Übung 7

Give answers to the following questions about yourself.
was für = 'what sort of'

1   Wohin fahren Sie gewöhnlich in Urlaub?
2   Was machen Sie abends zu Hause?
3   Was machen Sie am Wochenende?
4   Haben Sie einen Job? Was für einen Job?
5   Was für Hobbys haben Sie?
6   Wie oft gehen Sie ins Kino?

 ## Übung 8

Interview a class partner using the above questions, and note down the responses. Then write a brief description in German:
X fährt gewöhnlich nach ..., etc.

  ## Text 1

Read the following passage carefully, without looking up any words in the dictionary at this stage:

[handwritten: teuer und billig]

[handwritten: dich und dunn — thick & thin]

Urlaub im All: Tickets ab 200 000 Euro!

[handwritten: likely] *[handwritten above Allerdings: However]*

[handwritten left margin: in space only]

Urlaub (im All?) In 15 bis 20 Jahren ist das gut möglich, glauben Experten. Allerdings nur für jemanden, der eine dicke Brieftasche hat. Professor Jesco von Puttkamer (NASA): 'Die ersten Tickets werden teuer sein.' *[handwritten: expensive]* So rechnet Hartmut Müller (Space Tours GmbH) mit 200 000 bis 280 000 Euro pro Person für einen Vier-Tage-Trip. Die japanische (Raumfahrt)agentur Nasda (will die Kosten später auf rund 40 000 Euro (reduzieren.) *[handwritten: want]* Interesse ist jedenfalls da. In den USA gibt es schon einige 100 feste Buchungen. *[handwritten: fixed]* Experten: Wenn die ersten Touristen fliegen, wird die Nachfrage steigen. Es könnte ein Milliarden-Markt werden. *[handwritten: demand]*

[handwritten left: space travel]

[handwritten: in anycase]   *[handwritten: Es gibt — there is/are]*

✍ Übung 9

Try to find equivalent German expressions in the text for the following words. The first letter is given to help you.

holiday	(U_____)
wallet	(B_____)
space	(A_____)
space travel	(R_____)
bookings	(B_____)
to reckon with	(r_____)
demand	(N_____)
ltd company	(G_____)

✍ 🎤 Übung 10

Answer the following questions on the text:

1 What is the unusual holiday destination being discussed here?
2 What kind of people will go on this holiday?
3 How long will a typical holiday of this kind last?
4 When will we be able to take this kind of holiday?
5 What evidence do we have that the idea is already popular in the USA?

✍ Übung 11

Using your dictionary, make a list of the *nouns* in the above passage, together with their meanings. Make a note of the *gender*, and the *plural* form, of each of the nouns.

🎧 Before you read the written version which is given below, listen carefully to this interview with Herr and Frau Wolff.

Dialogue 6

These words will help you understand what you hear:

die Südküste	south coast
mieten	to rent
die Dörfer	the villages
die Berge	the mountains
eine Ferienwohnung	holiday apartment
eine Pension	guest house

Übung 12

✍ Now you have heard the dialogue, answer the following questions:

1 Herr und Frau Wolff waren zwei Wochen an der Südküste in Spanien.	Richtig oder falsch?
2 Wie lange waren sie in Madrid?	10. (4 in
3 Was haben sie in den Bergen besucht?	
4 Sie waren die ganze Zeit in einem Hotel.	Richtig oder falsch? falsch
5 Wohin fahren Herr und Frau Wolff normalerweise?	Greece
6 Das Wetter war die ganze Zeit schön.	Richtig oder falsch?

📖 Now you have heard the dialogue and done the exercise, read carefully through this written version: (last year)

Interviewer:	Was haben Sie letztes Jahr im Sommer gemacht?
Herr Wolff:	Gewöhnlich fahren wir mit Freunden nach Griechenland, aber letztes Jahr waren wir in Spanien, an der Südküste.
Interviewer:	Und wie lange waren Sie dort?
Frau Wolff:	Wir waren zehn Tage da, und dann noch vier Tage in Madrid.
Interviewer:	Und was haben Sie im Urlaub gemacht?
Frau Wolff:	Wir haben ein Auto gemietet, und haben die kleinen Dörfer in den Bergen besucht. Das war herrlich.
Herr Wolff:	Ja, das Wetter war auch meistens schön – es hat aber ab und zu geregnet – in den Bergen, meine ich.
Interviewer:	Waren Sie in einem Hotel?
Frau Wolff:	Nein, wir haben an der Küste eine Ferienwohnung gemietet. In Madrid waren wir in einer Pension.

Übung 13

Dialogue 7

Listen to the following people describing what they do on holiday, and complete the grid below. There might be odd words which you have not yet met, but you should be able to get the required information.

	Goes to?	For how long?	With?
Marion	America	3	sister
Anton	France	3 whs	friend
Michael	Aust.	4 whs	brother

Dialogue 8

Ingrid works in a travel agent's office. She is helping a customer find a package holiday.

Ingrid:	Guten Tag, wie kann ich Ihnen helfen?
Frau Fleming:	Guten Tag. Ich habe gestern diesen Prospekt bekommen – ich möchte einen Urlaub buchen.
Ingrid:	Schön. Wohin wollen Sie denn fahren?
Frau Fleming:	Wir interessieren uns für diese Pauschalreise nach Südafrika – auf Seite 63.
Ingrid:	So ... Ja, sehe ich. Also, wann wollen Sie genau fahren?
Frau Fleming:	Wenn möglich, Mitte bis Ende Mai.
Ingrid:	Für zwei Wochen?
Frau Fleming:	Zwei Wochen, ja.
Ingrid:	Und sie wollen von welchem Flughafen abfliegen?
Frau Fleming:	Von Hamburg wenn möglich.
Ingrid:	Moment bitte – ich schaue mal nach ... Ja, das geht. Kein Problem. Es gibt einen Flug ab Hamburg am 11. Mai nach Kapstadt.
Frau Fleming:	Direkt, oder müssen wir umsteigen?
Ingrid:	Direkt nach Kapstadt. Und da haben Sie ein Doppelzimmer in einem Luxushotel. Und, wie Sie sehen, ist der Preis besonders günstig.
Frau Fleming:	Ja. Ich muss das zuerst mit meinem Mann besprechen.
Ingrid:	Also, wenn Sie wollen, kann ich das bis morgen für Sie reservieren.
Frau Fleming:	Das wäre nett von Ihnen. Ich komme morgen wieder vorbei – gegen 11 Uhr.
Ingrid:	Schön – also bis morgen.
Frau Fleming:	Bis morgen. Auf Wiedersehen.

Vocabulary

Prospekt (der)	brochure
buchen	to reserve, book
Pauschalreise (die)	package holiday
Kapstadt	Cape Town
nachschauen	to check
günstig	favourable (here = good value)
umsteigen	to change (flight)
besprechen	to discuss
ich komme vorbei	I'll call by, call in

Language notes

1   **ich möchte** – 'I should like'. This is one use of **mögen**, the *modal* verb you met in chapter 3.

2   **wir interessieren uns für** ... – 'we are interested in ...'. This is an example of a reflexive verb in German. They often indicate an action done to oneself:

   ich wasche mich   I wash (lit: I wash myself)

 Übung 14

After reading the dialogue once again, answer the following questions:

1   Where does Frau Fleming want to go? SA .
2   When would she like to travel? May
3   For how long does she want to book? 2 wks
4   When will she leave, and from which airport? 11 Nov Hamburg
5   When is she going to call in to the travel agent again? in the morning

 Übung 15

Perform the following role-play with a partner from the class:

Customer:	(Would like holiday in Greece)
Travel Agent:	(Travelling when?)
Customer:	(Around end of August)
Travel Agent:	(Flight from?)
Customer:	(Give preferred airport)
Travel Agent:	(For how long?)
Customer:	(Ten days)

Travel Agent: (One possibility – flight to Athens – give dates – hotel half board for 10 nights)

Customer: (Check cost and make booking)

Dialogue 9

Listen to the following four people talk about their departure dates and destinations, and take notes as you listen.

✍ Übung 16

Complete the gaps, based on the information you have heard in the recording:

1   _17 April_ is going to Rome.
2   Ute is going to _a Zurich_ on the _2_____ April.
3   Walter is flying to _15 Sept_ on the _____ of _Moscow_.
4   Sabine is flying to _France_ on the _fifteen_ October.

Text 2

Read the following account of Frau Wolff's holiday:

we went

Voriges Jahr waren wir zehn Tage in der Türkei, an der Küste. Das war für uns das erste Mal dort – normalerweise bleiben wir in Deutschland, oder wir fahren nach Frankreich zu unseren Bekannten in Paris. Das Wetter war wirklich heiß, und das Hotel war schön, ein großes Hotel direkt am Strand. Aber es war ein echter Horror-Urlaub. Der Flug (ein Charterflug) hatte sieben Stunden Verspätung. Vom Flughafen in der Türkei bis zum Hotel waren wir noch 3 Stunden im Bus. Wir haben also das Hotel um 5 Uhr Morgens erreicht, nach einer Fahrt von 16 Stunden. Wir waren beide total kaputt. Dann gab es noch ein Problem: neben dem Hotel war eine Baustelle. Es gab zu viel Lärm. Schlafen war unmöglich. Wir waren so froh, nach einer Woche wieder zu Hause zu sein.

Vocabulary

voriges	last	
das erste Mal	the first time	_echt._
Bekannte	friends, acquaintances	
kaputt	shattered, tired	
es gab	there was	
Baustelle	building site	

✍ Übung 17

Try to answer the questions in German, but if this is too difficult at this stage give answers in English.

1   Wo war diese Dame letztes Jahr auf Urlaub?
2   Wie lange war sie dort?
3   Wie war das Hotel?
4   Wie war das Wetter?
5   Wohin fährt sie normalerweise auf Urlaub?
6   Wie lange hat die Reise letztes Jahr gedauert?
7   Warum hat sie so wenig Schlaf gehabt?

Text 3

Read the following passage without using your dictionary. Read it several times to try to understand the main points. You will not be expected at this stage to be able to understand everything, but you will understand a surprising amount on careful reading.

Urlaub und Ihre Gesundheit

Endlich Urlaub – aber das ist allzu oft eine Gefahr für die Gesundheit. Für zwei oder drei Wochen keine Arbeit mehr!

Aber Vorsicht! – in den Tagen vor dem Urlaub haben Sie noch eine Menge Aufgaben (Urlaubseinkäufe machen; Koffer aus dem Dachboden oder dem Keller holen; einpacken, Nachbarn mitteilen; dass Sie wegfahren, und, und, und …)

Und wenn Sie endlich am Urlaubsziel sind, fühlen Sie sich schlapp, *weak* und werden manchmal *even* sogar krank. Kein Wunder, denn Pyschoanalytiker warnen: Man kann Angst, Kopfweh, Depressionen und sogar Herzrythmus-Störungen bekommen. Der Flug, ein anderes Klima und andere Nährung – alles kann unser Immunsystem belasten. Wir reagieren oft sehr *sensitive* empfindlich auf die Umstellung.

Zwei wichtige Tips für einen gesunden Urlaub:

- In der Woche vor dem Urlaub schalten Sie sich ab –keine Überstunden!
- Am Wochenende vor der Abreise nicht 1000 Dinge erledigen!

✍ **Übung 18**

After reading the text, give the German equivalent (with gender in the case of nouns) of the following English expressions:

departure	~~vorsicht~~ abfahrt	loft	Dachboden ✓
neighbour	Nachbarn ✓	flight	der Flug ✓
to inform	mitteilen ✓	overtime	Überstunden
food	Nährung ✓	healthy	Gesunden
climate	Klima ✓		
change (from one thing to another)	Umstellung (umsteigen)		

📚 ✍ Übung 19

Now look up the remaining words which you do not know. In the case of nouns, make a list of their plural and singular forms.

✍ Übung 20

Try to match the picture with the weather description:

1   Es schneit.
2   Es regnet.
3   Die Sonne scheint.
4   Es friert.
5   Es ist sehr windig.

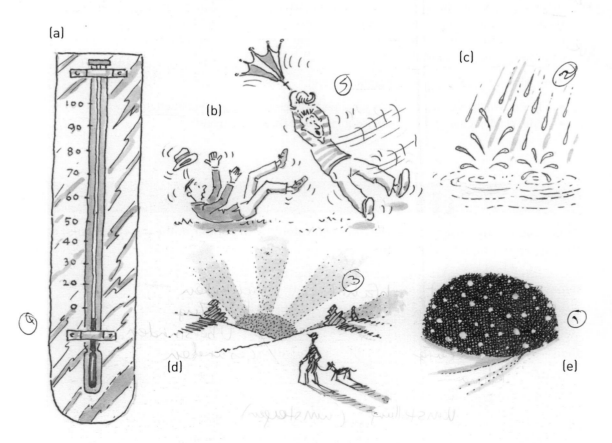

(a)

(b)

(c)

(d)

(e)

Text 4

Das Wetter

An der Ostsee bis zu acht Grad – im Süden kommt es örtlich zu Glatteis. Im Westen gibt es ein paar sonnige Stunden, und im Osten bleibt es trübe und bedeckt.

  Text 5

Wetterlage

Südbayern
Zu Tagesbeginn scheint noch die Sonne, später bilden sich immer mehr Wolken, und die Schauer- und Gewitterwahrscheinlichkeit steigt. 26 bis 28 Grad.

Aussichten
Der Montag beginnt freundlich, später ziehen Schauer und Gewitter heran. Am Dienstag wechselt sich Sonnenschein mit zahlreichen Wolken ab.

Wind
Der Wind wäht zunächst mäßig aus Südost. Später kommt er schwach aus Nordost.

Grammar

1. The perfect tense

If you re-read Dialogue B you will see that there are two new forms of the verb:

hast ... gemacht
habe ... gearbeitet

These are the perfect tenses of the verbs **machen** and **arbeiten**.

The perfect tense of regular, weak verbs in German is formed by using the present tense of **haben** together with the past participle:

We form the past participle by:

* Adding **ge-** to the beginning of the verb stem.
* Adding **(e)t** to the end.

For example:

Infinitive	Past participle
arbeiten (to work)	**gearbeitet**
machen (to do)	**gemacht**
sammeln (to collect)	**gesammelt**
stecken (to put in)	**gesteckt**
stellen (to put)	**gestellt**
kaufen (to buy)	**gekauft**
ich arbeite	I work
ich habe gearbeitet	I worked, I have worked
sie kauft	She buys
sie hat gekauft	She bought, has bought

Note that verbs which end in **-ieren** or which begin with:

be-
ent-
er-
ver-
zer-

do NOT add **ge-** to the stem to form the past participle:

studieren to study
Ich habe in Köln studiert

erreichen to reach, catch
Sie hat den Zug nicht erreicht

bestellen to order
Er hat ein Glas Wein bestellt

---

2. The genitive and dative cases

In the preceding chapter you have already met the accusative (and nominative) case.
German has two more cases: genitive and dative.

GENITIVE

Used to indicate *possession.*

The English expression 'the woman's book' (= 'the book of the woman') is rendered in
German by the use of the genitive case:

of the
Das Buch **der Frau**

Similarly,

the man's car = **der Wagen des Mannes**   *the car of the man*
the girl's lamp = **die Lampe des Mädchens**

DATIVE

Used to indicate the *indirect object*:

English: We give the newspaper *to the dog*. ('the dog' is the indirect object)
German: **Wir geben *dem Hund* die Zeitung.**

English: He gives the woman the ticket. (lit: gives the ticket to the woman)
German: **Er gibt der Frau die Fahrkarte.**

Note that if we have two German nouns together, the dative precedes the accusative.

3. Word order after dass

Dass is known in German as a 'subordinating conjunction'. After **dass**, the verb is placed at the end of the sentence:

Tina und Andrea gehen ins Kino. (Tina and Andrea go to the cinema)
Ich weiß, dass Tina und Andrea ins Kino gehen.

Du arbeitest im Supermarkt. (You work in the supermarket)
Ich weiß, dass du im Supermarkt arbeitest.

4. Adjective endings after the definite article (**der**, **die**, **das**)

So far in the course you will have noted that the adjectives have had various endings. They follow a set pattern, in accordance with:

*   what precedes them
*   the gender of the noun which follows them
*   the case of the noun which follows them
*   the 'number' of the noun which follows them (i.e. is it singular or plural).

The pattern is set out in the tables below:

SINGULAR

	Masculine	Feminine	Neuter
Nominative	**der rote Wagen**	**die neue Lampe**	**das alte Kino**
Accusative	**den roten Wagen**	**die neue Lampe**	**das alte Kino**
Genitive	**des roten Wagens**	**der neuen Lampe**	**des alten Kinos**
Dative	**dem roten Wagen**	**der neuen Lampe**	**dem alten Kino**

PLURAL

Nominative	**die neuen Häuser**
Accusative	**die neuen Häuser**
Genitive	**der neuen Häuser**
Dative	**den neuen Häusern**

5. Plurals of nouns

Nouns in German *tend* to follow a pattern in the plural form, but there are many exceptions to this rule, so the only safe method is to learn the plural at the same time as you learn the gender and meaning of a noun!

The 'standard' patterns are as follows:

MASCULINE NOUNS

Add an Umlaut to the vowel if possible, then add **-e**.

Plural

der Lohn (wage)	**die Löhne**
der Stuhl (chair)	**die Stühle**
der Tisch (table)	**die Tische**
der Vorhang (curtain)	**die Vorhänge**
der Bahnhof (station)	**die Bahnhöfe**
der Fluss (river)	**die Flüsse**

*Note that masculine nouns ending in **-n** or **-l** do not add **-e** in the plural:*

der Garten (garden)	**die Gärten**
der Sattel (saddle)	**die Sättel**

FEMININE NOUNS

Add **-(e)n**:

Plural

die Lampe (lamp)	**die Lampen**
die Torte (tart)	**die Torten**
die Frau (woman)	**die Frauen**
die Wohnung (flat)	**die Wohnungen**
die Diskette (floppy)	**die Disketten**
die Decke (ceiling)	**die Decken**

NEUTER NOUNS

Adds **-er** (and an Umlaut to the vowel if possible):

das Brett (board)	**die Bretter**
das Haus (house)	**die Häuser**
das Dach (roof)	**die Dächer**
das Tuch (cloth)	**die Tücher**

ɔ. Reflexive verbs

Many verbs in German are used reflexively – they imply an action done to oneself:

ich wasche mich	I wash (myself)
ich rasiere mich	I shave (myself)
ich ziehe mich um	I get changed
ich setze mich	I sit down (I seat myself)

The **mich** in these examples is the reflexive pronoun (in this case of **ich**).

The full range of reflexive pronouns is:

Personal pronoun		*Reflexive pronoun*
ich	I	**mich**
du	you	**dich**
er/sie/es	he/she/it	**sich**
wir	we	**uns**
ihr	you	**euch**
sie	they	**sich**
Sie	you	**sich**

Examples in use

ich setze mich
du setzst dich
er/sie/es setzt sich
wir setzen uns
ihr setzt euch
sie setzen sich
Sie setzen sich

A commonly heard example is:

Bitte setzen Sie sich!   Please take a seat!

Language in use

✍ Übung 21: perfect tense

Put the following sentences into the perfect tense:

Example

1   Ulli hat heute abend gearbeitet.

1   Ulli arbeitet heute abend.   *house jobs*
2   Walter macht seine Hausaufgaben nach 10 Uhr.   *Walter hat s.*
3   Annie und Tina spielen am Samstag Tennis.
4   Wir wohnen bis September in der Klarastraße.   *earn*
5   Tina verdient nicht viel Geld im Supermarkt.
6   Das Eis mit Sahne kostet nur 2 Euro.

✐ Übung 22: perfect tense

Complete each of the following sentences with the appropriate form of the given verb:

Example

Am Samstag haben wir beide bis 9 Uhr _____ (arbeiten)
Am Samstag haben wir beide bis 9 Uhr *gearbeitet*.

Tip: be particularly careful with numbers 2 and 6!

                                                          to prepare
1   Anton hat das Abendessen schon *bereitet* (bereiten)
2   Tina hat im Hotel ein Einzelzimmer *reserviert* (reservieren)
3   Johann hat seine Prüfungen schon *gemacht* (machen)
4   Der Supermarkt hat am Samstag um 8 Uhr *geöffnet* (öffnen) *?*
5   Ich habe das Auto schon *verkauft* (verkaufen)
6   Tinas Vater hat an der Universität Heidelberg *studiert* (studieren)

✐ Übung 23: perfect tense   *Me - to do*

Using the vocabulary from this and earlier chapters, write 10 sentences in the perfect tense.

                     to do.

✐ Übung 24: word order

Insert **Ich weiß, dass** at the start of each of the following sentences, and rearrange the word order to make it correct.

                In order know that

Example
Deine Mutter arbeitet in der Stadtmitte.
Ich weiß, dass deine Mutter in der Stadtmitte arbeitet.

                                              Dass
1   Ursula spielt jeden Samstag Tennis.   *Ich weiss, dass Ursula in*
2   Markus fährt jeden Sommer nach Spanien.   *Samstag tennis spielt*
                                                        spielen

Ich weiß, dass Markus in Sommer nach Spanien fährt.

3   Wolfgang geht nicht so oft ins Kino. *Ich weiß, dass Wolfgang ins Kino nicht geht.*
4   Er geht gerne ins Theater. *Ich weiß, dass er gerne ins Theatre geht.*
5   Tina hat ihre Prüfungen schon gemacht. *Dass, Tina ihre Prü" gemacht hat!*
6   Das ist nicht sein Auto. *Ich weiß, dass es nicht sein Auto nicht.*
7   Sie wohnt jetzt in Stuttgart.
8   Er studiert Philosophie in Freiburg.
9   Sie möchte hier bleiben.
10   Sie suchen eine neue Wohnung.

✎ Übung 25: adjective endings

You might find it necessary to refer to the table in the **Grammar** section when completing the first few of these. You will find that you have to rely on this less and less as you get more practice.

Insert the appropriate adjective endings in each of the following sentences:

1   Wir haben gestern den neu_en_ Wagen gekauft.
2   Mein Bruder arbeitet in dem groß_en_ Geschäft neben dem Bahnhof.
3   Wo ist meine Jacke? Auf dem rot_en_ Stuhl.
4   Der alt_e_ Computer funktioniert nicht mehr.
5   Hast du das neu_e_ Buch über Südafrika gelesen?
6   Ich weiß, dass das klein_e_ Chinarestaurant in der Hauptstraße sehr gut ist.
7   Viele Deutsche fahren jedes Jahr mit dem eigen_en_ Auto in Urlaub.
8   Wollen Sie den rot_en_ Bleistift?

✎ Übung 26

NOUN PLURALS

Using your dictionaries if necessary, give the gender, and the plural, of the following nouns:

das	Buch	das	Radio	das	Bett	das	Auto
die	Straße	der	Bleistift (m)		Regenschirm	der	Wagen
der	Computer	der	Zug	das	Maus	die	Uhr
der	Apparat	der	Flug	die	Jacke	der	Bildschirm (screen)
das	Gerät	der	Sessel	der	Haus	der	Hose

bettdecke – blanket
bettuch – sheet
umbrella

✍ Übung 27

NOUN AND VERB PLURALS

Rewrite the following sentences in the plural: *[handwritten] 1*

1 Die Flasche ist leer. — *[handwritten] Die Flaschen sind leer (empty).*
2 Das Radio ist auf dem Tisch. *[handwritten] Die Radios sind auf dem Tisch*
3 Die Jacke ist blau. *[handwritten] Die Jacken sind blauen (blauen)*
4 Das Auto ist neu. *[handwritten] Die Autos(er?) sind neuen*
5 Die Dame kauft die Zeitung. *[handwritten] Die Damen kaufen die Zeitungen*
6 Der Junge kauft die Zeitschrift. *[handwritten] Die Jungen kaufen die Zeitschrift (magazine)*
7 Das Buch ist nicht sehr interessant. *[handwritten] Die Bücher sind nicht sehr interessant.*

📖 ✍ Übung 28

USE OF CASES

Read the following sentences very carefully, and in the table which follows each one indicate which component is in which case.

[handwritten] NOM = subject of verb
ACC = Direct obj. of verb
GEN = possession
DAT = Indirect object of a verb

Example
Der Mann sieht den Hund.

Nominative	Accusative	Genitive	Dative
der Mann	den Hund		

1 Wir kaufen den Wagen morgen. *[handwritten] We buy / the car / in the morning*

Nominative	Accusative	Genitive	Dative
Wir (kaufen)	den morgen		morgen

2 Der Verkäufer gibt der Dame die Zeitung. *[handwritten] The shopseller gives the lady the newspaper*
[handwritten] (Direct) (Indirect)

Nominative	Accusative	Genitive	Dative
Der Verkaufer	der Dame		die Zeitung

3. Die Werkstatt repariert den Wagen des Mannes. *[handwritten] The garage repairs the cars of men.*

Nominative	Accusative	Genitive	Dative
Die Werkstatt	den Wagen	des Mannes	des Mannes

[handwritten] Garage (workshop).

4. Walter verpasst den Zug und kauft eine Zeitung.

(missed) (train not plane) (equal.)

Nominative	Accusative	Genitive	Dative
Walter	den Zug		eine Zeitung

5. Die Leiterin der Firma gibt den Arbeitern eine Lohnerhöhung. (This is a difficult one!)

the Leader (of the firm) gives (the workers) a payrise

pay rise

workers are subject of verb (?)

Nominative	Accusative	Genitive der Firma	Dative den Arbeitern
den Arbeitern		Die Leiterin	eine Lohnerhöhung.

Die Leiterin.

Test your knowledge

🎙 ✍ Übung 29

Give suitable responses to these questions:

1 Wie komme ich bitte zum Theater? *Ich komme mit dem Bus.*
2 Ist es weit von hier? *Nein, Es ist nicht weit von hier.*
3 Wann ist der nächste Zug nach Saarbrücken? *Der nächste Zug ist am 10 uhr.*
4 Wann kommt er an? *Er kommt in 30 minuten an.*
5 Fährt der Zug direkt? *Jah*

Par

📚 Übung 30

What do the following mean?

1 eine einfache Fahrkarte – *one way ticket*
2 das Gleis – *platform*
3 Nichtraucher – *non smoking*
4 umsteigen – *get down/ change flights*
5 die Ankunft – *arrival*
6 planmäßig *Scheduled*
7 dringend – *urgent*

✍ 🎙 Übung 31

Give the German for:

1 luggage *der Koffer*
2 station *der bahnhof*

3   supermarket   *der Supermarkt*
4   cinema   *Kino*
5   the second street on the left   *die zweiten strasse zum links*
6   the third street on the right   *die dritten strasse zum links*
7   I am a stranger here   *Ich bin Ausländer hier*
8   I don't know my way around
9   straight on – *geradeaus*
10 next to – *neben*
11 lunch – *Mittagspause*
12 Singapore
13 to check in
14 boarding card – *die Bordkarte*
15 delay *die Verspätung*

fremd
auskennen – to know way around.
Ich kenne mich nicht aus.

✎ Übung 32

Fill the gaps with words from the list:

1   Ich _____ bitte einen Kaffee.
2   Er _____ nicht hier bleiben.
3   Wir _____ gleich fahren.
4   Ich _____ das nicht verstehen!
5   _____ Sie noch länger bleiben?

---

darf   müssen   wollen   möchte   kann

✎ Übung 33

Give the German equivalent of the following:

probably		Greece	
to watch TV		approximately	
to telephone		to meet	
flowers		tired	
to inform someone		shop	
piano		demand for sth.	

✍ Übung 34

Put the following sentences into the perfect tense:

1   Ich reserviere zwei Einzelzimmer.
2   Jeden Abend spielt Angela Klavier.
3   Ich besuche ihn am Samstag.
4   Steffi arbeitet von Freitag bis Sonntag in dem Geschäft.
5   Sie mieten ein Auto.
6   Wir besuchen die kleinen Dörfer in den Bergen.
7   Die Familie Wolff wohnt in der Bergstraße.
8   Meine Mutter bestellt ein Glas Wein.
9   Ich reserviere einen Tisch im China-Restaurant.
10 Am Montag kauft sie eine neue Jacke.

✍ Übung 35

Give suitable German equivalents of the following statements:

1   Where do you go on holiday?
2   What do you do in your free time?
3   She works every Saturday in the supermarket.
4   I worked there last year.
5   Wolfgang has worked there since Monday.
6   We are going to Spain this year.

✍ Übung 36

Using the language you have learned so far, write a brief essay (100–150 words) about yourself and your leisure pursuits. This can all be written mainly in the present tense, but try to use the perfect tense whenever you can.

Unit 5
Ein Einzelzimmer, bitte!

TOPICS	• Hotel accommodation
	• Ordering food and drink
GRAMMAR	• Use of prepositions
	• Adjective endings (indefinite article)

🎧 📖 Dialogue 1

IM HOTEL

Frau Kramer books two rooms.

Empfangsdame:	Guten Abend.
Frau Kramer:	n'Abend. Haben Sie bitte zwei Einzelzimmer frei?
Empfangsdame:	Für heute Abend?
Frau Kramer:	Ja, ich brauche ein Zimmer gleich – für mich – und meine Kollegin kommt gegen 20.00 Uhr an.
Empfangsdame:	Verstehe, einen Moment bitte. Ja – zwei Zimmer haben wir – beide mit Bad und Dusche.
Frau Kramer:	Und der Zimmerpreis?
Empfangsdame:	Pro Zimmer 210 Euro – einschließlich Frühstück.
Frau Kramer:	Gut – dann nehme ich die, bitte.
Empfangsdame:	Und auf welchen Namen?
Frau Kramer:	Mein Name ist Kramer – und meine Kollegin heißt Dietrich – Ulrike Dietrich.
Empfangsdame:	So, ich brauche bitte Ihre Kreditkarte, Frau Kramer.
Frau Kramer:	Bitte. (*Hands her the credit card*)
Empfangsdame:	Moment bitte. So, danke. (*Gives her the card back.*) Also Frau Kramer, da ist Ihr Zimmerschlüssel – Zimmer 248 auf der zweiten Etage. Den Aufzug finden Sie hier links. Und Zimmer 250 ist für Ihre Kollegin reserviert.
Frau Kramer:	Danke schön.
Empfangsdame:	Bitte sehr. Und schönen Abend noch!

Vocabulary

das Einzelzimmer	single room
gleich	straight away
die Kollegin	colleague
die Dusche	shower
einschließlich	including
das Früstück	breakfast
auf welchen Namen?	in what name?
der Schlüssel	key
der Aufzug	lift
schönen Abend noch!	have a good evening!

ausschließlich – exclusive

modisch (fashionable)

altmodisch (un ").

✍ Übung 1

1   What booking does Frau Kramer want to make?
2   What sort of rooms are available?
3   What is included in the price?
4   When is Frau Dietrich arriving?
5   Where is the lift?

  Dialogue 2

IM HOTEL

An hour later.

Empfangschef: Guten Abend!
Frau Dietrich: Ja, guten Abend. Ich glaube meine Kollegin, Frau Kramer, ist
                 schon im Hotel?
Empfangschef: Sekunde bitte – ja – sie ist im Zimmer 248.

Frau Dietrich:	Und sie hat auch ein Zimmer für mich reserviert? – Mein Name ist Dietrich.
Empfangschef:	Ja, Frau Dietrich. Ist schon reserviert. Zimmer 250 – zweite Etage. Und das ist Ihr Schlüssel.
Frau Dietrich:	Vielen Dank. Noch eine Frage bitte?
Empfangschef:	Ja?
Frau Dietrich:	Mein Auto ist jetzt vor dem Hotel – wo finde ich den Parkplatz?
Empfangschef:	Das Hotel hat eine Tiefgarage. Gehen Sie gleich rechts, wieder rechts, und Sie finden die Einfahrt. Brauchen Sie Hilfe mit dem Gepäck?
Frau Dietrich:	Danke, nein – ich habe nur eine kleine Reisetasche.

Vocabulary

Sekunde	just a second
der Parkplatz	car park
die Tiefgarage	underground car park
die Einfahrt	entrance
das Gepäck	luggage
die Reisetasche	hold-all, travel bag

Language note

1 **eine kleine Reisetasche** – note the ending of the adjective. Adjectives take slightly different endings after the indefinite article (**ein, eine**, etc.). See the **Grammar** section for more information on this.

2 **vor dem Hotel** – 'in front of the hotel'. This is the use of the *dative* (**dem** Hotel) after the preposition to indicate the location of something.

3 **die Einfahrt** – entrance (for vehicles – from 'fahren'). An entrance for 'humans' would normally be 'der Eingang' (from 'gehen'). German is often wonderfully logical!

✍ Übung 2

Match up the two halves of the sentences:

Frau Kramer ist	die Einfahrt zur Tiefgarage
Frau Dietrich kommt	sagt 'Guten Abend'
Frau Dietrich sucht	hat einen Parkplatz
Das Hotel	im Zimmer 250
Der Empfangsherr	arbeiten zusammen
Die beiden Frauen	etwas später an, als ihre Kollegin

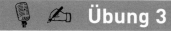 ## Übung 3

In welchem Zimmer – und in welcher Etage – sind Anton und seine Freunde?

 ## Übung 4

How do you say in German?

1   I would like a single room
2   Where is the car park?
3   When is breakfast?
4   Including breakfast
5   Room with shower

Übung 5

ROLE-PLAY

With a partner carry out the following role-play. You will need to do some preparatory work on the vocabulary first. After the first attempt, swap roles and run through the exercise again.

Receptionist	Guest
Greet	Need double room
For how long?	Two or three nights
Double room available	Bath or shower?
Yes – and with TV	Cost?
Give price	Agree to take room
Give room number and keys	

🛏 Hotel Bienenstock – Schubertallee 27 – 8000 München

'das gemütliche Hotel in der Stadtmitte'

(nur 500 Meter vom Bahnhof)

Im Familienbesitz seit 1951. 40 geschmackvoll eingerichtete Zimmer, alle mit Bad/ Dusche/WC und TV. Bar und intimes Restaurant mit erstklassiger Küche. Echt bayerische Spezialitäten. Parkplatz für 20 Autos nebenan.

Halb- oder Vollpension möglich.

Tarif
(alle Preise einschließlich Zimmer und Frühstück)

Einzelzimmer	140
Doppelzimmer	220
Kinder (bis zu 10 Jahren) im Zimmer der Eltern	frei.

(Preise schließen Bedienung und Mehrwertsteuer ein)

  ## Übung 6

Try to answer the questions before looking at the vocabulary list, to see how much information you can get from the advert.

1   What is the location of the hotel?
2   What do you know about the history of the hotel?
3   Give details of the facilities in the rooms.
4   What are we told about the possibilities for dining at the hotel?
5   What are the parking facilities?

Vocabulary

gemütlich	cosy
der Besitz	ownership, possession
geschmackvoll	tastefully
eingerichtet	equipped, furnished
nebenan	neighbouring, next door
echt	genuine
die Bedienung	service
die Mehrwertsteuer	VAT

 Gasthaus Schlick (garni)

Liebigstrasse 28

Gießen

Direkt am Bahnhof

- Familienbetrieb
- Günstig gelegen
- Alle Zimmer mit Dusche/Farbfernseher/Telefon
- Reichhaltiges Frühstücksbuffet

☕ Hotel Seeblick

Wemmetsweiler

in der Vulkaneifel

das Luxus-Hotel für den Feinschmecker

Hallen- und Freibad (beheizt)

Sauna und Solarium

Terrasse

Erstklassiges Restaurant mit internationaler Küche

Weinstube

Wochenend-Angebote zu Ostern und Weihnachten (Kinderermäßigung)

Silvester-Feier mit Sektempfang, Gala-Büfett und Tanz

Luxus-Appartements für Familien

Language note

Seeblick would translate as 'lake view' not 'sea view' – **See** can mean either lake or sea in German:

die See   sea
der See   lake

  ## Übung 7

Read the adverts for the **Schlick**, **Bienenstock** and **Seeblick** hotels, and find the German expressions for:

English	German
cuisine	
connoisseur	
situated	
Easter	
breakfast buffet	
indoor pool	
reduction	
heated	
offer	
colour TV	
view	
beehive	
lake	

 ## Übung 8

Read the following travel brochure descriptions of two hotels, and list the key features of each.

or

If you prefer (and this is a more difficult exercise) you can listen to the recorded version, and then check the written version later.

Text 1

Das Hotel Adria liegt an einem langen feinen Sandstrand, etwa 8 Kilometer von der Stadtmitte. Es hat 250 schön ausgestatte Zimmer auf 4 Etagen. Das Hotel bietet Ihnen drei Spezialitätenrestaurants: türkisch, italienisch und französisch. Es hat ein grosses Freibad und ein Kinderbecken, und Sonnenterrassen mit Liegen und Sonnenschirmen. Für Sportfreunde gibt es vier Tennisplätze, Wasserski, Bananaboot, und Verleih von Mountainbikes.

Das Hotel Medklub ist im Familienbesitz seit 50 Jahren. Es liegt direkt am Strand – zum Stadtzentrum sind es etwa 4 Kilometer. Alle Zimmer haben Telefon, Klimaanlage, Farbfernseher, Bad/WC, und Minikühlschrank. Die meisten haben Balkon oder Terrasse. Zur Unterhaltung bieten wir unseren Gästen Shows, Cabarett und auch Sprachkurse. Das Hotel hat 6 Tennishartplätze, zwei Pools (beide mit Kinderbecken) und einen 9-Loch Golfplatz.

 Übung 9

Working with a partner in class, create a simple advert in German for a hotel, listing the main features. You will find the vocabulary from the adverts you have already seen very useful.

 Übung 10

Role-plays: hotel bookings

With a partner use the following outlines for work in pairs. In all cases start and end the exchange appropriately, and ensure that the price is given and agreed.

1   Visitor: Wants a single room for one week. Must have colour TV. Needs a car park also.   *Könten wir — können wir .*
    Receptionist: Only double rooms left – but can have one for 150 Euros. All rooms have colour TV. Car park is 800 yards away.

2   Visitor: Two rooms – one single, one double, for family of three. Wants dinner if possible (does hotel have restaurant?). Needs early breakfast (6.00). Staying for 4 nights.
    Receptionist: Two rooms okay – but one on second floor, one on fourth floor. No hotel restaurant, but there is one (very good!!) next door. Breakfast from 05.30–09.00 daily.

3   Visitor: Two rooms for tonight – one for self, other for colleague arriving later
    – possibly after midnight. No breakfast – have to leave 5a.m. next morning.
    Receptionist: No problem with rooms. One on first floor, one on third. Name of
    colleague? Can have cold breakfast if they wish – at 4.30.

  ## Dialogue 3

Frau Kramer and Frau Dietrich are in the restaurant. Frau Kramer is already seated,
Frau Dietrich is just arriving.

Frau Kramer:	Guten Abend Ulrike! Wie war die Reise?
Frau Dietrich:	Danke, ja – eine kleine Verspätung in Düsseldorf, aber kein Problem.
Frau Kramer:	Was trinkst du?
Frau Dietrich:	Ich möchte bitte einen Rotwein.
Frau Kramer:	Herr Ober!
Kellner:	Ja, bitte schön?
Frau Kramer:	Ein Glas Rotwein – Spätburgunder, bitte.
Kellner:	Gerne.

Language note

1   **Herr Ober** – a common and polite way to address a waiter in German. The word
    for waiter is **der Kellner**, but you would never address the waiter as **Kellner**.
2   Note that the two ladies use **Du** when speaking to each other – they are work
    colleagues, but also personal friends. In a standard business context – where
    for example colleagues might have worked together for many years in the same
    office, but are not friends outside of work, **Sie** would be preferred.

  ## Dialogue 4

They order food.

Frau Kramer:	Also Doris, was möchtest du essen?
Frau Dietrich:	Ich glaube, ich nehme die Scholle – und du?
Frau Kramer:	Fisch mag ich eigentlich nicht – ich nehme das Putensteak.
Kellner:	So, Rotwein. Und zum Essen?
Frau Kramer:	Das Putensteak für mich, bitte.
Kellner:	Und dazu? – Salat, Pommes, Gemüse?
Frau Kramer:	Nur einen kleinen Salat bitte.
Frau Dietrich:	Ich möchte bitte die Scholle – mit Pommes Frites.

Vocabulary

der Fisch	fish
die Scholle	plaice
ich nehme	I take (= I'll have)
das Putensteak	turkey steak
zum Essen?	to eat?
und dazu?	and with that?
das Gemüse	vegetables
Pommes (= **Pommes Frites**)	chips

 Dialogue 5

Twenty minutes later.
(The food arrives!)

Kellner:	So, einmal Putensteak, und einmal Scholle.
Frau Kramer/Frau Dietrich:	Danke schön.
Kellner:	Salat und Pommes hole ich gleich …
Frau Kramer/Frau Dietrich:	Danke sehr.
Kellner:	Bitte sehr. Guten Appetit!

Vocabulary

Einmal …	one …
holen	to bring
guten Appetit!	enjoy your meal!

Language note

1 **einmal Putensteak** – literally 'once turkey steak'. **Einmal, zweimal** etc. are widely used in this context
2 **guten Appetit!** – like many other nationalities, Germans are more 'polite' than the British in terms of commencing meals. An alternative, used more informally, is **Mahlzeit!** (**die Mahlzeit** = 'meal').

  Dialogue 6

Getting the bill.

Kellner:	So, hat's geschmeckt?
Frau Kramer:	Ja, es war sehr gut, danke.

113

Möchten Sie einen Nachtisch?

...er: Nein, danke – wir möchten bitte zahlen.

Ja, sofort.

.guage note

1 **hat's geschmeckt** – 'did you like it, did it taste good'. 'Did you enjoy your meal?'
2 **wir möchten bitte zahlen** – 'we would like to pay'. You can also say:

die Rechnung, bitte ('the bill, please')
or
zahlen, bitte.

3 **sofort** = 'at once'.

✍ Übung 11

Fill the gaps with one of the given words:

mag	**isst**	**Putensteak**	**später**	**schon**	**trinken**

1 Frau Kramer ist _____ im Restaurant.
2 Sie _____ Fisch nicht.
3 Frau Dietrich kommt etwas _____ an.
4 Sie _____ beide Weißwein.
5 Mit ihrem _____ hat Frau Kramer einen kleinen Salat.
6 Frau Dietrich _____ Pommes Frites.

Other useful expressions

die Rechnung bitte	the bill please!
zahlen, bitte	the bill please!
Mahlzeit!	bon appetit (more colloquial)
das Fleisch	meat
das Obst	fruit
die Vorspeise	starter
der Nachtisch/die Nachspeise	dessert
der gemischte Salat	mixed salad
durch (or **durchgebraten**)	well done (steak, meat)
das Rindfleisch	beef
das Lammfleisch	lamb

geldtasche/porte monraie.

- handtasche   - gepäck
- etui makeup bag

Plaste tüte - plastic bags (+chips)
ice tüte
Beutel - bag. - koffer

das Schweinefleisch	pork
das Kalbfleisch	veal

Note: eating habits in Germany

Most Germans will take their main evening meal (**Abendessen**) between 6 and 7 in the evening, but for many this consists of a selection of cold meat, cheeses and bread (called **der Aufschnitt**), since they will have eaten a hot meal at lunchtime (**Mittagessen**). Germans are also inveterate 'snackers', and a bewildering variety of hot and cold food outlets can be found on all city centre streets, ranging from simple 'hotdogs' (much bigger than the English equivalent) to more elaborate stews or stirfries.

The Germans are not, however, 'big' on after-meal desserts, and the dessert menu in standard German restaurants is quite restricted. Instead, a very civilised custom is that of mid-afternoon **Kaffee und Kuchen** ('coffee and cake') taken in a café or the cafeteria/restaurant of the larger department stores. Even the smallest German town is likely to have its café (often linked to a family-run bakery/pastry outlet) – with very comfortable and plush fittings.

Food and the preparation and serving of it is a serious business in Germany, and it takes several years to train as a fully qualified baker (**Bäcker**) or confectioner (**Konditor**).

The downside of all this is that the German diet is not without its health consequences, and there are real concerns about the high fat/high cholesterol intake. **Kreislaufstörung** ('circulatory disease') is a commonly reported ailment.

Snacking!

die Bäckerei	bakery
die Konditorei	confectioners (cakes and sweets)
die Imbiss-Stube	snack bar, stand
der Imbiss	snack
die Wurst	sausage
die Currywurst	sausage (in curry sauce)
das Gulasch	stew
das Wurstbrot	roll with sliced cold sausage
das Käsebrot	cheese roll

 ## Übung 12

Using the vocabulary you have met, and your dictionary, compose a simple restaurant menu, ensuring that you include starters, and fish and meat dishes.

Übung 13

Making use of a suitable search engine on the web, see if you can list some of the main wine-producing areas of Germany, and some of the wines produced.

Text 2: Rezept

Eier mit Mangochutney und Curryjogurt

Zutaten:
- zwei Eier
- ein kleiner Becher Naturjogurt
- Pfeffer
- Salz
- zwei Teelöffel Currypulver
- zwei Teelöffel Mangochutney

Zubereitung:

Den Jogurt mit dem Currypulver und einer Prise Pfeffer verrühren. Die Eier acht bis zehn Minuten hart kochen. Dann die Schalen entfernen und die Eier in Scheiben schneiden. Die Eierscheiben unter den Curryjogurt mischen. Eine kleine Schlüssel mit dem Salatblatt auslegen, Eier einfüllen und Mangochutney darüber geben.

Text 3: Rezept

Nudelsalat

Zutaten:

250 g Farfalle
120 g Paprikasalami
3 Tomaten
1 rote Paprika
1 gelbe Paprika
1 rote Chillischote
1 Zwiebel
1 Knoblauchzehe
150 g Feta
80 g schwarze Oliven (ohne Stein)
4 Esslöffel Rotweinessig
6 Esslöffel Öl
1 Teelöffel Honig
1 Teelöffel Paprika (mild)
1 Teelöffel Oregano
Salz
Pfeffer

Zubereitung:

Farfalle bissfest garen und abgießen. Salami in Würfeln schneiden. Paprika waschen und in schmale Streifen schneiden.

Chilischote halbieren, entkernen und fein hacken. Zwiebel in Ringe, Knoblauch in Stücke schneiden. Oliven halbieren. Aus Essig, Öl, Honig, Paprika, Oregano, Salz und Pfeffer eine Soße rühren. Zutaten mischen, und mit Feta bestreuen.

 Übung 14

In the recipes above, see if you can spot the German equivalent of:

chop up	ingredients	stir, mix	slices
'de-seed'	clove of garlic	'al dente'	cut
strips	honey	vinegar	drain
remove	shell	egg	boil

🔍 Grammar

1. Prepositions

In German a noun or a pronoun following a preposition has to be in a particular case (accusative, genitive or dative).

The following prepositions are always used with the *accusative*:

bis	until
durch	through
entlang	along
für	for
gegen	against (in time: about)
ohne	without
um	around

Examples

Wir gehen durch den Park.	We go through the park.
Er geht ohne mich in die Stadt.	He goes into town without me.

This group is always used with the *dative*:

aus	out, out of
außer	except
bei	with, by
entgegen	against
gegenüber	opposite
mit	with
nach	after
seit	since
von	by, from
zu	to

Examples

Sie kommt aus dem Kino.	She comes out of the cinema.
Er schreibt mit dem Bleistift.	He writes with the pencil.

2. Expression of 'place' or 'movement'

Certain prepositions (e.g. **in** and **auf**) can take either the accusative or the dative case.

To express *movement* to/into a place, the *accusative* is used:

er geht in *das* Kino	he goes into the cinema
wir gehen in *das* Büro	we go into the office
sie geht in *das* Zimmer	she goes into the room
sie stellt das Buch auf *den* Tisch	she puts the book on the table
er steckt das Geld in *die* Tasche	he puts the money in his pocket

To express *location*, the *dative* is used:

er ist in *dem* Kino	he is in the cinema
wir sind in *dem* Büro	we are in the office
sie ist in *dem* Zimmer	she is in the room
das Buch ist auf *dem* Tisch	the book is on the table
das Geld ist in *der* Tasche	the money is in the (his) pocket

3. Abbreviations with prepositions

in, **an** and **zu** + the definite article are often abbreviated:

in das Hotel > ins Hotel
in dem Hotel > im Hotel
an dem Bahnhof > am Bahnhof
zu dem Supermarkt > zum Supermarkt
zu der Haltestelle > zur Haltestelle

4. Adjective endings after the indefinite article

After the indefinite article (**ein**, **eine**), the adjective which precedes the noun takes specific endings depending on the gender, number and case.

The full list of endings is given below:

SINGULAR

	Masculine	Feminine	Neuter
Nominative	ein guter Wein	eine gute Lampe	ein gutes Auto
Accusative	einen guten Wein	eine gute Lampe	ein gutes Auto
Genitive	eines guten Weins	einer guten Lampe	eines guten Autos
Dative	einem guten Wein	einer guten Lampe	einem guten Auto

PLURAL (SAME FOR ALL GENDERS)

Nominative	keine guten Weine
Accusative	keine guten Weine
Genitive	keiner guten Weine
Dative	keinen guten Weinen

*Note the **en** on the end of the noun in the dative plural.*

Language in use

✎ Übung 15

PREPOSITIONS WITH THE ACCUSATIVE

Insert the appropriate preposition from the table:

bis   für   durch   ohne   um   gegen

1   Wir haben _____ 9 Uhr gewartet.
2   Ich weiß nicht den genauen Preis, aber er liegt _____ 120 Euro.
3   Wir müssen _____ die Stadtmitte fahren.
4   Ich glaube, er trifft uns _____ 9 Uhr.
5   Ich kann _____ den Computer nicht arbeiten!
6   Hast du das Geschenk _____ mich gekauft?
7   Wir fahren nur _____ München.
8   Er geht schnell _____ die Ecke.
9   Ich habe eigentlich nichts _____ ihn.
10   _____ wieviel Uhr kommt sie an?
11   _____ diesen Torwart spielt die Mannschaft schlecht.

✎ Übung 16

PREPOSITIONS WITH THE DATIVE

Insert the correct form of the definite article. (*Note: You will also sometimes have to abbreviate* **zu der** *to* **zur**, *etc.*)

1   Er fährt mit _____ Taxi zu _____ Arbeit, weil es schon 8 Uhr ist.

2   Sie sitzt in _____ Zimmer und spielt mit _____ Katze.
3   Sie kommt erst nach 9 Uhr aus _____ Theater.
4   Frau Walter arbeitet bei _____ großen Unternehmen gegebüber _____ Bahnhof.
5   Der Intercity nach Köln fährt gleich ab. Vorsicht bei _____ Abfahrt!
6   Sie müssen gleich zu _____ Lebensmittelabteilung gehen.
7   Er kommt aus _____ Aufzug.
8   Klaus ist sehr faul. Er sieht ständig aus _____ Fenster.
9   Außer _____ Leiterin sind alle Kollegen hier neu.
10 Ich komme gleich von _____ Basketballspiel.
11 Seit _____ Examen bin ich sehr müde.
12 Ich glaube, wir bleiben heute in _____ Hotel.

✐ Übung 17

PREPOSITIONS

Make as many sentences as you can by using the prepositions and verbs in the boxes – and make sure that the nouns are in the correct case.

| mit   aus   von   zu   ohne   durch   für   um |

| treffen   arbeiten   gehen   kommen   bleiben   essen   sitzen   spielen |

✐ Übung 18

ACCUSATIVE OR DATIVE?

Complete the gaps with a suitable preposition, and the definite article in the correct case:

1   Maine Jacke ist _____ _____ Bett.
2   Das Auto fährt _____ _____ Garage
3   Er liest einen Artikel _____ _____ Abendzeitung.
4   Sie stellt die Tasse _____ _____ Tisch.
5   Meine Oma wohnt _____ _____ Schillerstraße.
6   Antworten Sie bitte _____ _____ Frage!
7   Das Haus liegt oben _____ _____ Hügel.

8 Doris sitzt _____ _____ Wohnzimmer.
9 Ich kann ihn nicht sehen. Er steht _____ _____ Mauer.
10 Wo ist denn mein Koffer? Dort _____ _____ Fenster.

✐ Übung 19

ADJECTIVE ENDINGS

Fill in the gaps with the appropriate adjective ending:

1 Ein klein___ Hund
2 Ein gut___ Freund
3 Ein alt___ Bier
4 Ein klein___ Haus
5 Eine alt___ Dame
6 Eine klein___ Küche
7 Er kauft einen neu___ Pullover.
8 Sie liest eine alt___ Zeitung
9 Ich möchte bitte ein kalt___ Bier!
10 Er sitzt in einem dunkl___ Zimmer
11 Sie wohnen in einem groß___ Haus
12 Sie hat einen neu___ Computer.
13 Ich kenne keine gut___ Filme.
14 Ein braun___ Hund sitzt vor dem Haus.

✐ Übung 20

Complete each sentence with a suitable adjective from the box, and ensure that the adjective is in the correct form:

> **blau   klein   kalt   neu   alt   best**

1 Einen _____ Wagen kann man sehr billig kaufen.
2 Die _____ Weine kommen aus Frankreich.
3 Ich möchte bitte ein _____ Bier!
4 Ich mag das _____ Hemd nicht.
5 Die _____ Häuser sind sehr schön.
6 Er kauft heute eine _____ Jacke.

Unit 6
Fitness und Gesundheit

TOPICS
- How to describe your state of health
- Some current health trends in Germany

GRAMMAR
- Perfect tense of strong verbs
- Relative pronouns

TEST YOUR KNOWLEDGE

Dialogue 1

AT THE DOCTOR'S

Marcus has got up late today as he doesn't feel at all well. He goes to the doctor's surgery.

Marcus: Guten Tag, Frau Doktor.
Ärztin: Guten Tag, Herr Feldbach. Also, was fehlt Ihnen?
Marcus: Ich habe Fieber, und mein Hals tut weh.
Ärztin: Seit wann?
Marcus: Seit gestern.
Ärztin: Was haben Sie gestern gegessen?
Marcus: Nicht viel – zum Frühstück Muesli, zu Mittag ein Käsebrot, und am Abend Steak mit Pommes.
Ärztin: Haben Sie auch Husten?
Marcus: Nein, Husten habe ich nicht.
Ärztin: Haben Sie Ohrenschmerzen?
Marcus: Die Ohren – ja, ein bißchen.
Ärztin: So, ich möchte zuerst Fieber messen, und dann den Hals untersuchen.

Vocabulary

was fehlt Ihnen?	what's wrong?
ich habe Fieber	I feel hot, have a temperature
der Hals	throat, neck
tut weh	hurts
Husten	cough
die Ohren	ears

Language note

was haben Sie gestern gegessen? – 'what did you eat yesterday?'. This is the *perfect* tense of a *strong* verb. Strong verbs change their vowel when forming different tenses, and the *past participle* (here: **gegessen**) ends in **-en** rather than **-t** or **-et**.

  Dialogue 2

A few minutes later.

Ärztin:	Also, ich glaube, Sie haben eine Halsentzündung. Sind Sie gegen Penizillin allergisch?
Marcus:	Ich glaube nicht.
Ärztin:	So, dann verschreibe ich Antibiotika – Sie müssen die Tabletten zweimal am Tag nehmen – gleich nach dem Essen. Und wenn möglich, viel Wasser trinken!
Marcus:	Danke sehr, Frau Doktor.
Ärztin:	Nichts zu danken – auf Wiedersehen.
Marcus:	Wiederschauen.

Vocabulary

die Halsentzündung	throat infection, inflammation
verschreiben	to prescribe
zweimal am Tag	twice per day

  ## Übung 1

1   What are Marcus's symptoms?
2   What is the diagnosis?
3   What is the treatment?

 ## Übung 2

Rewrite the following as a description of someone (e.g. **er ist krank**, etc.).

Ich stehe spät auf. Ich fühle mich krank. Ich gehe zum Arzt. Ich habe eine Halsentzündung. Ich muss viel Wasser trinken.

  ## Übung 3

Which of the following pictures fits which description?

1   Ich bin erkältet.
2   Ich habe Ohrenschmerzen.
3   Ich habe Magenschmerzen.
4   Öffnen Sie bitte den Mund!
5   Tief einatmen!
6   Ich messe den Puls.

(a) (b) (c)

(d) (e) (f)

Beim Arzt: other useful expressions

mir ist übel/mir ist schlecht	I don't feel well
was sind die Symptome?	What are the symptoms?
ich friere	I'm cold, freezing
ich bin erkältet	I have a cold
ich habe Halsschmerzen	my throat hurts
ich habe Ohrenschmerzen	I have earache
den Blutdruck messen	take the blood pressure
ich gebe Ihnen eine Spritze	I'll give you an injection

 Übung 4

ROLE-PLAY

With a partner from the class, perform the following role-play:

Patient	**Doctor**
Temperature, stomach pains	For how long?
Just today	Take temperature, and blood pressure
Also earache	Need antibiotics – no work, stay at home

Übung 5

Ich fühle mich krank.

Ich muss:

	Ja / Nein
1 schwimmen gehen	
2 viel Wasser trinken	
3 zum Arzt gehen	
4 zum Zahnarzt gehen	
5 wenig schlafen	
6 Alkohol trinken	

Text 1

Read this text carefully. There are some constructions you have not met, and you will not understand every word, but you should be able to grasp the key information.

Schokolade macht munter!

Schokolade enthält weniger Coffein als Kaffee oder schwarzer Tee, aber ihre anderen Inhaltsstoffe wirken auf das Nervensystem, wie zum Beispiel das Serotonin. Dieses Hormon kann im Körper die Bildung von Glückshormonen anregen. Vielleicht aus diesem Grund haben wir besonders große Lust auf Schokolade an dunklen Winterabenden.

Aber nicht alle können Schokolade essen: Serotonin und andere Stoffe in der Schokolade können bei migräne-anfälligen Menschen zum Problem werden. Auch glauben einige Experten, dass Nickelallergiker auf Schokolade verzichten sollten, weil der Nickelgehalt hoch ist.

Vocabulary

der Inhaltsstoff	ingredient
der Körper	body
-anfällig	susceptible to
der Allergiker	allergic person
verzichten auf (+ Acc)	to do without
verbrauchen	consume, burn off

 **Übung 6**

1   What are we told about the caffeine content of chocolate?
2   When do people prefer to each chocolate?
3   Who should avoid eating chocolate?

 **Übung 7**

Write down the infinitive form of all of the verbs in the above passage, and then give the **ich** form of the perfect tense of each one.

 **Text 2**

Fett reduzieren

Weniger Fett macht schlank und kann das Leben verlängern. Gesättigte Fettsäuren aus tierischen Produkten sollte man nur gelegentlich genießen. Ungesättigte pflanzliche Fettsäuren sind aber lebenswichtig. Hier einige Tips:

- Obst, Gemüse, Kartoffeln, und Salat haben bis auf geringe Spuren kein Fett.
- Reis, Nudeln und Getreide enthalten Fett nur in Spuren.
- Bei Fleisch, Fisch und Würsten sollte man nur magere Sorten essen.
- Toast auskühlen lassen – sonst saugt er viel Fett auf. Auch Butter mit Zimmertemperatur kann man dünner verstreichen als direkt aus dem Kühlschrank.
- Gummibären, Fruchteis und Salzstangen haben kaum oder überhaupt kein Fett.

 **Übung 8**

In the above text, find German equivalents for the following English expressions:

English	German
to spread	
saturated	
traces	
to prolong	
grains	
fat	
fatty acids	
lean	
fridge	

 Übung 9

Find, and check the gender and plural of, all the nouns in the above two texts.

 Übung 10

Based on the information in the preceding text, match up the halves of the following sentences:

Obst und Gemüse	nur mageres Fleisch essen.
Heißer Toast	haben kaum Fett.
Man sollte	haben fast kein Fett.
Gummibären	saugt viel Fett auf.

 Text 3

Regeln für eine erfolgreiche Diät

Viel trinken –. Mindestens zwei Liter täglich – das fördert den Stoffwechsel und hilft, Giftstoffe auszuschwemmen. So kann man Kopfschmerzen und Hautunreinheiten verhindern.

Fettkonsum einschränken – man sollte kritisch auf versteckte Fette in Speisen (z.B. in Wurst) achten. Mindestens einmal wöchentlich eine Fleischmahlzeit durch ein Fischgericht ersetzen.

Vitamine und Kohlenhydrate – Vitamine sind während einer Diät besonders wichtig, und Kohlenhydrate verhindern Hunger. Der Körper braucht jeden Tag mindestens 50 Gramm Kohlenhydrate für den Fettstoffwechsel.

Bewegung steigern – mehr Kalorienverbrauch durch körperliche Bewegung. Besonders geeignete Sportarten sind: Joggen, Fahrrad fahren, Schwimmen, Aerobic. Die Regelmäßigkeit ist sehr wichtig.

Vocabulary

Giftstoffe	poisons/toxins
ausschwemmen	to flush out
Unreinheiten	impurities
Fettkonsum	fat consumption
versteckt	hidden

ersetzen	to replace
Kohlenhydrate	carbohydrates
der Kalorienverbrauch	calorie consumption

✍ Übung 11

Write a brief summary of the key points of the above text.

✍ Übung 12

Select suitable words from the list to fill the gaps. (The list contains more words than you need!)

1 Man muss mindestens zwei Liter _____ pro _____ trinken.
2 _____ in der Woche sollte man _____ essen.
3 Während einer Diät sind _____ sehr _____.
4 _____ Bewegung ist für die Gesundheit auch sehr wichtig.

Fleisch   Wasser   Vitamine   körperliche   einmal

wichtig   Tag   Fisch   Bonbons

🎧 📖 Dialogue 3

A telephone conversation.

Marcus:	Hallo?
Rita:	Marcus – du warst heute nicht an der Uni?
Marcus:	Ach, Rita! – nein – ich habe verschlafen.
Rita:	Warum? Du bist nicht krank?
Marcus:	Doch – ich bin zur Ärztin gegangen – ich habe eine Halsentzündung.
Rita:	Was hat sie verschrieben?
Marcus:	Antibiotika – zweimal täglich. Ich muss auch viel Wasser trinken.
Rita:	Du weißt, dass wir heute ausgehen? – Max hat Geburtstag.
Marcus:	Das habe ich völlig vergessen! – ich muss noch eine Karte und ein Geschenk kaufen.
Rita:	Kein Problem – ich muss sowieso in die Stadt – ich kann dir das besorgen. Kommst du dann heute Abend mit?

Marcus: Sicher – aber ich darf keinen Alkohol trinken – wegen der Tabletten!
Rita: Das schadet nichts – du hast am Wochenende zuviel getrunken – heute
             kannst du bei Wasser bleiben!
Marcus: Danke! Also, wir treffen uns vor dem Rathaus?
Rita: Ja – um acht.
Marcus: Also, bis später – und danke für den Anruf!
Rita: Bis später.

Vocabulary

sich verschlafen	to oversleep
verschreiben	to prescribe
das Geschenk	present
sowieso	in any case
ich kann dir das besorgen	I can get that for you
das schadet nichts	that won't do any harm
bei Wasser bleiben	to stick with water

Language note

1 **du warst** – 'you were'. This is actually the *imperfect* form (you will meet this in
   more detail in later chapters)
2 **ich bin zur Ärztin gegangen** – 'I went to the doctor's'. This is an example of the
   perfect tense of a strong verb (one which changes its vowel, and whose past
   participle ends in **-en**). The verb **sein** (**ich bin**) is used as the *auxiliary* verb,
   because this is a verb indicating change of *position* or change of *state*. See the
   Grammar section for more information.

✍ Übung 13

Fill the gaps with words from the list:

Marcus ist heute _____ und hat sich verschlafen. Er ist zur Ärztin _____,
und sie _____ Antibiotika verschrieben. Obgleich er krank ist, _____ er
heute Abend mit Rita aus, aber er darf kein _____ trinken. Er trifft Rita später
vor dem Rathaus in der _____

---
geht   Bier   gegangen   Stadtmitte   krank   hat

 **Text 4**

Read the following text several times without checking the vocabulary, to try to understand the key points. For a more taxing exercise, listen to the recording first to see how much information you can grasp, and then read through the text.

Allergien bei Kindern

Allergische Erkrankungen bei Kindern und Jugendlichen gehören heutzutage zu den größten Gesundheitsproblemen. Die Häufigkeit bestimmter Allergien – zum Beispiel Asthma, Heuschnupfen, und Nahrungsmittelallergien – hat in den letzten Jahren stark zugenommen. Zwischen 20 und 30 Prozent der Kinder leiden an solchen Allergien – besonders in Industriestaaten. Ärzte rätseln über die Ursachen dieser Zunahme. Viele sehen die Ursache in unserem modernen Lebensstil: Die guten hygienischen Verhältnisse haben, glauben die Experten, das Allergierisiko gesteigert. Das Immunsystem ist sozusagen 'arbeitslos' und weil es einen Mangel an schädlichen Substanzen gibt, bekämpft es harmlose Stoffe, wie zum Beispiel Pollen. Deswegen leiden so viele Kinder an Heuschnupfen.

Es gibt zur Zeit kein Medikament, das Allergien heilen kann, aber moderne Präparate – Antiallergika und Steroide – können die Symptome bekämpfen. Wichtig ist, dass die Eltern so bald wie möglich eine mögliche allergische Erkrankung bei Ihrem Kind feststellen. Ihre Beobachtungen, welche Symptome auftreten, können die Diagnose erleichtern.

Language note

kein Medikament, das Allergien heilen kann = 'no medicine, which can …'
(See the **Grammar** section for the use of relative pronouns.)

✍ Übung 14

Match up the meanings of the words in the text:

illness	**erleichtern**
frequency	**Zunahme**
hay fever	**feststellen**
increase	**Erkrankung**
to increase	**schädlich**
to make easier	**Beobachtungen**
to notice	**Häufigkeit**
harmful	**Heuschnupfen**
observations	**steigern**

Übung 15

Richtig oder falsch?

1 In den letzten Jahren hat man ein effektives Heilmittel für Allergien entwickelt.
2 Es gibt heute mehr allergische Erkrankungen als vor vielen Jahren.
3 Experten wissen die Ursachen vieler Allergien.

Übung 16

Check the meaning of other words you do not know.

Übung 17

Text 5

Listen to the recording (based on the previous text) and fill in the missing words:

Heute _____ viele Kinder an _____, besonders in _____. Experten _____, dass die guten hygienischen Verhältnisse das _____ steigern.

Text 6

INFORMATION

Health insurance in Germany is delivered by companies called **Krankenkassen** which are generally private, competing organisations but under public scrutiny and control. The net result for Germans is a considerably higher level of health care and treatment than we are used to in the UK, but the costs are high. There are concerns, particularly with an ageing population, about the rapidly increasing costs of the system, and there are national debates about the benefits and disadvantages of increasing the contribution rates in order to guarantee a continuing high level of service.

It is possible for Germans to go directly to a specialist, rather than to have to wait for referral from a GP. Many Germans also take advantage of a **Kur** – a treatment or series of treatments sometimes lasting two or three weeks – at a **Kurort** (often a spa town with specialist facilities to treat a variety of modern-day ailments). This practice of course adds to the high costs of the health care system.

The following text deals with some aspects of this problem.

> **Gesundheitskrise in Deutschland?**
>
> *Ja, glauben viele Experten:*
>
> Wie in anderen Staaten wird die deutsche Bevölkerung älter, und immer weniger junge Leute zahlen für immer mehr Alte und Kranke. Der Staat selbst zahlt weniger für die Gesundheit der Arbeitslosen. Die Kosten der neuen Behandlungsmethoden steigen ständig. Ohne eine Reform des ganzen Systems werden die Krankenkassenbeiträge bis 2010 auf 18% steigen. Bereits heute liegen die Beiträge im Durchschnitt über 13%.

Vocabulary

die Bevölkerung	population
Kranke	patients, sick people
der Staat	state
die Krankenkasse	health insurance fund/company
die Beiträge	contributions

Übung 18

Richtig oder falsch?

1   Die Deutschen werden in Zukunft weniger für die medizinische Behandlung zahlen.
2   Die Bevölkerung in Deutschland und in anderen Ländern wird allmählich älter.
3   Für die Erwerbslosen ist die Lage nicht so schlimm.

  ## Text 7

Topfit werden – im Krankenhaus!

Ein Berliner Krankenhaus bietet jetzt 'Fitness- und Wellness-Training' in seinem neuge-
bauten Gesundheitszentrum. Hier trainieren nicht Patienten, sondern Männer und
Frauen, die keine Patienten werden wollen. Das Stammpublikum in den Gymnastik- und
Geräteräumen will kein Waschbrettbauch haben, sondern nur fit und gesund bleiben. Die
meisten sind zwischen 40 und 60 Jahren alt. Sie bekommen individuelle Beratung und einen
persönlichen Trainingsplan. Das Zentrum hat 20 staatlich geprüfte Physiotherapeuten. Es
gibt auch ein beheiztes Hallenbad (mit Aqua-Training) und eine Sauna. Noch ein Vorteil:
Die Preise sind sehr niedrig. Kein Wunder, dass das Gesundheitszentrum fast immer
ausgebucht ist.

Vocabulary

bieten	to offer
neugebaut	newly built
das Stammpublikum	regular clientele
das Waschbrett	washboard
die Beratung	advice
ausgebucht	booked up, fully booked
staatlich geprüft	lit: state-tested (= state qualified)

 ## Übung 19

Write a brief summary of the main points of the above text.

  ## Übung 20

Re-read the text, and then match up the halves of the following sentences to create
statements which make sense:

Die 'Patienten' trainieren,	gibt es individuelle Beratung für die 'Kunden'.
Das Schwimmbad	sind nicht junge Leute.
Die meisten Kunden	hat qualifiziertes Personal.
Im Gesundheitszentrum	um fit zu werden.
Das Zentrum	ist beheizt.

 # 'Bekanntschaftsmarkt'

♥ Beate, 34 J. ein romantisches Wesen, möchte ihr Herz verschenken. Mehr über mich wähle Info-Band Tel: …

♥ Karl, 46 J. Betriebsleiter, sympathisch, gefühlvoll. Wähle Info-Band. Tel: …

♥ Regina, 22 J., hübsch und natürlich, aber etwas schüchtern. Wähle Info-Band. Tel: …

♥ Theodor, 36 J., Rechtsanwalt, kinder- und tierlieb. Mehr über mich wähle Info-Band. Tel: …

 ## Ihr Horoskop

 ### Löwe (23/7 – 23/8)

Liebe: Sie müssen sich die Sorgen von der Seele reden.
Sie brauchen einen verständnisvollen Zuhörer.
Geld: Mehr Bescheidenheit!

Jungfrau: (24/8 – 24/9)

Liebe: Sie haben endlich mehr Zeit für Privates.
Geld: Großeinkäufe am besten jetzt erledigen!

 # Grammar

1. Perfect tense of strong verbs

You have already met the formation of the perfect tense of weak verbs:

ich arbeite – ich habe gearbeitet
er reserviert – er hat reserviert

The perfect tense of strong verbs is formed by the use of **haben** (or occasionally **sein** – see later) as the auxiliary verb, together with the past participle. The difference between strong verbs and weak verbs is that the former have a past participle ending in **-en**, and frequently have a vowel change:

lesen (to read)	**ich lese**	**ich habe gelesen**
schreiben (to write)	**ich schreibe**	**ich habe geschrieben**
trinken (to drink)	**ich trinke**	**ich habe getrunken**
singen (to sing)	**ich singe**	**ich habe gesungen**

Strong verbs which indicate a change of position, or change of state (a typical example being verbs indicating motion from one place to another) take **sein** as the auxiliary verb:

fahren (to go, travel)	**ich fahre**	**ich bin gefahren**
kommen	**ich komme**	**ich bin gekommen**
steigen (to climb)	**ich steige**	**ich bin gestiegen**

It is always 'safer' to learn the different patterns of strong verbs (they are indicated in any good dictionary, and can also be found in grammar references), but here are some of the more common ones:

Infinitive	Third person present	Perfect
lassen (leave)	er lässt	er hat gelassen
schreiben (write)	er schreibt	er hat geschrieben
bitten (ask)	er bittet	er hat gebeten
gehen (go)	er ging	er ist gegangen
lesen (read)	er liest	er hat gelesen
essen (eat)	er isst	er hat gegessen
trinken (drink)	er trinkt	er hat getrunken
sehen (see)	er sieht	er hat gesehen
schwimmen (swim)	er schwimmt	er ist geschwommen
laufen (run)	er läuft	er ist gelaufen
gebären (be born)	er gebar (rare)	er ist geboren
sterben (die)	er stirbt	er ist gestorben
steigen (climb)	er steigt	er ist gestiegen
sitzen (sit)	er sitzt	er hat gesessen
bleiben (stay)	er bleibt	er ist geblieben
liegen (lie)	er liegt	er hat gelegen

2. Relative pronouns

In English, relative pronouns are fairly simple:

The lady *who* works here.
The man *whom* I saw yesterday.
The lamp *which* I bought.

In German, the form of the relative pronoun depends on the *number* and the *gender* of the noun to which it refers.

The table of forms of the relative pronouns is as follows:

	Masculine	*Feminine*	*Neuter*
Singular			
Nominative	der	die	das
Accusative	den	die	das
Genitive	dessen	deren	dessen
Dative	dem	der	dem
Plural			
Nominative	die	die	die
Accusative	die	die	die
Genitive	deren	deren	deren
Dative	denen	denen	denen

Some examples in practice:

Der Mann, *der* **hier wohnt** (*masculine singular*, because **der Mann** is masculine singular; *nominative*, because **der** is the subject of the verb **wohnt**)

Der Computer, *den* **ich kaufe** (*masculine singular*, because **der Computer** is masculine singular; *accusative*, because **den** is the object of the verb **kaufe**)

Die Dame, mit *der* **ich arbeite** (*feminine singular*, because **Dame** is feminine singular; *dative*, because **der** is governed by the preposition **mit**, which takes the dative)

Der Junge, *dessen* **Mutter hier arbeitet** … (*masculine singular*, because **der Junge** is masculine singular; *genitive*, because the reference is to the boy's mother)

Die Leute, mit *denen* **wir arbeiten** … (*plural*, because **die Leute** is plural; *dative*, because the pronoun is dependent on **mit**).

Language in use

✎ Übung 21

STRONG VERBS: PERFECT TENSE

Put the following into the perfect tense. These verbs all require **haben** as the auxiliary verb.

1   Sie liest die Zeitung mit Interesse.
2   Er findet einen sehr interessanten Artikel.
3   Der alte Mann bittet mich um Geld.
4   Der Autor schreibt einen sehr langen Roman.
5   Wir sehen die kleine Ameise nicht.
6   Er sitzt studenlang auf der Bank in dem Park.
7   Das Buch liegt oben auf meinem Tisch.
8   Julia trifft ihre Kolleginnen im Restaurant.
9   Sie trinken alle Weißwein.
10 Wir schreiben einen Brief an Peter.

✎ Übung 22

STRONG VERBS: PERFECT TENSE

Put the following sentences into the perfect tense. This time, the verbs all require **sein** as the auxiliary verb.

1   Wir bleiben bis Mitternacht, dann gehen wir.
2   Der Bus fährt um 9 Uhr pünktlich.
3   Sie fährt nicht mit der Straßenbahn in die Stadt.
4   Der Apfel fällt vom Baum.
5   Er läuft die Straße entlang.
6   Die Preise steigen ständig.
7   Er geht vor 8 Uhr zur Arbeit.
8   Sie schwimmt zum anderen Ufer.
9   Wir fliegen am Samstag von Paris nach Rom.
10 Walter kommt am Freitag.

✎ Übung 23

Compose ten sentences in the *present* tense using components from the lists below.

NOUNS

das Abendessen   der Laden   der Arbeiter   die Freundin   Marcus   der Zug

die Schokolade   die Geburtstagskarte   das Magazin   die Stelle   die Ärztin

das Geschenk

VERBS

geben   verlieren   essen   kommen   vergessen   laufen   fahren   lesen

stellen   besuchen   steigen   bleiben

✐ Übung 24

Now rewrite the sentences you have just produced, but this time in the *perfect* tense.

✐ Übung 25

RELATIVE PRONOUNS (DER, DIE, DAS, ETC.)

Put the appropriate relative pronoun in each of the following sentences:

1   Die alte Dame, _____ hier wohnt, ist sehr nett.
2   Das ist nicht der Man, _____ ich kenne.
3   Das Buch, _____ ich gelesen habe, ist in meinem Zimmer.
4   Die Zeitung, _____ ich gekauft habe, ist nicht sehr interessant.
5   Der Mann, _____ hier arbeitet, kennt meinen Vater.
6   Die Stühle, _____ ich gekauft habe, sind im Wohnzimmer.
7   Das Auto, _____ er fährt, ist sehr alt.
8   Die Städte, _____ ich gut kenne, sind in Südfrankreich.

✐ Übung 26

Match up the two halves of these sentences:

Die Bücher,	den ich letzte Woche gekauft habe, war nicht sehr teuer.
Meine Tante,	die er auf der Bank gefunden hat.
Der Computer,	die wir in diesem Semester lesen, sind nicht sehr interessant.
Die Kollegen,	den wir gestern probiert haben, war ausgezeichnet.
Er liest die Zeitung,	die in der Schweiz wohnt, besucht uns nächste Woche.
Der Wein,	die in diesem Büro arbeiten, sind sehr nett.

Test your knowledge

 Übung 27

Match up the words with their correct meaning:

key	**die Dusche**
luggage	**gemütlich**
floor (of building)	**das Frühstück**
service	**die Reisetasche**
breakfast	**der Schlüssel**
lift	**die Einfahrt**
cosy	**das Gepäck**
holdall	**die Etage**
shower	**der Aufzug**
entrance (vehicles)	**die Bedienung**

Übung 28

Put an appropriate preposition from the list into the gaps:

> **mit   ohne   nach   neben   seit   auf   durch   gegen**

1   Er geht _____ mich in die Stadt
2   Wir kommen _____ 9 Uhr zurück.
3   Ich laufe sehr schnell _____ das Zimmer.
4   Wir fahren _____ dem Zug nach Münster.
5   Die neuen Bücher sind _____ dem Tisch _____ dem Fenster.
6   Wir treffen dich _____ 8 Uhr.
7   Ich arbeite _____ gestern dort.

✎ Übung 29

Take a simple hotel advertisement from your local paper or from a brochure and produce a simple word-processed version in German, listing the main facilities. Your version need not be a word-for-word translation of the original, as this would be too difficult – you should try to make it as 'naturally' German as you can.

✎ Übung 30

Put appropriate endings on the adjectives:

1   Sie arbeitet in einem groß__ Büro.
2   Er hat einen neu__ Computer.
3   Heidelberg ist eine schön__ alt__ Stadt.
4   Sie liest ein__ alt__ Zeitung.
5   Sie wohnen in einer ganz modern__ Wohnung.
6   Das ist ein neu__ Pullover!
7   Er muss mit einem später__ Zug fahren.
8   Ich möchte in einer ander__ Stadt wohnen.

🎤 ✎ Übung 31

Give English equivalents for:

1   What's wrong with you?
2   I feel ill.
3   I have a temperature.
4   My ears hurt.
5   inflammation
6   injection

📖 Übung 32

What do the following German words/expressions mean?

1   Ich bin erkältet.
2   Tief einatmen!
3   Ich messe den Puls.
4   Ich verschreibe Antibiotika.
5   Ich friere.
6   der Blutdruck
7   Jugendliche
8   Heuschnupfen

9   die Ursache
10 der Körper
11 das Fett
12 einschränken
13 die Krankenkasse
14 die Bevölkerung

Unit 7
Studentenleben

TOPICS	• German student life • The German University system • Finding student accommodation
GRAMMAR	• Use of **dieser** • Imperfect tense of weak verbs • Use of the subjunctive (present tense) • Use of the passive (present tense)

 **Text 1**

Astrid kommt aus Saarbrücken im Saarland. Sie machte dort ihr Abitur, aber sie will nicht dort studieren. Deshalb hat sie sich um einen Studienplatz in Essen beworben. Sie will Englisch und Französisch studieren – im Fachbereich Literatur- und Sprachwissenschaften. In den ersten Wochen gibt es viel zu tun – sie muss sich für die Grundkurse an der Universität einschreiben und auch eine Wohnung finden – zur Zeit wohnt sie bei einer Freundin. Da sie kein Bafög bekommt, ist es wichtig, dass sie einen Teilzeitjob findet.

Vocabulary

das Abitur	(equivalent of) A level
sich bewerben	to apply for
Grundkurse	introductory courses
sich einschreiben	to register
Bafög	grant (see below)

Language note

sie machte dort ihr Abitur – machte is an example of the *imperfect* tense ('she did her Abitur there').

The other imperfect forms of **machen** are:

ich machte	wir machten	Sie machten
du machtest	ihr machtet	
er/sie/es machte	sie machten	

The **Grammar** section gives further details on the formation of this tense.

Information

The **Abitur** is the German equivalent of the Advanced level examination.

Bafög is the term used for the student financial assistance system in Germany. The word is an abbreviation of the **Bundesausbildungsförderungsgesetz**, which was the law passed to set up the student grants system. It is intended to assist those whose own income, or parental or partner's income, is insufficient to support their study. The system is means-tested, is quite complex, and has been subject to recent modifications. The financial assistance is for a limited period, depending on the subject studied (a maximum assistance period of 9 semesters is the norm). It is also not a grant, since a proportion of the financial support must be paid back later.

📚 ✍ Übung 1

1 Where did Astrid take her Abitur?
2 What does she want to study now?
3 Why does she need a part-time job?
4 Where is she living at the moment?

🎧 📚 Dialogue 1

Marlene introduces her friend Astrid to Otto.

Marlene:	Tag, Otto!
Otto:	Grüß dich, Marlene. Wie geht's?
Marlene:	Gut, danke – Otto, kennst du Astrid?
Otto:	Nein – Hallo, Astrid, freut mich!
Astrid:	Freut mich!
Otto:	Was studierst du hier?
Astrid:	Ich studiere Englisch und Französisch als Hauptfächer.
Otto:	In welchem Semester bist du?
Astrid:	Im ersten – ich bin vor zwei Wochen angekommen.
Otto:	Wo kommst du her?
Astrid:	Aus Saarbrücken – aber ich wollte nicht dort studieren.
Otto:	Und wo wohnst du?
Marlene:	Zur Zeit bei mir – sie sucht eben eine Wohnung.
Otto:	Noch nichts gefunden?
Astrid:	Leider nicht – ich habe schon ein paar Wohnungen gesehen, aber sie waren entweder zu klein oder zu teuer.
Otto:	Dann müssen wir mal mit Dieter sprechen – ich glaube, seine Vermieterin hat andere Wohnungen frei – und die sind gar nicht teuer!

Vocabulary

grüß dich!	hello! (informal greeting)
freut mich!	pleased to meet you
das Hauptfach	main subject
entweder ... oder	either ... or
die Vermieterin	landlady

Language note

Although Astrid does not yet know Otto, they use **du** to address each other. This is the norm among students and young people.

 ## Übung 2

These are brief descriptions of some students. Try to put the information into the *imperfect* tense:

1   Max studiert Geschichte in Regensburg. Er wohnt bei seiner Großmutter.
2   Doris sucht eine billige Wohnung in Hamburg. Sie arbeitet am Wochenende.
3   Ute arbeitet in einem Kaufhaus. Sie verdient ziemlich viel Geld.

Übung 3

 Text 2

Without reading the text beforehand, listen to the descriptions of the following four students, and note down the following details:

• name
• where they are are studying
• what they are studying
• where they live
• in which year/semester they are
• what their part-time job (if any) is.

The vocabulary list will help you understand what you hear:

teilen	to share
die Tankstelle	petrol station
Germanistik	German (language and culture – as an academic subject)
gemütlich	cosy, friendly
die Dozenten	the lecturers

Now read the written version to check your answers:

Mein Name ist Friedrich Altmeier. Ich bin seit 3 Jahren Student an der Technischen Universität in Berlin. Ich studiere Geschichte und Philosophie. Zur Zeit wohne ich bei meinen Eltern etwa 20 Kilometer von der Universität, aber ich will für nächstes Semester eine kleine Wohnung mit meinem Freund teilen. Am Wochenende arbeite ich an einer Tankstelle. Ich bekomme kein Bafög.

Hallo! Andrea Kiesinger ist mein Name. Ich studiere Germanistik in der philosophischen Fakultät an der Universität Gießen. Ich bin im ersten Semester und kenne mich noch nicht an der Uni aus. Ich wohne in Gießen, nicht weit von der Uni. Ich habe eine Dreizimmerwohnung mit zwei anderen Studentinnen. Ich suche noch einen Job.

Ich heiße Max Dürer, und ich bin Student an der Universität Regensburg. Ich bin Münchener, aber es gibt zu viele Studenten dort, und ich finde Regensburg viel gemütlicher. Ich studiere Mathematik und Physik, und ich bin im vierten Semester. Es gibt nicht so viele Studenten hier, und die Dozenten sind sehr nett. Abends und am Wochenende arbeite ich in einem kleinen Restaurant in der Stadtmitte. Ich wohne im Studentenwohnheim, nur 3 Kilometer von der Uni.

Guten Tag! Ich bin Carola Frenker. Ich komme aus Rostock in Mecklenburg-Vorpommern, und ich studiere seit 4 Jahren Mathematik in Hamburg. Ich wohne bei meinen Grosseltern nicht weit von der Stadtmitte – aber nächstes Jahr werde ich meine eigene Wohnung haben. Ich suche einen Teilzeitjob, aber bisher habe ich leider keinen gefunden.

Information

GERMAN UNIVERSITIES

Most German universities are controlled by the **Land** and are funded at regional level. There is no system of student fees as we know it in the UK – and this 'fee-free' status applies to both German students and to students from overseas. Unlike in the UK, there is not an end-of-year examination as a means of progression to the next stage, and there is a very wide variation in assessment methods: some modules/units might require written and oral examinations, some one or the other, some have none. The UK concept of a firmly established syllabus is not very widespread in the German system.

German universities in the main do not have 'bachelor's degrees' in the same way as UK institutions. Instead there is a system of diplomas and masters' level quali-fications, as well as state examinations (**Staatsexamen**) for certain professions, for example law and medicine. Bachelor's degrees have been introduced in a number of **Fachhochschulen** (see below).

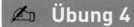 ## Übung 4

Write a description of yourself, including:

- place of study
- what you study
- your part-time job (if any)
- where you live (inc. distance from university/college).

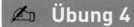 ## Übung 5

Now write a description of a friend of yours who is studying at another university.

Information

FACHHOCHSCHULEN

There are also in Germany many **Fachhochschulen** which specialise in more vocationally orientated subjects such as applied sciences, business studies and social sciences. They tend to be smaller than the traditional universities, and they do have more precisely determined periods of study (typically 4 years or 8 semesters to a Diploma (**Diplom**)).

The class contact hours and therefore the teaching hours for staff tend to be higher in the **Fachhochschule** than in the traditional university system.

  ## Text 3

Das Studium an der Fachhochschule

Besondere Kennzeichen der Fachhochschule sind: Praxisbezug, schnelleres Studium. Was die Studenten dabei verlockt, ist vor allem der schnellere Weg in den Beruf. Denn das Studium an Fachhochschulen ist sehr praxisorientiert. Straff organisierte Studiengänge, Unterricht in kleinen Gruppen und studienbegleitende Prüfungen ermöglichen kürzere Durchschnittsstudienzeiten, als an den Universitäten. Die vorlesungsfreien Zeiten ("Semesterferien") sind auch meist kürzer.

An Fachhochschulen wird nicht nur gelehrt, sondern ebenso geforscht. Aber diese Forschung orientiert sich ebenfalls vorrangig an praktischen Bedürfnissen. Daraus folgt, daß sogenannte Orchideenfächer und rein theoretisch ausgerichtete Studiengänge an der Fachhochschule nicht zu finden sind. Der Studienabschluss an einer Fachhochschule ist das Diplom.

Vocabulary

das Kennzeichen	feature, characteristic
besonder	particular, special
der Praxisbezug	practical orientation
verlocken	attract
straff	tight, tightly
der Studiengang	course (academic)
ermöglichen	make possible
der Durchschnitt	average
die Studienzeit	study time, duration of study
vorlesungsfrei	free of lectures
vorrangig	predominantly
das Bedürfnis	need
Orchideenfächer	'blue skies' subjects, purely theoretical subjects
ausgerichtet	orientated, aligned
der Studienabschluss	final qualification

Language note

an Fachhochschulen wird nicht nur gelehrt, sondern ebenso geforscht – 'it is not only teaching which is done in Fachhochschulen, but also research'.

This is an example of the *passive* in German: you will meet other examples and a full explanation later in this unit.

  Text 4

Content of an undergraduate course at a typical German **Fachhochschule**:

Inhalt des Bachelor-Studiengangs

Der Bachelor-Studiengang bietet folgende Kernbereiche an:

- Marktmanagement
- Finanzmanagement

- Informationsmanagement
- Personalmanagement

Bereits nach 6 Semestern erhalten die Absolventen den ersten berufsqualifizierenden Abschluss.

Information

THE VORLESUNGSVERZEICHNIS

The key source of information for German students at a German higher education institution is the **Vorlesungsverzeichnis**, a compendium of data on timetables for lectures and seminars, general university information, staff names and contact details. It is increasingly being duplicated (or even replaced) by on-line information.

  Text 5

Das Vorlesungsverzeichnis: ein Doppel-Klick?

Das Vorlesungsverzeichnis einer Universität ist ein bedeutsamer "Uni-Kompass". Inzwischen wird es mehr und mehr durch die virtuelle Präsentation der Universität im Internet ersetzt.

Wer **Adressen, Telefonnummern, Sprechzeiten usw.** von Dozenten und Einrichtungen der Universität sucht, blättert im **Vorlesungsverzeichnis** oder klickt mit der Maustaste durchs Internet.

Das Vorlesungsverzeichnis gibt Auskunft auf Fragen, wie z.B.

- Welche Fachbereiche/Fakultäten gibt es an der Universität?
- Welche Professoren und Dozenten lehren im Fachbereich?
- Welche Institute und Lehrstühle und Mitarbeiter hat ein Fachbereich?
- Welche Studiengänge/Studienprogramme betreut der Fachbereich?
- Welche Lehrveranstaltungen werden aktuell – wo, wann und von wem – angeboten?

Erfahren kann man aber auch

- Wer ist Rektor, Prorektor, Dekan usw.?
- Angebote und Öffnungszeiten der Serviceeinrichtungen des Zentralbereichs

Vocabulary

das Vorlesungsverzeichnis	lecture guide, lecture timetable
bedeutsam	significant, important
ersetzen	replace
usw. (und so weiter)	etc. (and so on)
Sprechzeiten	'surgery' hours, consultation times
die Einrichtungen	offices, departments (admin.)
blättern	to leaf through a book, look through
die Maustaste	mouse button
der Fachbereich	(equivalent of) department

Language note

welche Lehrveranstaltungen werden aktuell ... angeboten – 'which classes are currently offered'. This is another example of the *passive*.

In English it is formed by using the appropriate tense of the verb 'to be' and the past participle:

The car is (being) driven.
The car was driven.
The bank was robbed.
The woman was bitten by the dog.
The football team was beaten.

In German it is similarly easy to form: but in this case the appropriate tense of the verb **werden** is used:

das Haus wird gebaut	the house is (being) built
das Zimmer wird geputzt	the room is being cleaned

For a fuller explanation see the **Grammar** section later in this unit.

 Dialogue 2

Astrid discusses accommodation possibilities with Otto.

Otto: Nichts in der Zeitung?
Astrid: Wieder nichts – die Wohnungen sind zu teuer.
Otto: Wie gesagt – meine Vermieterin hat noch eine Wohnung frei.
Astrid: Was für eine Wohnung?
Otto: In der Fürstenstrasse – zweite Etage – Schlafzimmer, Badezimmer mit
          Dusche, und Einbauküche. Auch mit Gasheizung – gar nicht schlecht!

Astrid: Wann kann ich die Wohnung sehen?
Otto: Gleich, wenn du willst – ich habe mein Auto da – wir können in 5 Minuten
            dort sein. Ich weiß, dass Frau Dilling zu Hause ist – ich habe sie gerade
            angerufen.
Astrid: Schön – dann fahren wir gleich!

Vocabulary

wie gesagt	as I've said
was für eine?	what sort of?
die Einbauküche	fitted kitchen

  ## Dialogue 3

Otto and Astrid view the flat.

Otto: Frau Dilling, darf ich Ihnen Astrid Feldmann vorstellen?
Frau Dilling: Freut mich sehr, Fräulein Feldmann!
Astrid: Freut mich, Frau Dilling.
Frau Dilling: Sie wollten die Wohnung sehen?

(*Two minutes later.*)

Frau Dilling: Also, wie Sie sehen, ist alles neu möbliert. Da haben Sie das
                Schlafzimmer, und hier die Einbauküche. Dort gegenüber ist das
                Badezimmer.
Astrid: Eine sehr nette Wohnung, Frau Dilling. Ab wann ist sie frei?
Frau Dilling: Sofort – der letzte Mieter ist vor einer Woche ausgezogen. Es
                kommen noch zwei Leute heute, die an der Wohnung interessiert
                sind.
Otto: Dann mußt du dich schnell entscheiden!
Astrid: Ich glaube, ich nehme sie. Bis Mitte August – geht das?

Frau Dilling:	Ja, sicher – die Miete wissen Sie schon?
Astrid:	Ja. Darf ich übermorgen einziehen?
Frau Dilling:	Moment mal – ja, das geht – ich bin bis 11 Uhr da.

Vocabulary

darf ich ... vorstellen?	may I introduce?
möbliert	furnished
ist ... ausgezogen	has moved out
die Miete	rent

Language note

der letzte Mieter ist vor einer Woche ausgezogen – an example of a verb of change of position or state, therefore forming its perfect tense with **sein**. It is also a separable verb:

ausziehen
ich ziehe aus – 'I move out'

BUT in forming the past participle, the **-ge** is placed between the prefix and the rest of the past participle: **ausgezogen**.

Other examples:

umsteigen – to change (trains, buses, etc.)
ich steige um
ich bin umgestiegen

ausgehen – 'to go out'
ich gehe aus
ich bin ausgegangen

Übung 6

True or false?

1 The flat has new furniture.
2 The flat is available next week.
3 Astrid wants the flat until late August.
4 She wants to move in tomorrow.

Text 6

Zimmersuche

Wolfgang wohnt zur Zeit in einer sehr kleinen Wohnung nicht weit von der Stadtmitte. Er möchte gleich umziehen, weil er zusammen mit seiner Partnerin Ilse wohnen will, und sie brauchen eine größere, besser ausgestattete Wohnung. Wolfgang hat ein Auto. Er möchte nicht direkt in der Stadtmitte wohnen.

Text 7

Listen to the recording while you read the ads – this will help you understand the abbreviations used:

> Geräumige 2-Zimmer-Wohnung. DU+WC. Einbauküche und Balkon. Ruhige Lage. Ab sofort. Tel. 040/7 38 47 26

> Attraktive 1-Zimmer Wohnung, 45 qm, gut ausgestattet. Toplage mit Seeblick. EB, DU+WC. Stellplatz. Ab 1. September. Tel. 050/34 27 83

> 2-Zimmer-App. 60 qm. Hervorragend saniert. Bad, WC, Dusche. Einbauküche. Ruhige Lage. Stellplatz. Ab sofort. Tel. 060/3 86 73 48

> Helle, geräumige 2-Raum-Whg. in der Stadtmitte. Dielenboden, Vollbad und Küche. gr. Balkon. Keller. Ab 1. Dezember. Tel. 040/2 87 47 26

> 2-Zimmer-Wohnung (ca. 55 qm.) in rhg. Wohnlage. Keller, Terrasse, Einbauküche, Vollbad, Kabelanschl. Pkw-Stellplatz. Tel. 040/3 72 58 28

Übung 7

You have now read what Wolfgang's accommodation needs are – which of the above flats are suitable? Bear in mind that he does not wish to move later than early or mid-September.

✍ Übung 8

Write out in German in full – not abbreviated form – the descriptions of each of the flats.

✍ Übung 9

Working with a partner from the class, each write out a brief description of a flat in English. Now swap descriptions, and each of you produce a German version of the English outline you have been given.

🎧 📚 Dialogue 4

Renate and Wolfgang discuss a flat.

Renate:	Volker hat mir gestern gesagt, er habe eine Wohnung in der Augustinerstraße gefunden – aber sie sei nicht sehr groß.
Wolfgang:	Ja, stimmt. Ich habe die Wohnung auch gesehen – das Wohnzimmer ist viel zu klein. Volker hat auch gesagt, dass die Miete für ihn etwas zu hoch sei.
Renate:	Was will er jetzt tun?
Wolfgang:	Ich bin nicht sicher. Er hat aber gesagt, er bleibe bis Anfang September bei seinen Eltern.

Language note

er *habe* eine Wohnung ... gefunden

This is an example of the *subjunctive* in German, used in this case because this is an example of 'indirect' or 'reported' speech. **Habe** is the subjunctive form of the third person singular of the verb **haben**. The 'normal' form would of course be **hat**.

sie *sei* nicht sehr groß

Another example of the subjunctive used in reported/indirect speech. This is the subjunctive form of the verb **sein** (the normal version would be **sie ist**).

(For a fuller explanation of the formation and use of the subjunctive, see the **Grammar** section at the end of the unit.)

Text 8

Ein Haus baut man nicht für die Ewigkeit – im Laufe der Jahre werden Reparaturen und Modernierungsmaßnahmen fällig. Die Massivkonstruktion des Hauses sollte bei normaler Bauausführung 80 bis 100 Jahre alten, und die Dacheindeckung 20 bis 30 Jahre. Fenster sollte man nach 25 Jahren austauschen. Ein Außenanstrich hält fünf bis zehn Jahre. Die Haustechnik, wie Heizkessel und Warmwasserbereiter, muss man auch ab und zu durch neue ersetzen. Für all diese Investitionen muss ein Eigenheimbesitzer aufkommen.

Übung 10

In the above text, find German expressions for the English words in the table:

English	German
home owner	
eternity	
paint	
replace	
repairs	
boiler	
occasionally	

Übung 11

Give a summary in English of the key points of the above text.

Text 9

Obdachlose Studenten

Das Semester hat schon vor 4 Wochen begonnen, aber in vielen deutschen Hochschulstädten sind Studierende noch immer auf Wohnungssuche. Die Wohnsituation der deutschen Studenten hat sich in dem vergangenen Jahr dramatisch verschlechtert – so behauptet das Deutsche Studentenwerk.

In vielen Städten übersteigt die Nachfrage bei weitem das Angebot. Die Studentenwerke mussten in einigen Städten (z.B. Darmstadt, Frankfurt am Main, Düsseldorf) Notunterkünfte einrichten. Studenten müssen oft viele Wochen warten, bis sie eine geeignete Wohnung finden. Das Problem ist für ausländische Studenten besonders gravierend.

Vocabulary

obdachlos	homeless, without shelter
die Hochschule	university
sich verschlechtern	to get worse
das Studentenwerk	equivalent of students' union
übersteigen	exceed
die Nachfrage	demand
das Angebot	offer, supply

 **Übung 12**

Combine the two halves of the sentences to make sense:

Viele deutsche Studenten	gibt es nicht genug Wohnungen.
Die Wohnsituation ist	Notunterkünfte eingerichtet.
In einigen Städten hat man	dieses Jahr noch schlechter.
In vielen Städten	suchen noch eine Wohnung.

Text 10

Erhöhte Nachfrage in Informatik-Studiengängen

Zum Wintersemester haben sich mehr als 2000 Studenten für Informatikstudiengänge in Berlin beworben.

An den drei Berliner Universitäten hat man einen Numerus clausus eingeführt – deshalb werden nur 1000 Studenten zugelassen. Aber nicht alle zugelassenen Bewerber nehmen ihren Studienplatz in Anspruch – viele Studenten bewerben sich 'parallel' in mehreren Bundesländern.

Vocabulary

Numerus clausus	(lit. 'restricted number') quota admissions system
einführen	to introduce
zugelassen	admitted
Bewerber	applicants
in Anspruch nehmen	claim, take up

Übung 13

1   What has happened at the three universities in Berlin?
2   Why have some students not taken up their places?

Information

NUMERUS CLAUSUS

In theory German students are free to study the subject of their choice at the University of their choice (provided they have passed the Abitur), but on account of the popularity of a number of subjects (for example medicine, dentistry, veterinary science) limitations on entry have been imposed, with a quota system. The Abitur grades demanded for these subjects are very high. The generic term used to describe this system is the **Numerus clausus**.

  ## Übung 14

Making use of a suitable search engine, see if you can get further information on the subjects in German universities which have an entry quota imposed. Try also to get onto the website of a German university, to get general information about courses, facilities available, etc. You should find that entering keywords such as 'universities Germany' will produce links to the websites of numerous universities.

  ## Übung 15

Collect information about your own university/college (courses, accommodation available, social facilities), and make a list of these. Then, working in groups, produce a German version of this. You will find the information you obtained in the previous exercise particularly useful.

  ## Dialogue 5

Astrid's younger brother, Paul, visits her. He is currently in his Abitur year at school. Astrid meets Paul as he arrives at the station.

    (am Bahnhof)
Astrid: Du bist sehr früh angekommen! Gut, dass ich mein Handy dabei hatte!

Paul:	Ja – ich bin um 11 Uhr abgefahren. Das Wetter war unglaublich heiß – wir hatten also hitzefrei.
Astrid:	Das hat man als Student nicht! Heute hatte ich zwei Vorlesungen und ein Seminar. Und nächste Woche habe ich eine Klausur.
Paul:	Ja, ja. Wo ist denn deine neue Wohnung? Die würde ich mal sehen!
Astrid:	Nur zehn Minuten im Auto.
Paul:	Du hast doch kein Auto!
Astrid:	Nein, aber Otto bringt uns dorthin.
Paul:	Ach ja, der Otto …
	(lacht)

Vocabulary

das Handy	mobile phone
die Vorlesung	lecture
das Seminar	seminar
die Klausur	test
unglaublich	incredibly
hitzefrei	(see below)

Language note

1 **abgefahren, angekommen** – two more examples of the past participles of separable verbs.
2 **ich hatte** – 'I had' – the (irregular) imperfect form of the verb **haben**.

Information

HITZEFREI

Slang term for the system whereby German headteachers are able to send pupils home from school early if the temperature is too high. In order for this to happen, the temperature should reach 30 degrees Celsius before noon.

Heads are also able to send pupils home in the event of heavy snow. This is referred to colloquially as **schneefrei**.

 # Grammar

1. Dieser

Means 'this' – and takes different endings according to the gender and case of the following noun:

dieser Mann
diese Dame
dieses Auto

The full list of endings is indicated below:

	Masculine	*Feminine*	*Neuter*
Nominative	dieser Mann	diese Dame	dieses Auto
Accusative	diesen Mann	diese Dame	dieses Auto
Genitive	dieses Mannes	dieser Dame	dieses Autos
Dative	diesem Mann	dieser Dame	diesem Auto

2. Imperfect tense: weak verbs

The imperfect tense of weak verbs is formed by:

* removing the **-en** or **-n** from the infinitive
* adding the following endings (this is done here with the verb **tippen** (to type):

    ich tipp*te*
    du tipp*test*
    er, sie, es tipp*te*
    wir tipp*ten*
    ihr tipp*tet*
    sie tipp*ten*
    Sie tipp*ten*

Another example – **setzen**:

ich setz*te*
du setz*test*
er, sie, es setz*te*
wir setz*ten*
ihr setz*tet*
sie setz*ten*
Sie setz*ten*

3. The subjunctive

We can describe verbs as having different 'moods', two of which are the *indicative* mood and the *subjunctive* mood.

Most of the time we make statements about what actually is reality as far as the speaker is concerned – we talk about things which have actually happened or which we know will happen. To do this we use the *indicative* mood.

Sometimes however we might wish to express things which are less certain, for example:

1   To express a wish for something that has yet to happen
2   To express hypothetical situations
3   To express something someone else has said.

In German the *subjunctive* mood is used to express the above situations.

The *present subjunctive* of regular verbs is formed as follows:

spielen
ich spiel*e*
du spiel*est*
er, sie, es spiel*e*
wir spiel*en*
ihr spiel*et*
sie spiel*en*
Sie spiel*en*

(Remove the **-en** from the infinitive, and add the above endings.)

Thus the present subjunctive of **haben** is:

ich hab*e*
du hab*est*
er, sie, es hab*e*
wir hab*en*
ihr hab*et*
sie hab*en*
Sie hab*en*

You will see that this varies only slightly from the standard/*indicative* form.

The present subjunctive of **sein** ('to be') is as follows:

ich sei
du seiest
er, sie, es sei

wir seien
ihr seiet
sie seien
Sie seien

The present subjunctive of **haben** and **sein** (which are the auxiliary verbs for the formation of the perfect tense in German) are used to form the *perfect subjunctive*:

ich habe gespielt
du habest gespielt
er, sie, es habe gespielt
wir haben gespielt
ihr habet gespielt
sie haben gespielt
Sie haben gespielt

ich sei gegangen
du seiest gegangen
er, sie, es sei gegangen
wir seien gegangen
ihr seiet gegangen
sie seien gegangen
Sie seien gegangen

USE OF THE SUBJUNCTIVE IN INDIRECT/REPORTED SPEECH

This is one of the most common uses of the subjunctive in German.

Compare the following sentences:

"Ich komme um 9 Uhr", sagte Paul. (indicative)
Paul sagte, er *komme* um 9 Uhr. (subjunctive because it is reported speech)
Also possible: **Paul sagte, *dass* er um 9 Uhr *komme*.**

"Mein Vater wohnt in der Lessingstraße", sagte Wolfgang. (indicative)
Wolfgang sagte, sein Vater *wohne* in der Lessingstraße. (subjunctive because it is
    reported speech)
Also possible: **Wolfgang sagte, *dass* sein Vater in der Lessingstraße *wohne*.**

Note: In the above examples the <u>tense</u> *of the subjunctive is that of the* <u>original</u> *words spoken:*
Wolfgang's original words were in the present ('my father lives in . . .')
Paul's original words were also in the present ('I am coming at . . .')

Here are a few more examples to help you:

"Das Auto kostet zuviel", sagte Peter.

Peter sagte, das Auto koste zuviel.

(Peter sagte, dass das Auto zuviel koste.)

"Ich gehe um 10 Uhr aus", sagte Uschi.

Uschi sagte, sie gehe um 10 Uhr aus.

(Uschi sagte, dass sie um 10 Uhr ausgehe).

"Ich habe gestern bis 8 Uhr gearbeitet", sagte Renate.

Renate sagte, sie habe gestern bis 8 Uhr gearbeitet.

(Renate sagte, dass sie gestern bis 8 Uhr gearbeitet habe)

"Doris ist um 9 Uhr angekommen", sagte Ulrike.

Ulrike sagte, Doris sei um 9 Uhr angekommen.

(Ulrike sagte, dass Doris um 9 Uhr angekommen sei)

4. The passive

So far in the course you have met only verbs in the so-called *active* voice, in which an action is done by someone or something (the subject) to someone or something else (the object):

The student reads the book.
The woman drives the car.
The professor gives the lecture.
The girl uses the computer.

However, verbs can also be used in the *passive* voice, in which the action is done to the subject of the verb:

The apple *is eaten*.
The tree *is chopped* down.
The books *were bought*.
The lecture *was given*.
The car *was driven* too quickly.

You will note that in English the passive is formed by using the *appropriate tense* of the verb 'to be', together with the *past participle* of the verb in question.

In German the appropriate tense of the verb **werden** is used, together with the past participle of the required verb:

Das Auto wird gefahren.	The car is (being) driven.
Das Buch wird gelesen.	The book is (being) read.
Der Wagen wird repariert.	The car is (being) repaired.

Note that the English 'by' is rendered by the German **von**:

Das Auto wird von der Dame gefahren.	The car is being driven by the woman.
Das Buch wird von dem Lehrer gelesen.	The book is being read by the teacher.
Der Wagen wird von meinem Onkel repariert.	The car is being repaired by my uncle.

*Note also that **von** always takes the dative case.*

Language in use

✍ Übung 16

DIESER

Insert the appropriate form of **dieser**, etc. in the gaps:

1 Ich habe d_____ Buch gerade gelesen.
2 D_____ Firma ist eine der führenden Autohersteller der Welt.
3 Magst du d_____ Wein?
4 Ist es d_____ Haus?
5 D_____ Lehrerin ist sehr nett.
6 An d_____ Universität gibt es zu viele Studenten.
7 D_____ Studenten wohnen zusammen in einer Wohnung.
8 Ich wohne in d_____ Stadt seit vier Jahren.
9 Ich mag d_____ Fach nicht. Es ist sehr langweilig.
10 D_____ Musik is wunderschön.

✍ Übung 17

IMPERFECT TENSE

Rewrite the following in the imperfect tense:

1 Astrid sucht eine Wohnung in der Stadtmitte.
2 Sie hat einen Teilzeitjob.
3 Ihr Bruder besucht sie am Wochenende.
4 Marcus setzt sich auf den Stuhl.
5 Er tippt einen langen Brief.
6 Otto kauft einen neuen Pullover.
7 Marianna legt das Geschenk auf den Tisch.
8 Paul arbeitet heute nicht.

✍ Übung 18

IMPERFECT TENSE

Find an appropriate verb from the list and insert it, in its correct form of the imperfect, into the sentence:

> **regnen   hören   (sich) umdrehen   öffnen   kaufen   stellen**

1 Klara und Anna _____ gestern einen neuen Computer.
2 Maria _____ das Kissen auf die Sofa.
3 Er _____ sich plötzlich um.
4 Karl _____ die Tür.
5 Tut uns leid, aber wir _____ ihn nicht.
6 Gestern _____ es in Strömen.

✍ Übung 19

FORMATION OF THE SUBJUNCTIVE

Give the present subjunctive form of each of the following:

1 Sie geht
2 Ich schreibe
3 Er bleibt
4 Sie liest
5 Wir sprechen
6 Er spricht
7 Er hat
8 Sie schwimmt
9 Wir kommen
10 Er lacht

✍ Übung 20

USE OF THE SUBJUNCTIVE

Rewrite the following sentences in indirect speech, prefacing them with **Sie hat gesagt...**

You may use either normal word order (without **dass**), or use **dass** but change the word order as appropriate.

Two examples to help you:

Das Auto steht vor dem Haus.
Sie hat gesagt, das Auto stehe vor dem Haus./Sie hat gesagt, dass das Auto vor dem Haus stehe.

Der Bus kommt spät an.
Sie hat gesagt, der Bus komme spät an./Sie hat gesagt, dass der Bus zu spät ankomme.

1   Ihr Bruder arbeitet in dieser Fabrik.
2   Das Geschäft schließt um 7 Uhr.
3   Der amerikanische Präsident fliegt am Mittwoch nach Deutschland.
4   Sie hat die Arbeit sehr schwierig gefunden.
5   Sie fährt oft in die Stadt.
6   Die Hefte sind nicht auf dem Tisch.
7   Er ist letzte Woche zurückgekommen.
8   Morgen beginnt das Sommersemester.
9   Sie hat den Zug verpasst.
10 Sie ist den ganzen Tag im Bett geblieben.
11 Sie kauft bestimmt ein neues Auto.
12 Er hat das Examen bestanden.

✍ Übung 21

THE PASSIVE

Put the following sentences into the passive voice.

Example:

Meine Mutter tapeziert das Esszimmer.

becomes

Das Esszimmer wird von meiner Mutter tapeziert.

1   Die Leiterin diktiert den Brief.
2   Der Student schreibt den Aufsatz.
3   Mein Vater öffnet alle Fenster im Zimmer.
4   Der Hund beißt den Mann.
5   Herr und Frau Dilling kaufen die Fahrkarten.
6   Die Kinder pflücken die Blumen.
7   Sie bauen das Haus in der Stadtmitte.
8   Die vielen Fabriken zerstören unsere Umwelt.

Unit 8
Es geht ums Geld

 **Dialogue 1**

AT THE BANK

Astrid wants to open an account.

Bankangestellter:	Bitte schön?
Astrid:	Guten Tag – ich möchte ein Konto eröffnen.
Bankangestellter:	Ein Girokonto oder ein Sparkonto?
Astrid:	Ein Girokonto.
Bankangestellter:	Einen Moment bitte. Könnten Sie bitte diesen Antragsvordruck ausfüllen?
Astrid:	Ja – soll ich das gleich tun?
Bankangestellter:	Ja bitte – hier an diesem Tisch nebenan. Dort finden Sie auch einen Kugelschreiber. Ich werde auch Ihren Ausweis benötigen.
Astrid:	Danke.

Vocabulary

das Konto	account
das Girokonto	current account
das Sparkonto	savings account
der Antragsvordruck	application form
der Kugelschreiber	ballpoint pen
der Ausweis	ID card
ich werde ... benötigen	I shall need (future)

Language note

1   **eröffnen** – 'open': means to open for the first time. For example, the opening times (= regular opening times) of shops are **Öffnungszeiten**. If a shop were opening for the first time, its opening 'ceremony' might be referred to as an **Eröffnungsfeier**.
   Similarly, you would say: **öffnen Sie bitte die Tür** – 'please open the door' (not **eröffnen**.
2   **ich werde Ihren Ausweis benötigen** – 'I shall need your ID card'
   This is the future tense. It is very easy to form, simply taking the appropriate form of the verb **werden** ('to become') and using it with the infinitive:

ich werde schwimmen	I shall swim
du wirst arbeiten	you will work

Werden is an irregular verb – so check the **Grammar** section for more detailed information on the future.

 **Übung 1**

Select suitable words from the list to complete the gaps:

Astrid _____ in die Bank, weil sie ein _____ eröffnen _____. Sie möchte ein Girokonto eröffnen. Sie muss ein Formular _____, und sie _____ auch ihren _____.

Konto   Ausweis   braucht   will   geht   ausfüllen

Text 1

Girokonten

Es gibt heute viele Girokontenvarianten: fast alle Kreditinstitute bieten drei oder vier verschiedene Girokontenmodelle an. Viele bieten auch eine kostenlose Kontoführung – obwohl der Kunde bei diesen Konten oft für eine Kreditkarte bezahlen muss (die Kreditkarte ist oft bei kostenpflichtigen Konten inklusive). Finanzexperten haben die folgenden Tipps für Kunden:

Prüfen Sie, wofür das Kreditinstitut Geld verlangt, und wofür nicht.
Suchen Sie ein Konto, wofür Sie weniger als 80 Euro im Jahr bezahlen.
Nutzen Sie sooft wie möglich Geldautomaten – wenn Sie zur Filiale gehen, kostet es mehr.
Suchen Sie ein Konto, womit Sie an möglichst vielen Automaten kostenlos Geld abheben
   können.

Übung 2

In the text, find equivalent German expressions for:

- various
- customer
- account
- cash machine
- free of charge
- management of account

Übung 3

After re-reading the text, match up the two halves of the following sentences:

Die meisten Banken	Geld kostenlos von Automaten ab.
Für eine kostenlose Kontoführung	sollte man weniger als 80 Euro pro Jahr bezahlen.
Für die Kontoführung	bieten ihren Kunden verschiedene Konten an.
Am besten hebt man	muss man oft für eine Kreditkarte bezahlen.

Dialogue 2

Iris, an American visitor, wants to change travellers' cheques.

Bankangestellte:	Guten Tag. Bitte schön?
Iris:	Guten Tag. Ich möchte diese Reiseschecks einlösen.
Bankangestellte:	Ja, gerne. Können Sie bitte hier oben unterschreiben?
Iris:	So – und den Reisepass brauchen Sie auch?
Bankangestellte:	Ja, bitte. Und ich brauche auch noch die Unterschrift hier, bitte. So, Sie bekommen insgesamt 240 Euro. Gehen Sie bitte gleich zur Kasse 8 – und nehmen Sie bitte den Zettel mit.
Iris:	Danke sehr.
Bankangestellte:	Bitte schön. Wiederschauen – und einen schönen Tag noch!

Vocabulary

der Reisescheck	travellers' cheque
einlösen	to cash
der Reisepass	passport
die Unterschrift	signature
insgesamt	in total
der Zettel	slip

Information

1 Note that the American visitor needs her passport. Germans would usually carry an ID card with them (**der Ausweis**) – as Astrid does in the first dialogue.
2 **gehen Sie bitte zur Kasse 8** – it is the practice in many banks to process the paperwork at one counter, and then to go to another 'cash till' to collect money.

Some further useful expressions

Geld abheben	to draw money
Geld einzahlen	to pay in
der Kontoauszug	statement
überzogen	overdrawn
Geld auf ein Konto überweisen	to transfer money to an account
ein Konto löschen	to close an account
das Sparkonto	savings account
der Geldschein	bank note
die Münze	coin
der Wechselkurs	exchange rate

  ## Übung 4

Using expressions from the above list, complete the following sentences:

1 Ich habe leider keinen _____ bei mir – ich habe nur Münzen.
2 Marcus hat eine neue Stelle in Frankfurt – er will also sein Konto in Hamburg
   _____.
3 Ich gehe heute Abend aus – ich muss also Geld _____.
4 Otto gibt zu viel Geld aus – sein Konto ist _____.
5 Ich habe schon ein Girokonto – ich brauche auch ein _____.

 ## Übung 5

With a partner from the class, work through the following role-play:

Clerk:	(greeting – how can help?)
Customer:	(change travellers' cheques)
Clerk:	(how many?)
Customer:	(200 – US Dollars)
Clerk:	(ask for passport)
Clerk:	(asks customer to sign, and sends him/her to cash desk 15)

Übung 6

With a partner in the class, act out the following role-plays:

Partner A	Partner B
Is a student. Age 22. Wants to open an account – asks for advice. Asks about the charges. Decides to think about it and come back tomorrow.	Offers current account. Charges are about 150 Euros per year – but there is a special offer for students. Check age of customer. Free credit card up to age 25.
Wants to change travellers' cheques. Has forgotten passport and has no ID.	Greets customer and asks for travellers cheques. Asks for passport or other ID. Suggests customer returns with passport. Bank closes in one hour.
Wants to open savings account. Check on interest rates, and any special offers.	Good rate of interest, but better if customer also has a current account, and a credit card with same bank. Give written details and suggest customer come back for appointment with colleague.

 Übung 7

When you have carried out the role-plays, see if you can write down in German the 'script' of each – then exchange notes and check for accuracy.

  Text 2

PC-Nutzer

Der PC-Nutzer kann sein Konto ausschließlich per Computer von zu Hause führen. "Homebanking" ist viel besser für Bankkunden, die viel unterwegs sind. Sie haben kaum Zeit, eine Bank zu den normalen Öffnungszeiten zu betreten. Sie wollen aber zum Beispiel während einer Geschäftsreise rund um die Uhr Verbindung zu ihrem Bankkonto haben. Damit sparen Sie viel Zeit.

Vocabulary

ausschließlich	exclusively
unterwegs	travelling
betreten	to go to, visit

📚 ✍️ Übung 8

Match up the words with their meanings from the text above:

user	**Geschäft**
contact	**Kunden**
business	**ausschließlich**
customers	**Verbindung**
exclusively	**sparen**
to save	**der Nutzer**

Language note

während einer Geschäftsreise – 'during a business trip'

während is a preposition which takes the genitive case.

Other prepositions taking the genitive are:

wegen   because of
trotz   despite

(although in colloquial German both of these also take the dative).

🎧 📚 Text 3

Fachkräftemangel

In Berlin fehlen mehr als 8000 IT-Spezialisten

Laut einer Online-Befragung fehlen in der Hauptstadt mehr als 8000 Fachkräfte in den Bereichen Informationstechnologie und Multimedia. Der Bedarf ist doppelt so hoch wie in einer Studie im vergangenen Jahr. Die Unternehmen suchen vor allem junge Hochschulabsolventen mit Fachwissen: Die meisten Firmen sind nicht bereit, Auszubildende einzustellen. Experten glauben, dass sich die Lage nicht verbessern wird. Wegen der positiven Konjunktur und der demographischen Entwicklung wird die Nachfrage nach IT-Spezialisten in Zukunft noch stärker. Und wegen der Konkurrenz zwischen Unternehmen und der steigenden Gehälter wird es noch schwieriger,

 **Übung 9**

Find in the text corresponding German expressions for:

- the economic situation
- need, demand
- apprentice/trainee
- graduate
- to employ
- specialist knowledge.

  Übung 10

Richtig oder falsch?

1   Die Nachfrage nach IT-Experten ist in dem letzten Jahr gesunken.
2   Auszubildende finden es schwierig, eine Stelle im IT-Bereich zu bekommen.
3   Nächstes Jahr wird die Lage besser sein.
4   IT-Spezialisten können viel Geld verdienen.

Check all the other vocabulary in the text, and ensure you are familiar with the gender and plural of the nouns.

 Übung 11

Translate the text into English.

Übung 12

Listen to the recording, which uses vocabulary from the text you have just studied, and try to complete the gaps.

Text 4

In Berlin _____ man noch mehr als 8000 _____ in Informationstechnologie und Multimedia. Firmen suchen junge Leute mit Fachwissen. Die Lage wird auch nicht _____, glauben Experten. Es gibt viel _____ zwischen _____, und es ist deshalb _____, qualifiziertes Personal zu halten.

 **Text 5**

Der Bedarf an EDV-Spezialisten wuchs im vergangenen Jahr wieder. Wegen des Mangels an deutschen Fachkräften wollten viele Unternehmen ausländische Mitarbeiter anstellen. Firmen rekrutierten viele Mitarbeiter natürlich an Hochschulen, aber für Mittelmanagement-Stellen brauchten viele Firmen Headhunter. Sie boten auch Tausende von IT-Positionen im Internet. Wer heutzutage eine Führungsposition haben will, muss hervorragende EDV-Kenntnisse besitzen.

Vocabulary

EDV = **Datenverarbeitung**	data processing
wuchs = imperfect form of: **wachsen**	to grow, increase
vergangen	past (year)
boten = imperfect form of: **bieten**	to offer
die Führungsposition	leading position

Language note

wuchs and **boten** are *imperfect* forms of *strong* verbs. You have already met the imperfect forms of *weak* verbs.

Whereas weak verbs simply use the addition of **(e)t** and the appropriate endings (see chapter 7), strong verbs use a vowel change.

This is also the case in English.

Compare:

I walk, I walked (weak verb)

and

I run, I ran (strong verb)

For a full explanation of the formation and use of the imperfect form of strong verbs, see the **Grammar** section later in this chapter.

 **Text 6**

Topverdiener

Im Verkauf und Marketing sind Spitzengehälter zu verdienen. Allerdings muss die Leistung stimmen. Leute mit hoher fachlicher Kompetenz sind gefragt und steigen schnell in Spitzenpositionen auf. Topverkäufer im IT-Bereich haben ein Zieleinkommen von mehr als 80 000 Euro pro Jahr.

Die Einkommen sind aber je nach Branche unterschiedlich. Die größten Differenzen zwischen Mindestgehalt und Spitzenverdienst treten in den Branchen IT-Consulting und Software auf.

Vocabulary

Spitzengehälter	top salaries
Leistung	performance
stimmen	be appropriate, be right
fachlich	specialist
Zieleinkommen	target income
unterschiedlich	varied
Mindestgehalt	minimum salary
Spitzenverdienst	top earnings
auftreten	to occur, be found

Language note

sind Spitzengehälter zu verdienen – 'top salaries can be earned'. This use of **zu** with the infinitive to express a *passive* sense ('can be done') is quite a useful device in German.

  Übung 13

1   In which sectors are the highest salaries?
2   Which areas show the greatest differential in incomes?

 Text 7

Without reading the text first, listen to Max Fellbach's account of his working day and his job and salary:

Ich muss jeden Tag sehr früh – um 5.45 Uhr – aufstehen, weil ich bei einer großen Bank in Frankfurt arbeite, und ich wohne etwa 30 Kilometer außerhalb der Stadt. Obwohl Berlin die Hauptstadt Deutschlands ist, ist Frankfurt immer noch die sogenannte Finanzhauptstadt. Es hat mehr Banken als andere Städte, und in Frankfurt findet man auch die Börse. Ich bin vor 8 Uhr in der Bank, und ich arbeite normalerweise bis etwa 17.30 Uhr. Ich habe eine Mittagspause, und ich esse in einem kleinen Lokal neben der Bank. Die Arbeit ist anstrengend aber interessant – ich treffe jeden Tag viele Leute – Kunden und Kollegen. Früher musste ich viel reisen, aber jetzt nicht. Ich fahre ab und zu nach Berlin oder nach Hamburg – und dann übernachte ich dort. Gewöhnlich bin ich gegen 18.30 Uhr wieder zu Hause.

Übung 14

1   When does Max get up, and why?
2   Where does he work?
3   What does he say about the city he works in?
4   When does he get to work?
5   Where does he usually have lunch?
6   If he travels, where does he usually go?
7   What time does he get home in the evenings?

Übung 15

Complete the sentences with words from the above passage:

1   In Frankfurt gibt es viele _____.
2   Berlin ist die deutsche _____.
3   Max findet die Arbeit sehr _____ aber _____.
4   In der Bank kann Max viele Leute _____.
5   Er fährt manchmal nach _____ oder _____.

Text 8

Read the following passage carefully. You do not need to understand every word in the passage, but should ensure that you have understood the main points. This will require careful use of your dictionary. Some of the key words are given to help you.

An der Maus kommt niemand vorbei

Offerten bestehen auf DV-Wissen bei Fach- und Führungskräften

Nach der Stagnation des Bedarfs an DV-Spezialisten auf hohem Niveau im vergangenen Jahr geht der Run im neuen Jahr auf die Spezialisten dieser Branche wieder los. Der Bedarf an Software-Fachkräften wächst rasant. Die einen rufen nach Green Cards zur Beschäftigung ausländischer Kräfte. Andere fordern Fortbildung heimischer Kräfte und den Abbau der Technikfeindlichkeit.

Noch aber ringt die IT-Branche um Fach- und Führungskräfte auf einem leerer werdenden Markt. Die Rekrutierung an den Hochschulen gehört zum Alltag. Selbst für das Mittelmanagement wird bereits Headhunting eingesetzt. Groß kommt das Internet als Marktplatz ins Spiel, denn hier tummeln sich die, die man sucht. Zu Beginn des neuen Jahres bot die Jobbörse Jobs & Adverts 35 000 IT-Positionen, die Hälfte von Software-Firmen oder IT-Beratern. Auch die Telekommunikation gehts ins Netz, um Kräfte zu finden. Gut 20 Prozent der offerierten Posten stammen von ihr.

Vocabulary

der Bedarf an	the need for
wachsen	to grow
die Fortbildung	further training
der Abbau	removal
Führungskräfte	management staff, leading staff
Berater	consultants, advisors

 Übung 16

1   What was the situation with regard to IT specialists last year?
2   How has the situation changed this year?
3   Where is the recruiting of new staff being carried out?
4   What is surprising about the situation with regard to middle management posts?
5   What is said about the telecommunications sector?

 Übung 17

1   Make a list of all the verbs in this text.
2   Give the perfect form of each of the verbs in your list.

Grammar

1. The future tense

The future tense in German is formed by using **werden**, together with the infinitive:

ich gehe	ich werde gehen
du gehst	du wirst gehen
er/sie/es geht	er/sie/es wird gehen
wir gehen	wir werden gehen
ihr geht	ihr werdet gehen
sie gehen	sie werden gehen
Sie gehen	Sie werden gehen

The future tense is probably used less in German than its English equivalent. Essentially, if the future 'sense' of a sentence can be expressed in some other way (for example, by the use of an adverb), then the present tense is preferred:

Morgen fahren wir nach Paris.
Er kommt nächste Woche an.
Wir gehen heute Abend aus.

2. The imperfect tense of strong verbs

As described in the previous unit, weak verbs form the imperfect by adding **(e)t** to the verb stem, plus the appropriate endings, to form the imperfect.

A couple of examples to remind you:

arbeiten
ich arbeite   I work
ich arbeitete   I worked, was working

suchen
sie sucht   she looks
sie suchte   she looked, was looking

Strong verbs, however, form the imperfect by a change of vowel, and the endings are also rather different.

An example is the verb **bieten**, 'to offer':

Present tense = **ich biete**

Imperfect tense:

ich bot	I offered
du botest	you offered
er/sie/es bot	
wir boten	
ihre botet	
sie boten	
Sie boten	

A further example is the verb **fahren**

Present tense = **ich fahre**

Imperfect tense:

ich fuhr	I travelled, went
du fuhr(e)st	
er/sie/es fuhr	
wir fuhren	
ihr fuhr(e)t	
sie fuhren	
Sie fuhren	

Other examples are:

Present tense	**Imperfect tense**
ich lese (read)	**ich las** (read)
ich spreche (speak)	**ich sprach** (spoke)
es beginnt (begins)	**es begann** (began)
sie schreibt (writes)	**sie schrieb** (wrote)
er fliegt (flies)	**er flog** (flew)
es riecht (smells)	**es roch** (smelled)

You have now met the present, perfect and imperfect tenses of strong verbs, and will be aware that they are frequently 'irregular' in each tense.

A typical example is the verb **fahren**

Present
ich fahre
du fährst
er/sie/es fährt
wir fahren
ihr fahrt

sie fahren
Sie fahren

Perfect
ich bin gefahren

Imperfect
ich fuhr

The changes of vowel in the different tenses are often given in grammar books and in dictionaries in an abbreviated form, such as:

fahren (ä,u,a)

meaning that the singular second and third person in the present tense have an **ä** instead of a, the imperfect form takes the vowel **u**, and the past participle has **a**:

Present = **ich fahre, du fährst**
Imperfect = **ich fuhr**
Perfect = **ich bin gefahren**

sprechen (i,a,o)
Present = **ich spreche, du sprichst**
Imperfect = **ich sprach**
Perfect = **ich habe gesprochen**

Two very commonly used verbs which are also very irregular in the imperfect tense are:

sein (to be)
ich war
du warst
er/sie/es war
wir waren
ihr wart
sie waren
Sie waren

and

gehen (to go)
ich ging
du gingest

er/sie/es ging
wir gingen
ihr ginget
sie gingen
Sie gingen

The imperfect tense is very much used in written German, but, apart from some very common verbs like **sein**, it is not used in spoken German as much as the perfect tense, particularly in informal situations. Germans would be more likely to say, for example:

ich habe mit ihm gesprochen

rather than

ich sprach mit ihm.

Language in use

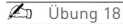 Übung 18

FUTURE TENSE

Put the following into the future:

1   Mein Bruder studiert in Heilbronn.
2   Alle Studenten suchen Teilzeitjobs.
3   Gehst du dorthin?
4   Sie fahren mit dem Zug nach München, und sie steigen in Frankfurt um.
5   Das glaube ich nie!
6   Er ist sehr krank.
7   Sie kaufen ein kleines Häuschen auf dem Lande.
8   Er fällt bei der Prüfung durch.
9   Er bekommt eine gute Note.
10   Er besteht ohne Zweifel das Abitur.

Übung 19

FUTURE TENSE/PRESENT TENSE

Put the following future sentences into the present. (Some are not as easy as they look!)

1   Er wird gleich fahren.
2   Sie wird mir helfen.
3   Wir werden uns ans Fenster setzen.
4   Sie werden das nicht tun.
5   Mein Kollege wird eine Gehaltserhöhung bekommen.
6   Sie wird nicht glücklich sein!

✎ Übung 20

IMPERFECT OF STRONG VERBS

Rewrite the following sentences in the imperfect tense. Use a dictionary to check the verb forms if you need to:

1   Wir gehen um 8 Uhr aus.
2   Ich fahre nur bis Hannover.
3   Sie steigt in Stuttgart um.
4   Sie lesen die Zeitung.
5   Er findet seine Schlüssel hinter dem Kissen.
6   Thomas wirft den Ball über die Mauer.
7   Vor 3 Uhr beginnt es immer zu regnen.
8   Der Wagen hält direkt vor der Garage.
9   Professor Liedtke spricht mit seinen Studenten.
10 Der Chef fliegt am Mittwoch nach Paris.

✎ Übung 21

IMPERFECT TENSE (STRONG AND WEAK VERBS)

Compose eight sentences in the imperfect tense using the following verbs and nouns:

Kino	Stadtmitte	Zeitung	Kollegen	Bierwurst	London	Auto	Bank

essen	sprechen	lesen	fahren	gehen	parken	sitzen	fliegen

Test your knowledge

 Übung 22

Interview a partner from the class in German, getting details of:

- what and where they are studying
- how long they have studied
- where they live
- their part-time job (if they have one)
- what they do in their free time
- what they intend to do after their studies.

Then produce a written account (also in German).

 Übung 23

What is the meaning of the following expressions? (Sometimes several words of explanation will be needed.)

1   Fachbereich
2   Grundkurs
3   Bafög
4   Numerus clausus
5   hitzefrei
6   Abitur
7   Hauptfach
8   Vermieter

 ✍ Übung 24

Give the German for:

1   to register (as student)
2   part-time job
3   hall of residence
4   gas heating
5   to move in (to a flat, house, etc.)
6   furnished
7   to move (house)
8   to apply (for a place)
9   demand (for places)

10   university (two different words)
11   to worsen (situation)
12   suitable

✍ Übung 25

Compose two ads in German for student flats – vary the vocabulary as much as you can. When you have done this, try to create another version of your ad using appropriate abbreviations in German.

📖 Übung 26

What do the following German expressions mean?

1   Kontoführung
2   Unterschrift
3   Reisescheck
4   Geld abheben
5   kostenlos
6   überweisen
7   Girokonto
8   Öffnungszeiten
9   sparen
10   Sparkonto
11   Bedarf
12   Konkurrenz
13   Gehalt
14   EDV
15   Spitzengehalt

🎙 ✍ Übung 27

Give equivalent German expressions for:

1   She lives outside the city.
2   They have to travel a lot.
3   My work is tiring but interesting.
4   He wants to close his account.
5   We would like to open a savings account.
6   He has a credit card.
7   Do you have an ID card?
8   Please fill in the form.

🐚 ✍ Übung 28

The text below is based closely on one you have already met. Put each of the verbs into the *imperfect* tense:

Klaus muss jeden Tag sehr früh – um 5.45 Uhr – aufstehen, weil er bei einer großen Bank in Frankfurt arbeitet, und er wohnt etwa 30 Kilometer außerhalb der Stadt. Er ist immer vor 8 Uhr in der Bank, und er arbeitet normalerweise bis etwa 17.30 Uhr. Er hat eine Mittagspause, aber er isst in einem kleinen Lokal neben der Bank. Die Arbeit ist anstrengend aber interessant – er trifft jeden Tag viele Leute – Kunden und Kollegen. Er fährt ab und zu nach Berlin oder nach Hamburg – und dann übernachtet er dort. Gewöhnlich ist er gegen 18.30 Uhr wieder zu Hause.

✍ Übung 29

Rewrite the following sentences in the future tense:

1 Wolfgang zieht am 1. August ein.
2 Marion arbeitet als Kellnerin in einem Restaurant in der Stadmitte.
3 Johann sucht einen Job an der Tankstelle.
4 Ulrike eröffnet ein Konto bei der Bank in der Nähe.
5 Unternehmen suchen vor allem Hochschulabsolventen.
6 Karl fährt mit der Straßenbahn zur Arbeit.
7 Uschi kauft einen neuen Computer.
8 Renate studiert Mathematik und Physik in Regensburg.
9 Doris arbeitet während der Semesterferien.
10 Er bleibt in seiner Wohnung in der Lessingstraße.

✍ Übung 30

The following sentences are all in direct speech. Put them into indirect speech, using the appropriate form of the subjunctive. (Some of these are quite tricky!)

1 "Ich gehe gleich nach Hause", sagte Peter.
2 "Die Prüfung ist sehr schwer", sagte Doris.
3 "Mein Bruder besucht uns heute", sagte Renate.
4 "Der Professor wohnt in dieser Straße", sagte Irmgard.
5 "Ich finde diesen Aufsatz zu schwierig", sagte Johann.
6 "Ich kaufe heute eine neue Jacke", sagte Dieter.
7 "Wir fahren sofort in die Stadt", sagten Uschi und Klara.
8 "Die Häuser in dieser Straße sind sehr alt", sagte Paul.
9 "Peter findet die Wohnung viel zu klein", sagte Wolfgang.
10 "Wir verpassen bestimmt den Zug", sagte Rita.

Unit 9
Arbeitssuche

TOPICS
- Job ads
- Applications
- Interviews

GRAMMAR
- Pluperfect tense
- Subjunctive (perfect and imperfect tenses)
- More about the passive

TEST YOUR KNOWLEDGE

Read the following job adverts carefully as you listen to the recording of each: listen particularly to the full version of each of the abbreviations.

  Text 1

Su. Bürokraft f. nachm. u. Urlaubsvertretung, g. Bezahlung.

Fahrschule H. Hammer. T. 85 74 63

  Text 2

Steuerfachangestellte/r für die Bearbeitung laufender Buchhaltung, Jahresabschlüsse und Steuererklärungen ges. Sie werden in modernen Räumen mit einem jungen Team arbeiten und laufend fortgebildet. Gehalt nach Vereinbarung. Herder Logistik.

T: 83 75 03

  Text 3

Wir suchen zum nächstmöglichen Termin eine/n Fachangestellte/n mit Datenverarbeitungskenntn.

Wir bieten angenehme Räume, mod. Aussttg., 37,5 Std./Wo, und angemess. Vergütung.

Tel: 870 45 39

  Text 4

Wir suchen zum 1. November eine Bürokauffrau. Wir bieten einen modernen Arbeitsplatz in einem jungen Team bei ansprechender Bezahlung. Wir erwarten umfangreiche Kenntnisse in Daten- und Textverarbeitung.

Bitte richten Sie ihre schriftl. Bewerbung an:
Hoffmann und Klinger
Doriusplatz 23
22457 Hamburg

Übung 1

Which of the advertised jobs:

1   Only requires someone for afternoons and occasional work?
2   Asks for written applications?
3   Wants someone to start as soon as possible?
4   Offers modern surroundings?
5   Mentions the age of your colleagues?
6   Offers training possibilities?

Übung 2

Listen to the recording once again, and write out in full the abbreviated words in each of the adverts.

Übung 3

In the adverts, find the equivalent German expression for each of the following English words:

application	
year-end reports	
(in the) afternoons	
to train	
pay, salary (three expressions)	
office worker/office staff	
specialist	
data processing	
word processing	
to offer	
to send (an application) to …	
as soon as possible	
to look for/seek	
tax	

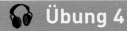 **Übung 4**

Without reading the printed version, listen to Herr Frenker's description of his work.

Complete the following sentences. You may need to listen to the recording at least once more to complete this exercise:

1   Herr Frenker ist _____.
2   Er arbeitet bei einer _____ Firma in _____.
3   Er arbeitet bei dieser Firma seit _____.
4   An der Uni hat er _____ und _____ studiert.
5   In seiner jetzigen Stelle gibt es wenige _____.
6   Er sucht eine Stelle mit besseren _____.
7   Er fährt oft nach _____.
8   Das Reisen ist für ihn _____ aber _____.
9   Wenn er eine neue Stelle findet, will er _____ _____ bleiben.
10 Er will nicht _____.

 Übung 5

Now try to transcribe the whole text exactly as it is in the recording.

When you have done this, compare your version with the original which follows.

Text 5

Ich bin Verkaufsleiter bei einer mittelgroßen Firma in Düsseldorf und bin seit etwa 15 Jahren dort. Ich habe an der Universität Bochum studiert und anschließend war ich zwei Jahre bei einem Maschinenbauunternehmen in Südfrankreich – ich habe Betriebswirtschaft und Französisch studiert. Ich mag die Arbeit bei meiner jetzigen Firma, aber es gibt nur wenige Beförderungsmöglichkeiten, und deshalb möchte ich eigentlich eine Stelle mit besseren Berufsaussichten finden.

Zur Zeit reise ich viel – ich bin für die Firma ständig unterwegs. Meistens nach Frankreich, aber auch ab und zu nach Kanada oder Südafrika. Das finde ich ermüdend aber sehr interessant. Meine Frau ist nicht begeistert! Wenn ich eine neue Stelle finde, ist es für mich sehr wichtig, dass ich im Ruhrgebiet bleibe. Ich bin hier aufgewachsen, und meine Familie und Verwandten sind auch hier. Ich reise gern, aber ich würde nicht gern umziehen!

Vocabulary

nicht begeistert   not enthusiastic

✍ Übung 6

The following are brief outlines of jobs. Write a short description of each one, in German OR give an oral desction to your colleague or tutor, who will prompt you with appropriate questions.

1. Sales representative

Company:	Large firm in Munich
Hours, conditions:	8 to 6, sometimes much later. Often weekends
	Travels in Germany – sometimes abroad
Education:	Studied finance at university
Time in this employment:	Seven years
Likes:	Travel and meeting people
Dislikes:	Boss, and hotel rooms!

2. Accountant

Company:	Small company in Bremen
Hours, conditions:	8 to 5.30.
	Pleasant environment and colleagues. Own office
Education:	Accountancy at universities in Germany and England
Time in this employment:	Ten years
Likes:	Place of work
Dislikes:	Travel to work (one hour by car)

3. University lecturer

Company:	Large university in south of Germany
Hours, conditions:	Very flexible. Own office. Generally pleasant colleagues
Education:	English and linguistics at University of Freiburg.
	Research at Augsburg.
Time in this employment:	25 years
Likes:	Research, and contact with students
Dislikes:	Students with mobile phones!

4. Secretary

Company:	Department store in Stuttgart
Hours, conditions:	8 to 4.30
Education:	School to Abitur
Time in this employment:	Four years
Likes:	Colleagues
Dislikes:	Routine of the job

5. Chef

Company	Large busy restaurant in central Frankfurt
Hours, conditions:	6.00 p.m. to 2 a.m.
Education:	School to Abitur. Professional training at **Berufsschule**
Time in this employment:	Three months
Likes:	Pressure of the job
Dislikes:	Difficult customers

✍ Übung 7

Compose adverts in German based on these English models. You need not translate literally.

We are looking for a colleague to take up duties as soon as possible in our new modern offices in the city centre.

You should have data processing skills and at least five years experience.

We offer in return a pleasant working environment with a young team, and a good salary. Apply in writing to:

Fraser and Turnbull
Unit 26
Hazelgrove Business Park
Birmingham B45 8JD

Small private firm requires a secretary for afternoon work. Experience in word processing essential.

You will be part of a young team in a modern office, and will have the opportunity for further training.

If interested contact:

Jennie Archibald
Personnel Manager
Light Electric
PO Box 2374
Southport

Here are a few tips in German on what to include in your curriculum vitae:

Checkliste für Ihren Lebenslauf:

- Persönliche Daten
- Schulabschlüsse
- Ausbildung/Studium
- Berufliche Praxis
- Berufliche Weiterbildung
- Interessen und Hobbys
- Foto nicht vergessen!

Text 6

Für ein dynamisches, mittelgroßes Unternehmen in der Elektronikbranche suchen wir ab sofort:

Eine/n Verkaufsleiter/in mit mindestens fünf Jahren Erfahrung in der Branche für unsere Zentrale in Essen (Stadtmitte)

Tätigkeit:
- Aufbau und Pflege von Geschäftsbeziehungen zu unseren Geschäftspartnern in Europa und Südostasien
- Erschließung neuer Marktpotentiale
- Leitung des Essener Büros
- Zusammenarbeit und Projektkoordination mit dem Pariser Büro

Gehalt nach Vereinbarung.

Bewerbung mit tabellarischem Lebenslauf, Foto und Zeugniskopien.

Ihr Ansprechspartner:

Ulrike Moser
Tel: 040 94 85 73

Übung 8

In the text above, find German equivalents for:

English	German
headquarters, head office	
office	
Asia	
cooperation	
CV	
experience	

Übung 9

1   What kind of post is advertised here?
2   What do we know of the person required?

3   Which customer markets will the successful candidate be responsible for?
4   What is said about the salary?
5   How should one apply?

CASUAL OR SUMMER JOBS?

Verkäufer/in als Teilzeitkraft ab sofort gesucht. Flexible Arbeitszeit – Bäckerei / Konditorei / Lebensmittel. Tel: …

Verkäufer/in gesucht. Ihre Aufgaben liegen in der Beratung und im Verkauf von Mobilfunkleistungen und Geräten in unserem Geschäft sowie in der Übernahme aller anfallenden administrativen Arbeiten. Tel: …

Ab 1. August – für unser erstklassiges Hotel im südlichen Schwarzwald suchen wir eine/n freundliche/n und engagierten Empfangsdame / -herrn. PC-Kenntnisse erforderlich.

Servicemitarbeiter/in sowie Küchenhilfe auf Aushilfsbasis gesucht. Arbeitszeiten vorwiegend abends und am Wochenende. Bitte sende Sie Ihre Kurzbewerbung an …

Read the following simple letter of application, and use your dictionary to check any new words or expressions:

| | Am Butenwall 19 |
| | Kiel |

Udo Fletzinger GmbH
Kastanienallee 45
Hamburg

                                                            5.8.2 ...

Sehr geehrte Damen und Herren

Ich habe Ihre Anzeige vom 1. August in der Handeslpresse gelesen und möchte mich um die Stelle als Verkaufsingenieur bewerben.

Wie Sie aus meinem beiliegenden Lebenslauf ersehen, habe ich das Gymnasium in Norddeich besucht, und anschließend Informatik und Betriebswirtschaftslehre an der Universität Ulm studiert. Als Teil meines Studiums habe ich ein Jahr als Praktikant bei einem englischen Unternehmen verbracht. Bereits vor meinem Studium hatte ich einige Zeit in England gewohnt. Ich spreche und schreibe Englisch und Französisch fließend.

Ich arbeite seit fünf Jahren als Verkaufsingenieur bei einem Hochbauunternehmen in Hamburg. Vorher war ich bei einer ähnlichen Firma in der Schweiz. Ich suche jetzt eine Stelle mit besseren Berufsaussichten bei einer größeren Firma.

Zu einem möglichen Vorstellungsgespräch stehe ich Ihnen jederzeit gerne zur Verfügung. Ich hoffe auf einen positiven Bescheid.

Mit freundlichen Grüßen

Dieter Escher

Language note

... hatte ich ... gewohnt – 'I had lived'. This is the *pluperfect* tense ('I had lived', 'I had worked' etc.)

In German it is formed by using the *imperfect* of **haben** or **sein** (depending on whether the verb is a verb indicating change of position or state – in which case **sein** is used) together with the *past participle*:

Examples:

ich wohne   **ich hatte gewohnt**   I had lived

sie arbeitet	sie hatte gearbeitet	she had worked
er geht	er war gegangen	he had gone

✍ Übung 10

Give the German for:

- to apply for
- business studies
- fluent
- similar
- career prospects
- consider.

✍ Übung 11

Write a translation of the letter.

✍ Übung 12

Using vocabulary you have already met, write a short letter (about 120 words) applying for summer work in a German hotel. Say a little about your education, and any part-time jobs you have already had.

✍ Übung 13

Write a description in German of the following individual:

Current post:	Manager of Export Department
Company:	IT firm, 150 employees
Experience:	Ten years export sales; six years with this company
Education:	School in Switzerland; university in Germany and France
	Wishes to move to Hamburg

📚 Stellengesuche

Here are some ads from people seeking employment:

1 Bürokauffrau, 42 J., Wiedereinsteigerin, Erfahrungen in manueller Buchhaltung, EDV, sucht Arbeit.
T: 0346 84 75 92

2 Sekretärin, Mitte 40, mit Büroerfahrung, Computer-Grundkenntnisse vorhanden, Englisch sehr gut in Wort und Schrift, Spanisch-Kenntn., sucht neuen Wirkungskreis
T.0837 653 87 37

3 Kreativer Küchenchef, 40 Jahre, 16 Jahre Erfahrung, sucht neuen Wirkungskreis in gehobener Hotelerie und Gastronomie
08763HC

4 Industrie-Kaufmann, M, 33 J., dynamisch und ehrgeizig, EDV-Kenntn. vorhanden, such Tätigkeit i.d. EDV-Branche od. im kfm. Bereich
T:0638 64 85 65

Übung 14

After reading the above ads, complete the checklist for the experience and/or career wishes of the people seeking employment:

	Advertisement number?
Returning to work	
Language skills	
Basic computer skills	
Data processing experience	
Ambitious	
Bookkeeping experience	
Wants work in hotel trade	

Übung 15

Without reading the text first, listen to the recording of Ute and Karl describing their jobs, then answer the questions:

1   Seit wann arbeitet Karl bei seiner Firma?

2   Wo arbeitet Ute vielleicht nächstes Jahr?
3   Was hält Karl von seinem Gehalt?
4   Was sagt Ute über ihr Gehalt?
5   Wo wohnt Karl?
6   Wielange arbeitet Ute schon in ihrem Büro?
7   In welchem Büro arbeitet Karl?
8   Wie ist die Leiterin von Ute?
9   Wie sind ihre Kollegen?

 Text 7

Ute

Ob ich meine Arbeit interessant finde? Ich würde 'Ja' sagen. Ich meine, ich finde sie ab und zu ziemlich langweilig, aber die Kollegen sind eigentlich meistens sehr nett. Die Leiterin ist manchmal schlechter Laune, und das ist dann nicht so gut – dann würde ich lieber zu Hause bleiben! Ich bin jetzt seit vier Jahren hier in demselben Büro, aber nächstes Jahr bin ich wahrscheinlich in der Exportabteilung – das wird für mich interessanter sein. Und das Gehalt? Ach, es könnte besser sein, aber ich komme klar!

Karl

Zur Zeit mag ich meine Arbeit nicht so sehr. Es gibt im Moment zu viel Druck, weil wir in der letzten Zeit Personal verloren und noch nicht ersetzt haben. Vor zehn Jahren, als ich hier angefangen habe, war alles leichter. Ich hoffe, es wird bald besser. Die Stelle selbst ist sehr gut, ich habe ein gutes Gehalt, und auch viel Verantwortung – ich bin Leiter der Buchhaltungsabteilung, mit mehr als zwanzig Mitarbeitern. Noch ein Nachteil für mich ist, daß ich täglich mehr als eine Stunde zur Arbeit fahren muss. Ich wohne nämlich fünfzig Kilometer außerhalb der Stadtmitte. Wir werden vielleicht bald umziehen, und dann wird es leichter sein. Oder aber ich suche mir eine neue Stelle.

Now read through the text carefully to check your answers.

 Übung 16

You are asked the question:

Warum suchen Sie eine neue Stelle?

Give a suitable response in German, based on the following prompts:

1   You want to move to another city.

2   You find your present job boring.
3   You want a more interesting job.
4   You want better prospects (e.g. for promotion).
5   You do not want to drive to work every day (takes you more than one hour).
6   You think you have been with your current company too long.
7   Your present company is small – you want to work for a larger firm.

🎧 📚 Dialogue 1

Herr Frenker has applied for a job with a company in Essen, and he is now at the interview. This is a part of his interview – Frau Kottbus is the personnel manager of the company.

Frau Kottbus:	Herr Frenker, Sie interessieren sich für die Stelle als Verkaufsleiter bei uns?
Herr Frenker:	Ja, ich bin an der Stelle sehr interessiert. Ich bin sehr froh, dass Sie mich zum Vorstellungsgespräch eingeladen haben.
Frau Kottbus:	Warum interessieren Sie sich für diese Stelle?
Herr Frenker:	In der Branche hat Ihre Firma einen hervorragenden Ruf. Ich weiß auch, dass Sie einen sehr guten Markt im Ausland haben.
Frau Kottbus:	Warum möchten Sie aber Ihre Firma verlassen?
Herr Frenker:	Ich bin schon seit einigen Jahren in der Firma. Im allgemeinen gefällt mir die Arbeit, und ich finde sie interessant, aber ich suche eine Stelle mit mehr Verantwortung und mit besseren Berufsaussichten.

Vocabulary

sich interessieren für	to be interested in
der Verkaufsleiter	sales manager
in der Branche	in the sector (of business, of industry)
hervorragend	outstanding
der Ruf	reputation
verlassen	to leave
die Verantwortung	responsibility
Berufsaussichten	career prospects

Language note

'to be interested in' can be expressed as **sich interessieren für** (+ accusative):

ich interessiere mich für diese Arbeit

or **interessiert sein an** (+ dative)

ich bin an dieser Stelle interessiert

  ## Dialogue 2

The interview continues.

Frau Kottbus:	Wir brauchen jemanden, der die Zusammenarbeit und die Projektkoordination mit unserem Büro in Paris führen kann. Wäre das für Sie ein Problem?
Herr Frenker:	Nein, gar nicht. In meiner gegenwärtigen Stelle fahre ich oft nach Frankreich – ich spreche fließend Französisch – und die Zusammenarbeit mit unseren französischen Geschäftspartnern ist ein besonders interessanter Teil meiner Arbeit.
Frau Kottbus:	Wenn Sie die Stelle hier bekommen, dann müssen Sie auch nach Südostasien fahren.
Herr Frenker:	Wie oft wäre das?
Frau Kottbus:	Schwer zu sagen, aber wahrscheinlich zwei- oder dreimal im Jahr.
Herr Frenker:	Kein Problem – ich würde mich darauf freuen.

Vocabulary

die Zusammenarbeit	cooperation
gegenwärtig	present
fließend	fluent
Südostasien	South-East Asia

Language note

1 **wir brauchen jemanden** – note the ending. This is the *accusative* form of **jemand** ('someone').
The dative form ends in **-em** – **mit jemandem**
2 **wie oft wäre das?** – 'how often would that be?'
(**wäre** is the *imperfect subjunctive* of **sein** ('to be'):

ich wäre	I would be
du wär(e)st	you would be, etc.
er/sie/es wäre	
wir wären	
ihr wäret	
sie wären	
Sie wären	

You have already met the present subjunctive form of various verbs. The imperfect subjunctive of weak verbs is exactly the same as the indicative form:

Indicative   **Subjunctive**
ich machte   ich machte
du machtest, etc. du machtest

For further details on the imperfect subjunctive and its formation, see the **Grammar** section of this chapter.

  ## Dialogue 3

At the end of the interview.

Frau Kottbus: Also, Herr Frenker, vielen Dank für Ihre Bewerbung. Wie Sie wissen, ich muss heute noch mit drei anderen Kandidaten sprechen, aber wir werden sie kontaktieren, sobald wir können – hoffentlich in den nächsten vier Tagen.
Herr Frenker: Vielen Dank. Es war ein Vergnügen, mit Ihnen zu sprechen.
Frau Kottbus: Auf Wiedersehen.
Herr Frenker: Auf Wiedersehen.

Vocabulary

es war ein Vergnügen   it was a pleasure

 ## Übung 17

Insert suitable verbs in the gaps from the list provided.

> **gefällt ist beworben muss spricht bekommt möchte wechseln**
>
> **will arbeiten fahren hat reist arbeiten**

Herr Frenker _____ seine Stelle _____. Er _____ sich um die Stelle als Verkaufsleiter bei einem anderen Unternehmen _____. Seine gegenwärtige Arbeit _____ ihm, aber er _____ für ein größerres Unternehmen _____.

Wenn er die Stelle _____, _____ er oft ins Ausland _____. Das _____ für ihn kein Problem, denn er _____ gerne, und er _____ auch fließend Französisch.

🎧 ✍ Übung 18

Listen to the recording of two people talking about their jobs, and then complete the grid.

Dialogue 4

	Job?	Where?	How long in this job?	Reason for wanting to move?
Maria				
Norbert				

🔍 Grammar

1. The pluperfect tense

The pluperfect tense (English examples: 'I had written'; 'He had worked') is formed by using the imperfect of **haben** or **sein**, together with the past participle.

In other words, the rules of formation are the same as for the perfect tense, except that the imperfect of the auxiliary verb (**haben** or **sein**) is used rather than the present tense.

Look at these examples:

Present	*Perfect*	*Pluperfect*
Ich arbeite	Ich habe gearbeitet	Ich hatte gearbeitet
Er schreibt	Er hat geschrieben	Er hatte geschrieben
Sie trinkt	Sie hat getrunken	Sie hatte getrunken
Wir gehen	Wir sind gegangen	Wir waren gegangen
Sie fährt	Sie ist gefahren	Sie war gefahren

2. The imperfect subjunctive

FORMATION OF THE IMPERFECT SUBJUNCTIVE

The imperfect subjunctive of weak verbs is exactly the same as the indicative form:

Indicative	*Subjunctive*
ich machte	ich machte
wir reservierten	wir reservierten
er arbeitete	er arbeitete

For strong verbs, the imperfect subjunctive is formed by taking the imperfect 'stem' (see the earlier chapter), then adding an Umlaut if the stem contains **a**, **o** or **u**, and then the subjunctive endings:

The verb **sprechen**:

Present indicative = **ich spreche**
Imperfect indicative = **ich sprach**

Imperfect subjunctive:

ich spräche
du sprächest
er/sie/es spräche
wir sprächen
ihr sprächet
wir sprächen
Sie sprächen

The imperfect subjunctive of two very common and very useful verbs (**haben** and **sein**) is as follows:

ich wäre
du wärest
er/sie/es wäre
wir wären
ihr wäret
sie wären
Sie wären

ich hätte
du hättest
er/sie/es hätte
wir hätten
ihr hättet
sie hätten
Sie hätten

USE OF THE IMPERFECT SUBJUNCTIVE

The imperfect subjunctive in German is commonly used to express *conditions*:

Wenn ich hier wäre   If I were here

Wenn er Geld hätte   If he had money

Wenn wir nach Hause führen   If we went home

The imperfect subjunctive is also very useful in the case of the verbs **werden** and **können** when they are used with a dependent infinitive:

In both cases the imperfect subjunctive is irregular:

ich würde   I would ...
du würdest
er/sie/es würde
wir würden
ihr würdet
sie würden
Sie würden

ich könnte   I could ...
du könntest
er/sie/es könnte
wir könnten
ihr könntet
sie könnten
Sie könnten

Examples of use:

Wenn ich könnte, würde ich hier bleiben. ('If I could I would stay here'.)

Wenn wir das tun könnten, wären wir sehr froh. ('If we could do that we would be very happy'.)

Ich könnte das nie tun. ('I could never do that'.)

Wenn ich genug Geld verdienen könnte, würde ich einen Wagen kaufen. ('If I could earn enough money I would buy a car'.)

CONDITIONAL SENTENCES

Look at the following conditional sentences in English:

If he *has* enough money, he *goes* out.
If he *had* enough money, he *would* go out.

If I *stay* at home, I *read* a book.
If I *stayed* at home, I *would read* a book.

You will see that there is a clear pattern: if the verb in the first clause is in the *present tense* ('if he has'), the verb in the second clause is also in the *present tense* ('he goes'.)

If the verb in the first clause is in the *past tense* ('if he had'), the verb in the second clause is in the *conditional* ('he would go out').

In German, the situation is similar in the case of the first clause being in the present tense:

Wenn er genug Geld *hat*, *geht* er aus.

However, if the *condition* is expressed in the *past*, German uses the *imperfect subjunctive* in *both parts* of the sentence:

Wenn er genug Geld *hätte*, *ginge* er aus.

(**hätte** is the imperfect subjunctive of **haben**)
(**ginge** is the imperfect subjunctive of **gehen**)

The above example is very formal German. A much more common alternative, particularly in spoken German, is to use the appropriate form of **würde** in the second clause:

Wenn er Genug geld *hätte*, *würde* er ausgehen.

(**würde** is the imperfect subjunctive form of **werden**)

Look at the following additional examples, and try to translate them into English:

Wenn ich zu Hause bleibe, lese ich ein Buch.
Wenn ich zu Hause bliebe, würde ich ein Buch lesen.

Wenn der Bus spät kommt, fahren wir mit der Straßenbahn.
Wenn der Bus spät käme, würden wir mit der Straßenbahn fahren.

Wenn er einen Job hat, kann er das Auto kaufen.
Wenn er einen Job hätte, könnte er das Auto kaufen.

Wenn Frau Meyer im Büro ist, können Sie mit ihr sprechen.
Wenn Frau Meer im Büro wäre, könnten Sie mit ihr sprechen.

Language in use

✍ Übung 19

PLUPERFECT TENSE

Put the following sentences into the pluperfect tense:

1 Er hat Marias Geburtstag völlig vergessen.
2 Wir haben den Bus nach Frankfurt verpasst.
3 Sie hat zwei Stunden auf ihre Freundinnen gewartet.
4 Meine Schwester hat in Freiburg studiert.
5 Markus ist allein ins Theater gegangen.
6 Johann hat sich um eine neue Stelle beworben.
7 Frau Kottbus ist nach Singapur geflogen.
8 Dieter ist um 6 Uhr aufgestanden.

✍ Übung 20

PLUPERFECT TENSE

Write ten sentences in the pluperfect using the infinitives listed below:

- suchen
- reservieren
- finden
- spielen
- sprechen
- lesen
- arbeiten
- verkaufen
- bestellen

✍ Übung 21

IMPERFECT SUBJUNCTIVE

Select appropriate verbs in the imperfect subjunctive from the list to complete the gaps.

würde   würden   hätten   könnten   möchten   könntest   hätten   könnte
wäre   hätte

1   Wenn ich hier bleiben _____, _____ ich froh.
2   Ich _____ gern ein Bier!
3   Das _____ wir nie tun!
4   Wenn der Chef hier _____, _____ er das nie erlauben.
5   _____ Sie das bitte gleich tun?
6   _____ Sie Zeit, mir zu helfen?
7   Wenn Ute und Wolfgang eine größere Wohnung _____, _____ du bei ihnen wohnen.
8   _____ Sie heute ausgehen?

✍ Übung 22

IMPERFECT SUBJUNCTIVE

Match up the two halves of each sentence correctly:

Wenn du nicht ausgehst	wären wir um 2 Uhr in Augsburg.
Wenn ich das wüsste	würde ich die Prüfung nie bestehen.
Wenn ich so langsam arbeitete	wären Sie nicht so geduldig!
Wenn der Zug pünktlich ankäme	kannst du mir mit meiner Arbeit helfen.
Wenn Sie an meiner Stelle wären	wäre ich nicht sehr glücklich.

Test your knowledge

✍ Übung 23

Give the imperfect subjunctive form of each of the following (you will probably need to use a dictionary for assistance with some of these):

ich kann
wir fahren
Sie bleiben
wir verdienen
er bringt
sie steigen
er ist
sie schreibt
wir lesen
ihr geht
wir können
sie darf

✍ Übung 24

Give the German equivalent expressions for the following:

application		career prospects	
to apply for		to consider (application)	
department		applicant	
curriculum vitae		pressure	
manager		responsibility	
sales manager		branch	
export department		sector (of industry)	
to invite		to look for	
company		to look forward to	

📖 ✍ Übung 25

What do the following German words mean?

- Erfahrung
- EDV
- Tätigkeit
- langweilig
- Personalleiterin
- Zusammenarbeit

✎ Übung 26

Write in German three brief descriptions of the following people and their jobs, based on the notes given:

	Johann	Maria	Renate
Age	35	48	38
Current post	Accountant	Manager of export department	Self-employed
First job	Sales manager	Buyer	Worked as trainee in IT company
Education	School in Hannover, university in Berlin, studied economics and accountancy	School in London, university in Paris and Munich	School followed by Berufsschule (studied IT)
Period in this job	6 years	8 years	4 years

✎ Übung 27

Write a simple letter of application for this advertised post:

Wir suchen zum nächstmöglichen Termin Computer-Verkäufer/innen für unser Geschäft in der Stadtmitte Hannover.

Wir brauchen dynamische, engagierte und teamfähige Mitarbeiter mit Erfahrungen im Verkaufsbereich.

Ihre Unterlagen senden Sie bitte an:

Frau Doris Müllbach
Postfach H8745

✎ Übung 28

Put the following sentences into the conditional – i.e. using the imperfect subjunctive.

Example:

Sie arbeitet bei dieser Firma. Sie verdient viel Geld.
Wenn sie bei dieser Firma arbeitete, würde sie viel Geld verdienen.

1   Ich gehe um 10 Uhr aus dem Haus. Ich verpasse den Bus.

2   Wir fahren mit der Straßenbahn um 11 Uhr. Wir kommen um 11.30 Uhr am
    Bahnhof an.
3   Wir reservieren einen Stellplatz. Wir kommen nach Mitternacht an.
4   Es regnet heute. Ich bleibe zu Hause.
5   Du hast genug Zeit. Du liest die Zeitung.
6   Es gibt eine neue Ölkrise. Die Benzinpreise steigen.
7   Das Restaurant ist billig. Ich esse oft dort.
8   Unsere Wohnung ist groß genug. Wir ziehen nicht um.
9   Meine Tante wohnt auch in der Stadtmitte. Ich besuche sie jeden Tag.
10 Sein Gehalt ist sehr gut. Er ist zufrieden.

Unit 10
Texts for aural and written comprehension

The following pages contain a number of texts which you may use to test your understanding of the written and spoken language. Each of the texts is recorded, so you can use them for aural comprehension, or for translation or summary. Some of the later texts are quite demanding, and you should concentrate on trying to understand the gist of these rather than every word. You should not attempt any of these texts until you have completed Unit 6 of the book.

You might wish to use these texts in the following ways:

1 'Gist' listening comprehension – listen to the recorded version before looking at the printed text, and try to list the main points of information. Then check the written version against your notes.
2 'Dictation' practice. Try to write down sections of the recorded text exactly as you hear them. This is very good practice for listening accuracy, and for spelling.
3 Written summary – produce a brief written summary of the key points.
4 Translation – either of sections of the text or of the whole text.
5 Working in pairs – one partner prepares the text carefully, and produces a list of comprehension questions relating to the points of information in the text. The other partner answers the questions. The roles are then exchanged for the next text.

The texts are, as far as possible, 'authentic' German which has not been modified to make it simpler. If you can read, listen to and understand some of these texts (or even all of them!) you have made very real progress.

To help you, the texts have been graded according to difficulty:

* reasonably straightforward
** quite difficult
*** difficult

 **Text 1**

Service im Zug*

- Wir bitten Sie, Ihre Fahrscheine im Zug stets mit sich zu tragen

- Bordbistro im Wagen 11

- Kleinkindabteil im Bereich der 2. Wagenklasse

- Rollstuhlplätze vorhanden

- Behindertengerechte Toilette vorhanden

- Sitzplätze für Schwerbehinderte im 1. und 2. Wagenklasse

 **Text 2**

Automarkt*

- Chrysler Neon. Baujahr 1999. 120000 km. 133 ps; Airbag; Zentralverriegelung; Metallic Lackierung; ABS; elektr. Fensterheber; Servolenkung

- Alfa Romeo 145. Erstzulassung: 01.06.01. 103 ps; Servolenkung; Airbag; Klimaanlage; TÜV neu. 48 000 km.

- Mitsubishi Runner. 1.8 Automatic; Katalysator; Klimaanlage; Alufelgen; Baujahr 1998; ZV; el. FH; 5Gg.

Restaurantführer*

'Klimbim'. Alte Rheinstraße 45, Köln.
Öffnungszeiten: Täglich 17–24h

Das Lokal ist komplett renoviert und im orientalischen Stil eingerichtet. Besonders zu empfehlen sind: Hähnchenfleisch süß-sauer mit einer Soße aus gemahlenen Walnüssen; Lammfiletspieß in Öl und Zwiebeln mariniert; gebratenes Hänchenfleisch in einer Soße aus Möhrenstreifen, Ingwer und Safran. Am Wochenende bietet das Lokal Veranstaltungen mit Bauchtanz und Live-Musik.

Pasta Pasta!
Hartmann-von-Aue Straße 24
Bonn (Innenstadt)

Öffnungszeiten 18–24h (Montags geschlossen)

Gemütliches italienisches Restaurant mit einer Terrasse im mediterranen Stil in der ersten Etage. Die 100 Plätze sind überdacht und können bei kaltem Wetter beheizt werden. Ein offener Kamin ergänzt die angenehme Atmosphäre.

Handy-Shop*

Hier bekommen Sie die neuesten Klingeltöne, Logos und Bildnachrichten!

- Ihr Handy können Sie individuell gestalten:

- Klingeltöne: Ihren Lieblingsklingelton können wir auf Ihr Handy senden.

- Betreiberlogos: Ersetzen Sie den Schriftzug Ihres Netzbetreibers durch ein neues Logo Ihrer Wahl.

Hotline jetzt anrufen und bestellen: Bestellhotline = 0190 27 37 49

Text 5

Wohnungen*

- Nachmieter gesucht – für schöne sanierte 3-Raumwohnung (120 qm) neben S- und U-Bahnhof. Ruhige Lage. Balkon, gefliestes Bad. tel: 030/28465869

- Nette 1 Zi-Wohnung mit Schlafnische. Hell, ruhig, großer Balkon. In direkter Nähe zum S-Bahnhof. 4 OG. Fahrstuhl. Tel: 239 47 5487

- Vermiete Zimmer in zweier-WG ab 9. September. 25 qm, teilmöbliert. Renoviert, sehr ruhige Lage, nahe Stadtmitte. Tel: 1829 3746

Text 6

Hartmann Fördertechnik**

Gabelstapler und Lagertechnik

Wir sind ein innovates Unternehmen und verkaufen seit über 50 Jahren Gabelstapler, Lagertechnik und Serviceleistungen.

Sie haben Führungsqualitäten und können Ihre Mannschaft zu Höchstleistungen motivieren. Sie haben eigene Erfahrung im Verkauf und verstehen den Verkaufserfolg als Teil Ihrer Persönlichkeit.

Interessiert?

Dann kommen Sie zu uns als Verkaufsleiter.

- Wir bieten Ihnen ein motiviertes Team, eine gute, leistungsbezogene Vergütung sowie einen Firmenwagen.

- Bitte senden Sie Ihre Bewerbungsunterlagen an unseren Geschäftsführer Herrn Peter Straub.

Hartmann Fördertechnik

Lastminute-Urlaub*

Jetzt können Sie bei uns online buchen – von jetzt bis zur Ihrer Urlaubsreise sind es nur wenige Mausklicks. In unserer Lastminute- und Charterflugdatenbank können Sie unter mehr als 1.2 Millionen Angeboten auswählen. Mit individuellen Suchkriterien stellen Sie schnell Ihr Urlaubspaket zusammen. Die Tickets werden anschließend direkt an Sie geschickt.

Frauen immer noch benachteiligt?**

Trotz besserer Schulabschlüsse werden Mädchen gegenüber männlichen Bewerbern auf dem Ausbildungsmarkt benachteiligt, glauben viele Experten. Mehr als 300 Ausbildungsberufe sind für junge Frauen zugänglich, aber zwei Drittel der Schulabgängerinnen werden in nur zehn Berufen ausgebildet. Viele Frauen beschränken sich auf Berufe wie Verkäuferin oder Frisörse.

Die Diät**

Der Frühling ist der beliebteste Zeitpunkt für die meisten Menschen, eine Diät zu beginnen. Wer seine Diät effektiv gestalten will, sollte auch moderaten Sport treiben. Langsames, langfristiges Training hilft, das körpereigene Fett an Bauch, Hüften und Oberschenkeln zu verbrennen. Experten raten: die Sportart ist nicht entscheidend, aber es ist wichtig, langfristig zu trainieren, wenn man abnehmen will. Am besten ist es, lebenslang Sport zu treiben. Man sollte zwei- bis dreimal in der Woche länger als eine halbe Stunde trainieren. Ausdauertraining ist gut für Herz und Kreislauf, und hilft, das eigene Gewicht zu reduzieren.

Text 10

Das Wetter*

Unsere Region
In der ersten Tageshälfte noch größere Wolkenlücken, am Nachmittag ziehen von Westen Schauer zu uns. Die Temperaturen erreichen 15 bis 18 Grad.

Windvorhersage
Nordwest 4 bis 5, abends um West, Böen um 6. Morgen West bis Südwest 5 bis 6, Böen 7 bis 8.

Aussichten
Morgen halten sich viele Wolken, und es gibt immer wieder Schauer. Die Temperaturen ändern sich kaum. Montag werden Werte um 20 Grad erreicht, und es bleibt wechselhaft.

Pollenflug
Die Belastung durch Pollen ist aufgrund der Wetterlage nur gering. Gräser- und Kräuterpollen fliegen schwach. Auch der Flug von Nesselpollen ist schwach.

Städtewetter von heute

Amsterdam	st. bew.	18 Grad
Athen	sonnig	35 Grad
Budapest	Schauer	25 Grad
Kopenhagen	st. bew.	17 Grad
Prag	Schauer	15 Grad
Wien	st. bew.	22 Grad

Text 11

Horoskop*

Widder
Bei Ihnen stellt sich ein Gefühl von Zufriedenheit ein und das mit Recht. Bald ist es aber aus mit der Ruhe, dann werden wichtige Entscheidungen verlangt.

Stier
Sie versuchen jetzt, unangenehme Aufgaben auf Schwächere abzuwälzen und sich aus der Affäre zu ziehen. Das ist aber nicht fein!

Zwillinge
Arbeiten Sie mehr mit den Kollegen zusammen – dann müssen Sie die Verantwortung nicht allein tragen. Sorgen Sie sich auch um Ihre Gesundheit.

Krebs
Durch Ihre beruflichen Belastungen laufen Sie Gefahr, Fehler zu begehen. Verscherzen Sie nicht die Sympathie von Vorgesetzten.

Text 12

Ihr Urlaubsdomizil*

Das gutbürgerliche Hotel Drei Adler befindet sich im Zentrum des Kurortes, in Strand- und Bahnhofsnähe. Das Haus verfügt über 40 Zimmer, alle mit Bad oder Dusche/WC, ein Restaurant, ein Café, eine Pizzeria, eine Weindiele sowie einen Aufenthaltsraum mit TV. Darüber hinaus stehen Ihnen Whirlpool, Solarium und das hauseigene Seebad zur Verfügung.

  Text 13

Hotel Steinhof**

Das familiär geführte und ansprechende 4-Sterne-Haus mit persönlichem Flair bietet Ihnen mehrere Aufenthaltsräume, Lift, Sauna, Solarium, einen Tennisplatz sowie ein Hallenbad mit direktem Zugang zum großen, schön angelegten Hotelgarten. Alle Zimmer sind mit Bad oder Dusche/WC, TV, Minibar und Telefon ausgestattet. Das Restaurant, die Sommerterrasse und die Bar laden zum Verweilen ein. Außerdem erwartet Sie an jedem Nachmittag ein Kuchenbüfett sowie dreimal in der Woche ein Unterhaltungsabend mit Musik.

  Text 14

Für jeden Rasen den passenden Mäher***

Jährlich werden in Deutschland mehr als eine Million Rasenmäher verkauft. Doch oft wählt man den falschen Mäher. Entscheidend ist die Rasengröße und die Topographie des Gartens. Aber die Einsatzzeit wird vom Gerätetyp bestimmt – Rasenmäher darf man nur werktags zwischen 7 und 19 Uhr betreiben, wenn sie lauter als 88 dB sind – und kein Benzinmäher unterschreitet diese Lärmgrenze.

Handrasenmäher sind umweltfreundlich und leise. Allerdings darf das Gras nicht zu hoch sein, und die Messer müssen scharf geschliffen sein, sonst wird das Hin- und Herschieben zur Qual.

Elektromäher eignen sich für alle mittleren Grundstücke bis 500 Quadratmeter Rasenfläche. Sie brauchen kaum Pflege, aber einen Stromanschluss im Garten. Das Kabel stört oft, wenn man um Bäume, Büsche oder Kinderspielgeräte herum mähen muss.

Benzin-Rasenmäher sind viel stärker als Elektro-Mäher und sind für höheres Gras und große Grundstücke geeignet. Nachteil: Sie sind laut und verursachen Abgase.

 **Text 15**

Die deutsche Autoindustrie***

Die deutsche Automobilindustrie reagiert mit harten Schnitten auf die derzeit schwache Nachfrage: Tausende von Arbeitsplätzen werden gestrichen. Allein in Europa werden in den nächsten 18 Monaten die Belegschaften um mehr als 5000 Beschäftigte gekürzt. Bei einigen Firmen versucht man, Stellen über Vorruhestand zu streichen.

Die guten Jahre in der Autoindustrie sind vorüber. Zum ersten Mal seit langem muss sich die Automobilindustrie auf magere Zeiten einstellen. Die Vorzeichen in den USA sind besonders ungünstig, und das hat Folgen für den deutschen Markt. Die deutschen Automobilmanager brauchen Geduld: Sie müssen die gegenwärtige Krise durchstehen und auf eine Belebung in zwei Jahren hoffen. Der Automobilabsatz wird im nächsten Jahr weltweit zurückgehen – um 4%, glauben einige britische Experten. Die deutschen Autofirmen rechnen mit einem Rückgang von rund 2%.

  Text 16

'Bullying'***

Viele kennen das aus der Schule: Ein Schwacher wird von einem (oder manchmal von mehreren) Stärkeren schikaniert, geschubst oder sogar geschlagen. Dann machen alle mit. Experten nennen das Phänomen Mobbing oder Bullying. Jedes siebte Kind wird ein- oder mehrmals pro Woche von anderen schikaniert. Der Täter erwartet vom Mobbing Vorteile – er wird dadurch von der Gruppe anerkannt und ist der Star. Die Mitläufer, die oben in der Hierarchie stehen, haben einfach Spaß. Die, die unten stehen, haben Angst, selbst Opfer zu werden, und machen deshalb mit. Es gibt unterschiedliche Formen von Mobbing: Mädchen machen es intelligenter und indirekter, und Jungen sind aggressiver. Die indirekte Aggression ist in der Regel leicht vor Lehrern zu verbergen, und wird kaum bestraft.

German grammar reference

CONTENTS

Imperfect tense
Perfect tense
9. **Days and months**
10. **Prepositions**
11. **Numbers**
12. **Dates**
13. **Time**

Note that this grammar reference is not intended to be exhaustive, but to give clear, easily comprehensible information on the elements of German grammar covered in this course. For more detailed explanations and for further examples, you should consult a separate grammar reference work.

1. Genders

German nouns have one of three genders:

Masculine (e.g. **der Wagen** – 'the car')
Feminine (e.g. **die Lampe** – 'the lamp')
Neuter (e.g. **das Haus** – 'the house')

*Note that gender is not determined by biological gender. For example, the German word for 'guard' or 'sentry' is **die Wache**, which is a feminine noun.*

2. Cases

There are four cases in German:

- Nominative (denotes the *subject* of a verb)
- Accusative (denotes the *direct object* of a verb)
- Genitive (indicates *possession*)
- Dative (indicates the *indirect object* of a verb)

Note that the accusative, genitive and dative cases are also used after certain prepositions.

[handwritten margin notes:]
① – Nom = subject
– Acc = direct ob
② – Gen = poss.
– Dat = indirect ob.
③

3. Nouns

Nouns in German have one of three genders (see above).

They are always written with an initial capital letter:

der Tisch	table
die Dame	lady
das Haus	house
der Computer	computer

German nouns form their plurals in a number of different ways – and 'patterns' can be determined, but the only safe rule is to learn the plural of a noun when you learn its gender and its meaning.

Here are some of the 'patterns' of plurals:

Masculine

Nouns which 'modify' the vowel (i.e. add an Umlaut), and add **-e**:

der Stuhl (chair)	**die Stühle**
der Fuchs (fox)	**die Füchse**
der Baum (tree)	**die Bäume**

Nouns which simply 'modify' the vowel:

der Vater (father)	**die Väter**
der Garten (garden)	**die Gärten**

Nouns which do not change in the plural form:

der Kellner (waiter)	**die Kellner**
der Fehler (mistake)	**die Fehler**
der Teller (plate)	**die Teller**

Most masculine nouns ending in **-el**, **-en**, or **-er** belong to this particular group.

Nouns which take an Umlaut and **-er** in the plural:

der Mann (man)	**die Männer**
der Wald (forest)	**die Wälder**

Feminine

Nouns which add **-n** or **-en** in the plural:

die Zeitung (paper)	**die Zeitungen**
die Lampe (lamp)	**die Lampen**

| **die Diskette** (diskette) | **die Disketten** |
| **die Lehrerin** (female teacher) | **die Lehrerinnen** |

(*Note the doubling of the 'n' in the last example.*)

Nouns which have an Umlaut and add **-e** in the plural (like some masculine nouns):

die Maus (mouse)	**die Mäuse**
die Stadt (city)	**die Städte**
die Wurst (sausage)	**die Würste**

Neuter

Nouns which have an Umlaut and add **-er**:

das Haus (house)	**die Häuser**
das Dach (roof)	**die Dächer**
das Dorf (village)	**die Dörfer**

Nouns which do not change in the plural (usually nouns ending in **-chen**, **-lein**, or **-er**):

das Zimmer (room)	**die Zimmer**
das Fräulein (young lady)	**die Fräulein**
das Mädchen (girl)	**die Mädchen**

Nouns which add **-en** in the plural:

| **das Bett** (bed) | **die Betten** |
| **das Hemd** (shirt) | **die Hemden** |

4. Definite article

Singular

	Masculine	*Feminine*	*Neuter*
Nominative	der Mann	die Frau	das Haus
Accusative	den Mann	die Frau	das Haus
Genitive	des Mannes	der Frau	des Hauses
Dative	dem Mann	der Frau	dem Haus

Plural

(The plural forms of the definite article are the same for all three genders.)

Nominative		die Frauen	
Accusative		die Frauen	
Genitive		der Frauen	
Dative		den Frauen	

5. The indefinite article

	Masculine	Feminine	Neuter
Nominative	ein Mann	eine Frau	ein Haus
Accusative	einen Man	eine Frau	ein Haus
Genitive	eines Mannes	einer Frau	eines Hauses
Dative	einem Mann	einer Frau	einem Haus

6. Pronouns

ich	I
du	you (intimate form)*
er	he
sie	she
es	it
wir	we
ihr	you (intimate form)*
sie	they
Sie	you (polite form)

* used with friends, children, and animals

The form of pronouns in German is determined by the gender, number and case of the noun they represent:

Das Haus ist neu. *Es* steht dort drüben.
Der Mann arbeitet hier. Ich kenne *ihn* aber nicht.
Die Dame wohnt in dieser Straße. *Sie* arbeitet in Frankfurt.

Singular

Nominative	ich	du	er	sie	es	Sie
Accusative	mich	dich	ihn	sie	es	Sie
Dative	mir	dir	ihm	ihr	ihm	Ihnen

Plural

Nominative	wir	ihr	sie	sie	sie	Sie
Accusative	uns	euch	sie	sie	sie	Sie
Dative	uns	euch	ihnen	ihnen	ihnen	Ihnen

7. Adjectives

If an adjective precedes a noun, it takes an ending which changes according to the gender, case and number of the noun.

An adjective which does not precede a noun does not take an ending: **Das Haus ist alt**.

The following tables indicate the endings of adjectives:

Endings after the *definite* article

SINGULAR

	Masculine	*Feminine*	*Neuter*
Nominative	der kleine Hund	die kleine Maus	das kleine Haus
Accusative	den kleinen Hund	die kleine Maus	das kleine Haus
Genitive	des kleinen Hundes	der kleinen Maus	des kleinen Hauses
Dative	dem kleinen Hund	der kleinen Maus	dem kleinen Haus

PLURAL (ALL GENDERS)

Nominative	die kleinen Häuser
Accusative	die kleinen Häuser
Genitive	der kleinen Häuser
Dative	den kleinen Häusern

Endings after the *indefinite* article

SINGULAR

	Masculine	Feminine	Neuter
Nominative	ein kleiner Hund	eine kleine Maus	ein kleines Haus
Accusative	einen kleinen Hund	eine kleine Maus	ein kleines Haus
Genitive	eines kleinen Hundes	einer kleinen Maus	eines kleinen Hauses
Dative	einem kleinen Hund	einer kleinen Maus	einem kleinen Haus

PLURAL (ALL GENDERS)

Nominative	keine kleinen Häuser
Accusative	keine kleinen Häuser
Genitive	keiner kleinen Häuser
Dative	keinen kleinen Häusern

Endings when the adjective and noun are not preceded by an article

SINGULAR

	Masculine	Feminine	Neuter
Nominative	guter Wein	gute Milch	gutes Bier
Accusative	guten Wein	gute Milch	gutes Bier
Genitive	guten Weins	guter Milch	guten Biers
Dative	gutem Wein	guter Milch	gutem Bier

PLURAL (ALL GENDERS)

Nominative	gute Weine
Accusative	gute Weine
Genitive	guter Weine
Dative	guten Weinen

8. Verbs

8.1 Infinitive form

The infinitive form of all German verbs ends in **-n** or **-en**:

lesen	read
fahren	go, travel
schreiben	write
arbeiten	work
lächeln	smile
klettern	climb

8.2 Present tense

Most verbs in German follow a regular pattern in the present tense:

ich schreibe	I write
du schreibst	you write
er/sie/es schreibt	
wir schreiben	
ihr schreibt	
sie schreiben	
Sie schreiben	

Note the formation of **sein** ('to be'), and **haben** ('to have'):

sein	*haben*
ich bin	ich habe
du bist	du hast
er/sie/es ist	er/sie/es hat
wir sind	wir haben
ihr seid	ihr habt
wir sind	sie haben
sie sind	Sie haben
Sie sind	

8.3 Irregular verbs (second and third person singular)

Certain (strong) verbs have a change of vowel in the second and third person singular.

Examples:

lesen
ich lese, du liest, er/si/es liest, wir lesen, ihr lest, sie lesen, Sie lesen

fahren
ich fahre, du fährst, er/sie/es fährt, wir fahren, ihr fahrt, sie fahren, Sie fahren

sprechen
ich spreche, du sprichst, er/sie/es spricht, wir sprechen, ihr sprecht, sie sprechen,
    Sie sprechen

essen
ich esse, du isst, er/sie/es isst, wir essen, ihr esst, sie essen, Sie essen

These are also verbs which undergo a vowel change to form the *imperfect* tense (see later in this reference)

8.4 Forming the negative

Verbs are made *negative* in German by the use of **nicht** ('not'):

er arbeitet = he works
er arbeitet nicht = he does not work

sie schreibt = she writes
sie schreibt nicht = she doesn't write

Note the word order in more complex sentences:

Sie darf nicht hier bleiben.
Er kann das nicht tun.
Wir dürfen nicht mit diesem Zug fahren.

8.5 Forming questions

Questions are formed in German by the inversion of subject and verb:

er arbeitet
arbeitet er?

sie schreibt
schreibt sie?

du bleibst hier
bleibst du hier?

wir dürfen das tun.
dürfen wir das tun?

sie ist um 9 Uhr abgefahren
ist sie um 9 Uhr abgefahren?

(avoir)

8.6 Perfect tense: weak verbs

The perfect tense of weak verbs is formed by using the *auxiliary verb* (usually **haben**) and the *past participle*, which is formed in the following way:

- remove the **-n/-en** from the end of the infinitive
- add **-t/-et** at the end
- add **ge-** at the front

Examples:

stellen – gestellt	put
arbeiten – gearbeitet	worked
lächeln – gelächelt	smiled
klettern – geklettert	climbed
kaufen – gekauft	bought

ich arbeite = I work
ich habe gearbeitet = I have worked, did work

sie lächelt = she smiles
sie hat gelächelt = she has smiled/did smile

(être) or (avoir)

8.7 Perfect tense: strong verbs

The perfect tense of strong verbs is formed by using the auxiliary verb (**haben** or **sein**: see below), together with the past participle.

The past participle of strong verbs is formed in a similar way to that of weak verbs, but it ends in **-en**, and frequently has a vowel change:

List of sein
– fahren
– bleiben

schreiben – geschrieben	written
trinken – getrunken	drunk
singen – gesungen	sung
frieren – gefroren	frozen

ich trinke = I drink
ich habe getrunken = I have drunk

er schreibt = he writes
er hat geschrieben = he has written / did write

Certain verbs, which indicate a change of position or change of state, take **sein** as the auxiliary verb:

Examples:

fahren	to travel
steigen	to rise, climb
kommen	to come

ich bin gefahren
er ist gestiegen
sie sind gekommen

8.8 Future tense

The future tense is formed by using the appropriate form of **werden**, and the infinitive:

ich fliege	I fly
ich werde fliegen	I shall fly
wir essen	we eat
wir werden essen	we shall eat

8.9 Imperfect tense: weak verbs

The imperfect tense of weak verbs is formed in the following way:

* remove the **-en** from the infinitive form
* add the endings as indicated below

arbeiten		*machen*	
ich arbeite*te*	I worked	**ich mach*te***	I made, I did
du arbeite*test*		**du mach*test***	
er/sie/es arbeite*te*		**er/sie/es mach*te***	
wir arbeite*ten*		**wir mach*ten***	
ihr arbeite*tet*		**ihr mach*tet***	
sie arbeite*ten*		**sie mach*ten***	
Sie arbeite*ten*		**Sie mach*ten***	

8.10 Imperfect tense: strong verbs

The imperfect tense of strong verbs is formed differently: it usually involves a change of vowel in the 'imperfect stem', and the endings are different from those of weak verbs.

Examples:

fahren		*bleiben*	
ich fuhr	I went	**ich blieb**	I stayed
du fuhr(e)st		**du blieb***(e)st*	
er/sie/es fuhr		**er/sie/es blieb**	
wir fuhren		**wir blieb***en*	
ihr fuhrt		**ihr blieb***t*	
sie fuhren		**sie blieb***en*	
Sie fuhren		**Sie blieb***en*	

The pattern of vowel changes of strong verbs (from present tense to imperfect tense to past participle) is indicated in any good German dictionary. Here are some common strong verbs:

Infinitive	Present tense	Imperfect	Perfect
lesen	ich lese	ich las	ich habe gelesen
schreiben	ich schreibe	ich schrieb	ich habe geschrieben
singen	ich singe	ich sang	ich habe gesungen
sprechen	ich spreche	ich sprach	ich habe gesprochen
fahren	ich fahre	ich fuhr	ich bin gefahren
bleiben	ich bleibe	ich blieb	ich bin geblieben
kommen	ich komme	ich kam	ich bin gekommen
steigen	ich steige	ich stieg	ich bin gestiegen

Note the irregular form of the *imperfect* of **sein** ('to be') and **haben** ('to have'):

sein		*haben*	
ich war	I was	**ich hatte**	I had
du warst		**du hattest**	
er/sie/es war		**er/sie/es hatte**	
ihr wart		**wir hatten**	we had.
wir waren	we were	**ihr hattet**	
sie waren		**sie hatten**	
Sie waren		**Sie hatten**	

8.11 Pluperfect tense

The pluperfect tense = in English 'I *had* gone', 'You *had* bought'.

In German it is formed by using the *imperfect* of the auxiliary verbs **haben** or **sein**, together with the *past participle*.

Examples:

Ich *hatte* das nicht *erwartet*.	I hadn't expected that.
Wir *hatten* diese Stadt nie *besucht*.	We had never visited this city.
Er *hatte* nie so schnell *gearbeitet*.	He had never worked so quickly.

As in the case of the perfect tense (see above), verbs indicating a change of condition, position or state use the auxiliary verb **sein**:

Sie *waren* in die Stadt *gefahren*.	They had gone into town.
Sie *war verschwunden*.	She had disappeared.
Er *war* um Mitternacht *angekommen*.	He had arrived at midnight.

8.12 Modal verbs

The German modal verbs are:

können	to be able to
wollen	to want to
mögen	to like to
sollen	to be supposed to
müssen	to have to
dürfen	to be permitted to

Modal verbs can take a dependent infinitive:

er kann heute kommen
ich darf nicht ausgehen
wir wollen hier bleiben

They are highly irregular, and the present tense forms are indicated below:

dürfen	_müssen_	_mögen_	_sollen_	_wollen_	_können_
ich darf	ich muss	ich mag	ich soll	ich will	ich kann
du darfst	du musst	du magst	du sollst	du willst	du kannst
er/sie/es darf	er/sie/es muss	er/sie/es mag	er/sie/es soll	er/sie/es will	er/sie/es kann
wir dürfen	wir müssen	wir mögen	wir sollen	wir wollen	wir können
ihr dürft	ihr müsst	ihr mögt	ihr sollt	ihr wollt	ihr könnt
sie dürfen	sie müssen	sie mögen	sie sollen	sie wollen	sie können
Sie dürfen	Sie müssen	Sie mögen	Sie sollen	Sie wollen	Sie können

8.13 Subjunctive: present tense

Verbs can be described as having '_moods_', and in German it is possible for verbs to be either in the _indicative_ mood, or the _subjunctive_ mood.

The indicative mood is the one we meet most frequently. It is used to describe fact, reality – things which we know to be true.

The subjunctive mood is used to express doubt and uncertainty, or hypothesis. There are relatively few obvious examples of the subjunctive mood in English. One example is:

If I _were_ a rich man ...

The present subjunctive is formed in German by removing the **-en** from the infinitive of the verb, and adding the following endings:

-e
-est
-e
-en
-et
-en
-en

For example:

schreiben

Indicative form	_Subjunctive form_
ich schreibe	ich schreibe
du schreibst	du schreibest
er/sie/es schreibt	er/sie/es schreibe
wir schreiben	wir schreiben

ihr schreibt	ihr schreibet
sie schreiben	sie schreiben
Sie schreiben	sie schreiben

Note that the **er/sie/es** form of the subjunctive is the one which differs most from the indicative form.

haben

Indicative form	*Subjunctive form*
ich habe	ich habe
du hast	du habest
er/sie/es hat	er/sie/es habe
wir haben	wir haben
ihr habt	ihr habet
sie haben	sie haben
Sie haben	Sie haben

The verb **sein** has an irregular subjunctive:

sein
ich sei
du seiest
er/sie/es sei
wir seien
ihr seiet
sie seien
Sie seien

8.14 Subjunctive: imperfect tense

The imperfect subjunctive of *weak* verbs is the same as the indicative.

The imperfect subjunctive of strong verbs is formed by taking the imperfect 'stem' of the verb, and adding the same subjunctive endings as for the present subjunctive:

schreiben
imperfect stem = schrieb
Imperfect subjunctive form
ich schriebe
du schriebest
er/sie/es schriebe
wir schrieben
ihr schriebet

sie schrieben
Sie schrieben

If the verb stem contains **a**, **o** or **u**, then an umlaut is added:

lesen
imperfect stem = las
add an Umlaut = läs
Imperfect subjunctive form
ich läse
du läsest
er/sie/es läse
wir läsen
ihr läset
sie läsen
Sie läsen

Three very useful verbs in their imperfect subjunctive form are **werden**, **können** and **mögen**:

ich würde	I would
ich könnte	I could
ich möchte	I would like

They are all irregular in their formation:

mögen	*können*	*werden*
ich möchte	ich könnte	ich würde
du möchtest	du könntest	du würdest
er/sie/es möchte	er/sie/es könnte	er/sie/es würde
wir möchten	wir könnten	wir würden
ihr möchtet	ihr könntet	ihr würdet
sie möchten	sie könnten	sie würden
Sie möchten	Sie könnten	Sie würden

Examples of use:

ich möchte heute ausgehen	I would like to go out today
könntest du mir helfen?	could you help me?
das würde sie nie tun.	she would never do that

8.15 Uses of the subjunctive

In German the subjunctive is more widespread than in English, and it is used particularly in expressing indirect speech, and in forming the conditional.

INDIRECT SPEECH/REPORTED SPEECH

Whereas the *indicative* is used in *direct speech*:

'Ich komme gegen 9 Uhr', sagte er.
'Ich fahre um10 Uhr in die Stadt', sagte sie.

In *reporting* the words, i.e. in *indirect* speech, the *subjunctive* is used:

Er sagte, er *komme* gegen 9 Uhr. (or: Er sagte, dass er gegen 9 Uhr *komme*,)
Sie sagte, sie *fahre* im 10 Uhr in die Stadt. (or: Sie sagte, dass sie um 10 Uhr in die
    Stadt *fahre*.)

In both of these note that the *present* subjunctive is used. The *tense* of the subjunctive is the same as the words *actually spoken*, whereas in English reported speech the verb is in the past tense:

He said he was coming at 9.
She said she was going into town at 10.

CONDITIONAL SENTENCES

In conditions expressed in the *present* tense, the *indicative* is used in German, as in English:

If he *comes* at 9 she *is going* out.
Wenn er um 9 Uhr *kommt*, *geht* sie aus.

In conditions expressed in the past, the subjunctive is used in German:

If he came at 9 she would go out.
Wenn er um 9 Uhr *käme*, *ginge* sie aus.

This form of the imperfect subjunctive is very formal, so the tendency, particularly in spoken German, would be to use **würde** + the infinitive in the second part of the sentence:

Wenn er um 9 Uhr *käme*, *würde* sie *ausgehen*.

Further examples:

Wenn er genug Zeit hätte, würde er die Zeitung lesen.
Wenn sie früher ins Bett ginge, würde sie vor 6 Uhr aufstehen.
Wenn das Auto nicht so teuer wäre, würde ich es sofort kaufen.

8.16 Passive

As in the case of English, German verbs have an 'active voice' and a 'passive voice'.

PRESENT TENSE

The active voice is the one we meet most frequently, in sentences in which the subject is the 'doer' of the action of the verb:

The woman buys the coat.	**Die Dame kauft den Mantel.**
The girl reads the book.	**Das Mädchen liest das Buch.**
The boy swims.	**Der Junge schwimmt.**
The bird flies.	**Der Vogel fliegt.**

In each of these sentences the verb is in the *active voice*.

There are however instances in which the action of the verb is actually 'done' to the subject:

The apple is eaten.
The man is bitten.
The book is read.

These are examples of the *passive voice*. In English we form it by using the verb 'to be' + the past participle, as in the above sentences.

In German, the verb **werden** is used, together with the past participle of the relevant verb:

Der Apfel wird von der Frau gegessen.	The apple is (being) eaten by the woman.
Das Buch wird von dem Mädchen gelesen.	The book is (being) read by the girl.
Der Mann wird von dem Hund gebissen.	The man is bitten by the dog.

Note the use of **von** to express the English 'by'.

IMPERFECT TENSE

To form a passive in the past tense, German uses the appropriate tense of **werden**, together with the infinitive, as before:

Das Buch *wurde* **gelesen**.	The book was read.
Das Hause *wurde* **gebaut**.	The house was built.
Der Brief *wurde* **diktiert**.	The letter was dictated.

PERFECT TENSE

The formation of the perfect passive in German is slightly irregular, in that a different form of the past participle of **werden** is used. The standard past participle is **geworden**, but to form the perfect passive, the form **worden** is used:

Das Haus ist gebaut *worden*.	The house has been built.
Der Computer ist gekauft *worden*.	The computer has been sold.
Der alte Bahnhof ist abgerissen *worden*.	The old station has been knocked down.

9. Days and months

Sonntag	Sunday
Montag	Monday
Dienstag	Tuesday
Mittwoch	Wednesday
Donnerstag	Thursday
Freitag	Friday
Samstag	Saturday
(Sonnabend)	Saturday

Note:

am Samstag = on Saturday
samstags = on Saturdays

Januar	January
Februar	February
März	March
April	April
Mai	May
Juni	June
Juli	July

August	August
September	September
Oktober	October
November	November
Dezember	December

Note:

im September = *in September*
Mitte September = *in the middle of September*
Anfang September = *at the beginning of September*
Ende September = *at the end of September*

10. Prepositions

In German, prepositions have to take the accusative, genitive or dative case (never the nominative).

The following prepositions are always followed by the accusative case:

bis (until)
durch (through)
entlang (along)
für (for)
gegen (against)
ohne (without)
um (around)

The following prepositions always take the genitive case:

trotz (despite)
statt (instead of)
wegen (because of)

The following prepositions always take the dative case:

aus (out of)
außer (except)
bei (with/alongside)
gegenüber (opposite)
mit (with)
nach (after)

seit (since)
von (from/by)
zu (to)

A number of prepositions take either the accusative or the dative, depending on the meaning of the sentence. These are:

in, an, auf, hinter, über, unter, vor, zwischen

Examples

sie geht in das Wohnzimmer – 'she goes into the living room' (accusative – indicates movement into the room)

sie steht in dem Wohnzimmer – 'she stands in the living room' (dative – indicates 'location')

er stellt das Buch auf den Tisch – 'he puts the book on the table' (accusative – indicates movement of the book onto the table)

das Buch ist auf dem Tisch – 'the book is on the table' (dative – indicates location of the book on the table)

11. Numbers

German	English	German	English
eins	one	dreißig	thirty
zwei	two	einunddreißig	thirty-one
drei	three	zweiunddreißig	thirty-two
vier	four	vierzig	forty
fünf	five	fünfzig	fifty
sechs	six	sechzig	sixty
sieben	seven	siebzig	seventy
acht	eight	achtzig	eighty
neun	nine	neunzig	ninety
zehn	ten	hundert	hundred
elf	eleven	hundertzwei	102
zwölf	twelve	hundertzehn	110
dreizehn	thirteen	hundertzwanzig	120
vierzehn	fourteen	hundertdreißig	130
fünfzehn	fifteen	hunderteinunddreißig	131
sechzehn	sixteen	hundertvierzig	140

siebzehn	seventeen	zweihundert	200
achtzehn	eighteen	dreihundert	300
neunzehn	nineteen	tausend	thousand
zwanzig	twenty	eine Million	one million
einundzwanzig	twenty one	eine Milliarde	one thousand million
zweiundzwanzig	twenty two		

Note:

Decimals: '2.5' ('two point five') is rendered in German as **zwei komma fünf**.

Percentages: 'four per cent' = **4 Prozent**

Ordinal numbers (first, second, etc.) are formed in German by adding **-(s)t** to the end of the number in question, and then the appropriate adjective ending:

zwei	der zweite Bus
vier	das vierte Auto
hundert	das hundertste Mal

Irregular ordinal numbers in German:

| **erst** | first | **die erste Straße** |
| **dritt** | third | **das dritte Haus** |

12. Dates

Dates are formed in German as in English, by using the ordinal number as an adjective:

der zweite Mai
der fünfzehnte April
der dreißigste Oktober

'On the . . .' = in German **am** . . . (with the dative):

am ersten Juli
am zehnten Februar
am sechzehnten September

13. Time

wieviel Uhr ist es? = what time is it?
wie spät ist es? = what time is it?

um neun Uhr = at nine o'clock
um elf Uhr = at eleven o'clock

There are various possibilities when giving the time in German:

13.10   = **acht Uhr zehn; zehn (Minuten) nach acht**
9.12 = **neun Uhr zwölf; zwölf (Minuten) nach neun**
10.20 = **zehn Uhr zwanzig; zwanzig Minuten nach zehn**

11.40 = **elf Uhr vierzig; zwanzig (Minuten) vor zwölf**
11.39 = **elf Uhr neununddreißig**

12.00= **Mittag** (noon) or **Mitternacht** (midnight)

'quarter past' = **Viertel nach** (**Viertel nach elf**) (11.15)
'quarter to' = **Viertel vor** (**Viertel vor zehn**) (09.45)

'half past' = **halb** but note the difference between English and German:
'halb acht' = 07.30 ('half way to eight')
'halb zehn' = 09.30

Note also:

Viertel zwei = 1.15
dreiviertel zwei = 1.45

Vocabulary

The following lists are not exhaustive, but give most of the words you will meet in this book. They are intended to help you understand the texts and exercises, but they are no substitute for a good dictionary – you should always, if in doubt, double check the meaning of a word or phrase in a dictionary.

Key to abbreviations

nf	feminine noun
nm	masculine noun
nn	neuter noun
npl	plural noun
v	verb
vr	reflexive verb

German–English Vocabulary

ab und zu		now and then
Abend	nm	evening
Abendessen	nn	dinner
aber	prep	but
abfahren	v	depart
Abfahrt	nf	departure
abheben	v	withdraw money
Abitur	nn	A level equivalent
Abreise	nf	departure
abschalten	v	switch off
abstellen	v	set down
acht		eight
Achtung	nf	attention, caution
achtzehn		eighteen
achtzig		eighty
Agentur	nf	agency
ähnlich	adj	similar
all		all
All	nn	space
allein		alone
allerdings	conj	of course
Allergie	nf	allergy
allergisch	adj	allergic
allmählich	adj	gradual
als		as, then
also	conj	well, therefore
alt	adj	old
Ameise	nf	ant
Amerika	nn	America
anbieten	v	offer
ander	adj	other
anderthalb		one and a half
Angebot	nn	offer
angemessen	adj	appropriate
Angestellte/r	nf/nm	clerk
ankommen	v	arrive
Ankunft	nf	arrival
anregen	v	trigger
Anruf	nm	telephone call
anrufen	v	telephone, call
anschalten	v	switch on
anschließend	conj	then, next
Anschluss	nm	connection
anstrengend	adj	strenuous
Anstrich	nm	paint
Antrag	nm	application
Antragsvordruck	nm	application form
Anwalt	nm	lawyer
Apfel	nm	apple
Apparat	nm	apparatus, machine

Arbeit	nf	work
arbeiten	v	work
Arbeiter	nm	worker
arbeitslos	adj	unemployed
Arm	nm	arm
arm	adj	poor
Armbanduhr	nf	wrist watch
Artikel	nm	article
Arzt	nm	doctor
Ärztin	nf	doctor (female)
auch		also
auf	prep	on
auf Wiedersehen		goodbye
Aufgabe	nf	task, job
aufgeben	v	give up, register
aufsaugen	v	soak up
aufstehen	v	get up
Aufzug	nm	lift
August	nm	August
aus	prep	out, out of
außer	prep	except
außerhalb	prep	outside of
Ausbildung	nf	training
Ausfahrt	nf	exit (for vehicles)
ausfüllen	v	fill out (form)
Ausgang	nm	exit (pedestrian)
ausgebucht	adj	booked up
ausgehen	v	go out
ausgestattet	adj	equipped
auskühlen	v	cool off
ausländisch	adj	foreign
ausschlafen	v	lie in
ausschließlich		excluding, exclusively
Ausstellung	nf	exhibition
Australien	nn	Australia
australisch	adj	Australian
Auswahl	nf	selection
Ausweis	nm	identity card
ausziehen	vr	get undressed
ausziehen	v	move out
Auszubildende/r	nf/nm	trainee, apprentice
Auto	nn	car
backen	v	bake
Bäcker	nm	baker
Bäckerei	nf	baker's shop
Bad	nn	bath
Badezimmer	nn	bathroom
Bafög	nn	grant (student)
Bahn	nf	railway
Bahnhof	nm	station

Bahnsteig	nm	platform
bald	adv	soon
Banane	nf	banana
Band	nn	belt (conveyor)
Bank	nf	bank
bauen	v	build
Baum	nm	tree
Baumwolle	nf	cotton
Baustelle	nf	building site
Bayern	nn	Bavaria
Bedarf	nm	need
bedecken	v	cover
bedeckt	adj	cloudy, dull
Bedienung	nf	service
befinden	vr	positioned, located
Beförderung	nf	promotion
Befragung	nf	enquiry, poll
begeistert	adj	enthusiastic
behandeln	v	treat
Behandlung	nf	treatment
beheizt	adj	heated
bei	prep	with
beide	adj	both
Bein	nn	leg
Beispiel	nn	example
Beitrag	nm	contribution
bekämpfen	v	combat, fight
Bekannte	npl	acquaintances
bekommen	v	get, obtain
belasten	v	burden
Belgien	nn	Belgium
belgisch	adj	Belgian
benötigen	v	need, require
Berater	nm	adviser, consultant
Beratung	nf	consultancy, advice
Bereich	nm	area
bereit	adj	ready
bereiten	v	prepare
Berg	nm	mountain
Beruf	nm	profession, occupation
Berufsaussichten	npl	career prospects
besetzt	adj	occupied
Besitz	nm	possession, ownership
besitzen	v	possess
besonders		especially
besorgen	v	get, acquire
besprechen	v	discuss
besser	adj	better
best	adj	best
bestellen	v	order

bestimmt	adj	definite
besuchen	v	visit
Betriebswirtschaft	nf	economics, businesss studies
Bett	nn	bed
Bevölkerung	nf	population
Bewegung	nf	movement
bewerben	vr	apply
Bewerber/in	nm/nf	applicant
bezahlen	v	pay
Bezahlung	nf	payment
Biene	nf	bee
Bienenstock	nm	beehive
Bier	nn	beer
Bildschirm	nm	screen, monitor
Bildung	nf	formation
billig	adj	cheap
bis	prep	until
bisher	adv	up to now
bissfest	adj	al dente
bitte		please
bitte schön		please, don't mention it
bitten	v	request, ask
blau	adj	blue
bleiben	v	stay
Bleistift	nm	pencil
Blick	nm	view, sight
Blume	nf	flower
Bluse	nf	blouse
Blut	nn	blood
Blutdruck	nm	blood pressure
Börse	nf	stock exchange
Boden	nm	floor, ground
Bordkarte	nf	boarding card
brauchen	v	need
Brett	nn	board
Brief	nm	letter
Brieftasche	nf	wallet, case
Brot	nn	bread
Brötchen	nn	(bread) roll
Brüssel	nn	Brussels
Buch	nn	book
buchen	v	book, reserve
Buchhaltung	nf	bookkeeping
Buchung	nf	booking
Büro	nn	office
Bürokraft	nf	office staff, assistant
Bus	nm	bus
Butter	nf	butter
Champagner	nm	champagne
Computer	nm	computer

da		there, since
Dach	nn	roof
Dachboden	nm	loft, Attic
Dacheindeckung	nf	roof cover
Dame	nf	lady
danke		thank you
danken	v	thank
dazu		additionally
Decke	nf	ceiling
dein	adj	your
deshalb	conj	therefore
deutsch	adj	German
Dezember	n	December
Diagnose	nf	diagnosis
dick	adj	thick
Dienstag	nm	Tuesday
diese/r	pron	this
Ding	nn	thing
Diskette	nf	diskette, floppy
Donnerstag	nm	Thursday
Doppelzimmer	nn	double room
Dorf	nn	village
dort		there
Dozent	nm	lecturer
drei		three
dreißig		thirty
dreizehn		thirteen
dringend	adj	urgent
dritt	adj	third
du	pron	you
Dünkirchen	nn	Dunkirk
dünn	adj	thin
dürfen	v	may (be allowed to)
dunkel	adj	dark
Durchsage	nf	announcement
durchschnittlich	adj	average, on average
Durschnitt	nm	average
Dusche	nf	shower
echt	adj	genuine
Ecke	nf	corner
ehrgeizig	adj	ambitious
Ei	nn	egg
eigen	adj	own
ein		a
einatmen	v	breathe in
Einbauküche	nf	kitchen (fitted)
einfach	adj	simple, single (ticket)
Einfahrt	nf	entrance (for vehicles)
einführen	v	introduce

Eingang	nm	entrance (pedestrian)
eingerichtet	adj	equipped, furnished
einige		few
Einkäufe	npl	purchases
einkaufen	v	shop, go shopping
Einkommen	nn	income
einlösen	v	cash (cheques)
einmal		once
einpacken	v	pack
einrichten	v	set up, establish
eins		one
einschließlich		including
einschreiben	vr	register
einzahlen	v	pay in
Einzelzimmer	nn	single room
einziehen	v	move in
Eis	nn	ice cream
Eiscafe	nn	ice cream parlour
elf		eleven
Eltern	npl	parents
empfindlich	adj	sensitive
Ende	nn	end
endlich		at last
englisch	adj	English
entfernen	v	remove
entgegen	prep	towards
enthalten	v	contain
entlang	prep	along
entschuldigen	v	excuse
Entschuldigung	nf	excuse, excuse me
Entzündung	nf	inflammation
er	pron	he
erfahren	adj	experienced
Erfahrung	nf	experience
Erhöhung	nf	increase
erkältet	adj	cold, having a cold
erledigen	v	do, carry out
erleichtern	v	relieve, make easy
Ermäßigung	nf	reduction
ermüdend	adj	tiring
eröffnen	v	open (account)
erreichen	v	reach
Erschließung	nf	opening up
ersetzen	v	replace
erwarten	v	expect
erwerbslos	adj	unemployed
es	pron	it
Essen	nn	meal

essen	v	eat
Essig	nm	vinegar
Etage	nf	floor, storey
etwa		approximately
etwas		something
euer	adj	your
Euro	nm	Euro
ewig	adj	eternal
Ewigkeit	nf	eternity
Examen	nn	exam
Fach	nn	subject
Fachbereich	nm	department (University)
Fachkräfte	npl	skilled workers
Fahrschule	nf	driving school
faul	adj	lazy
Feinschmecker	nm	gourmet
Fest	nn	celebration, festival
fest	adj	firm, solid
feststellen	v	establish, ascertain
Fett	nn	fat
Fieber	nn	fever
Filiale	nf	branch (company)
Firma	nf	firm, company
Fisch	nm	fish
Fleisch	nn	meat
fließend	adj	fluent
frei	adj	free
Freibad	nn	swimming pool (open air)
freuen	v	please
freuen (auf)	vr	look forward to
frieren	v	freeze
froh	adj	happy
Frühling	nm	spring
Frühstück	nn	breakfast
führen	v	lead
Führung	nf	leadership
Führungsposition	nf	leading job
für	prep	for
Fuß	nm	foot
Fußboden	nm	floor
garni	adj	bed and breakfast
Garten	nm	garden
Gas	nn	gas
geboren werden	v	be born
Geburt	nf	birth
Geburtstag	nm	birthday
geeignet	adj	suitable

Gefahr	nf	danger
gefährlich	adj	dangerous
Gehalt	nn	salary
Gehaltserhöhung	nf	salary increase
gehen	v	go
gelb	adj	yellow
Geld	nn	money
Geldautomat	nm	cash machine
gelegentlich	adv	occasionally
gemischt	adj	mixed
gemütlich	adj	cosy, comfortable
genau	adj	exact, precise
genießen	v	enjoy
geräumig	adj	spacious
Germanistik	nf	German language and culture
Geschäft	nn	shop, business
Geschäftsreise	nf	business trip
Geschenk	nn	present
Geschichte	nf	history
Geschmack	nm	taste
geschmackvoll	adj	tasteful
gestern	adv	yesterday
gesund	adj	healthy
Gesundheit	nf	health
gewöhnlich	conj	usually
Giftstoff	nm	poison
Girokonto	nn	current account
Glas	nn	glas
Glatteis	nn	black ice
glauben	v	believe
gleich	adv	immediately
Gleis	nn	track, platform
GmbH		limited company
Gott	nm	God
Grad	nm	degree
grau	adj	grey
gravierend	adj	serious (problem)
Griechenland	nn	Greece
griechisch	adj	Greek
groß	adj	big, large
Großmutter	nf	grandmother
Großvater	nm	grandfather
grün	adj	green
Grund	nm	reason
Grundkenntnisse	npl	basic knowledge
Grundkurs	nm	basic course
Gruß	nm	greeting
grüß Gott!		hello!
günstig	adj	favourable
Gulasch	nn	stew, goulash

Gummibär	nm	jelly bear	Hotel	nn	hotel
gut	adj	good	hübsch	adj	pretty
			Hund	nm	dog
Haar	nn	haar	hundert		hundred
Haarbürste	nf	hairbrush	Husten	nm	cough
Händler	nm	dealer	husten	v	cough
hässlich	adj	ugly			
haben	v	have	ich	pron	I
Halbpension	nf	half board	Ihr		your
halbtrocken	adj	medium dry (wine)	ihr		your, their
			Imbiss	nm	snack
Hallenbad	nn	swimming pool (indoor)	Inhalt	nm	content
			Inhaltsstoffe	npl	ingredients
Hals	nm	neck	insgesamt		in all, all together
halten	v	stop, hold			
Haltestelle	nf	stop (bus, tram)	interessant	adj	interesting
Hammelfleisch	nn	mutton			
Handel	nm	trade	Jacke	nf	jacket
handeln	v	trade, do business	Jahr	nn	year
			jährlich	adj	annual
Handelspresse	nf	trade press	Januar	nm	January
Handy	nn	mobile phone	Japan	nn	Japan
häufig	adj	frequent	japanisch	adj	Japanese
Häufigkeit	nf	frequency	jede/r		each
Hauptstadt	nf	capital city	jemand		someone
Haus	nn	house	jetzig	adj	current
heiß	adj	hot	jetzt	adv	now
heißen	v	called, be called	Job	nm	job
Heizkessel	nm	boiler	Jugendliche	npl	young people
Heizung	nf	heating	Juli	nm	July
helfen	v	help	Juni	nm	June
hell	adj	light			
hellblau	adj	light blue	Kaffee	nm	coffee
Herbst	nm	autumn	Kalbfleisch	nn	veal
Herr	nm	gentleman, Mr	kalt	adj	cold
herrlich	adj	splendid	Kapstadt	nn	Cape Town
herstellen	v	manufacture	kaputt	adj	useless, not working
Hersteller	nm	manufacturer			
hervorragend	adj	outstanding	Karte	nf	card
Herz	nn	heart	Kartoffel	nf	potato
herzlich	adv	hearty	Kasse	nf	cash desk, payment point
Heuschnupfen	nm	hay fever			
heute	adv	today	Katze	nf	cat
hier	adv	here	kaufen	v	buy
Hilfe	nf	help	Kaufhaus	nn	department store
hin		there, to there			
Hobby	nn	hobby	kein		none
hoch	adj	high	Keller	nm	cellar
Hochbauunternehmen	nn	construction company	Kellner	nm	waiter
			Kellnerin	nf	waitress
Hochschulabsolvent	nm	graduate	kennen	v	know
Hochschule	nf	university	Kenntnisse	npl	knowledge
holen	v	fetch, get	Kilo	nn	kilo
Honig	nm	honey	Kilometer	nm or nn	kilometre
Hose	nf	trousers	Kind	nn	child

Kino	nn	cinema	ledig	adj	single
Kirche	nf	church	leer	adj	empty
Klasse	nf	class	legen	v	lay, put
Klausur	nf	test	Lehrer	nm	teacher
Klavier	nn	piano	Lehrerin	nf	teacher (female)
Klima	nn	climate	leicht	adj	easy
Klimaanlage	nf	air-conditioning unit	leider		unfortunately
			Leistung	nf	achievement, performance
Klub	nm	club			
Knoblauch	nm	garlic	leiten	v	lead, manage
kochen	v	cook	Leiter	nm	manager
Koffer	nm	suitcase	Leiterin	nf	manageress
Kollege/in	nm/nf	colleague	lesen	v	read
Köln	nn	Cologne	Leute	npl	people
komisch	adj	funny	Liebe	nf	love
kommen	v	come	lieben	v	love
Konditor	nm	pastry chef	Liege	nf	recliner, bed
Konditorei	nf	patisserie	liegen	v	lie
können	v	can, be able to	links	adj	left
Konto	nn	account	Loch	nn	hole
Kontoführung	nf	maintenance of account	Löffel	nm	spoon
			Lohn	nm	wage, salary
Kopfweh	nn	headache	Lokal	nn	pub, inn
Körper	nm	body	Lust	nf	desire, wish
kosten	v	cost	Lüttich	nn	Liège
kostenlos	adj	free	Luxus	nm	luxury
Kotelett	nn	chop, cutlet			
krank	adj	ill	machen	v	do, make
Krankenhaus	nn	hospital	Magazin	nn	magazine
Krankenkasse	nf	health insurance company	Magen	nm	stomach
			mager	adj	lean, low fat
Kreditkarte	nf	credit card	Mahlzeit	nf	meal
Krise	nf	crisis	Mai	nm	May
Küche	nf	kitchen, cooking	man		one
Kugelschreiber	nm	ballpoint pen	Manager	nm	manager
kühl	adj	cool	manchmal		sometimes
Kühlschrank	nm	fridge	Mann	nm	man, husband
Kunde/in	nm/nf	customer	Mannschaft	nf	team
Kurs	nm	course, rate of exchange	Markt	nm	market
			Maschinenbau	nm	engineering
Küste	nf	coast	Maus	nf	mouse
			Mechaniker	nm	mechanic
lachen	v	laugh	Meer	nn	sea
Lage	nf	position	mein		my
Lammfleisch	nn	lamb	meistens		mostly
Lampe	nf	lamp	Menge	nf	crowd, amount
langweilig	adj	boring	Messe	nf	trade fair, mass
Lärm	nm	noise	messen	v	measure
lassen	v	let, allow	mieten	v	rent
laufen	v	run	Milch	nf	milk
Leben	nn	life	Milliarde	nf	thousand million
leben	v	live	Million	nf	million
Lebenslauf	nm	curriculum vitae	Mindestgehalt	nn	minimum salary
Lebensstil	nm	life style	Minute	nf	minute
Leder	nn	leather	mit	prep	with

Mitarbeiter	nm	colleague, co-worker		neun		nine
Mittag	nm	midday		neunzehn		nineteen
Mittagessen	nn	lunch		neunzig		ninety
Mittagspause	nf	lunch break		nicht		not
Mitte	nf	middle		Nichtraucher	nm	non-smoker
mitteilen	v	inform		nichts		nothing
mittelgroß	adj	medium size		niedrig	adj	low
Mittelmeer	nn	Mediterranean		Nizza	nn	Nice
Mitternacht	nf	midnight		noch		still
Mittwoch	nm	Wednesday		Not	nf	need, distress
Möbel	npl	furniture		November	nm	November
möbliert	adj	furnished		Numerus clausus	nm	entry restriction (university)
mögen	v	like to				
möglich	adj	possible		nutzen	v	use
Möglichkeit	nf	possibility		Nutzer	nm	user
Moment	nm	moment				
Monat	nm	month		öffnen	v	open
monatlich	adj	monthly		Öffnungszeiten	npl	opening times
morgen	adv	tomorrow		obdachlos	adj	homeless
Moskau	nn	Moscow		oben		top, at the top
müde	adj	tired		Ober	nm	waiter
München	nn	Munich		Obst	nn	fruit
Mund	nm	mouth		oft	adj	often
Münze	nf	coin		ohne	prep	without
müssen	v	must, have to		Ohr	nn	ear
Mut	nm	courage		Oktober	nm	October
mutig	adj	brave		Onkel	nm	uncle
Mutter	nf	mother		Osten	nm	east
				Ostsee	nf	Baltic
nach	prep	after		Park	nm	park
nach Hause		home (to home)		Parkplatz	nm	car park
nach links		left, to the left		Passagier	nm	passenger
nach rechts		right, to the right		pauschal	adj	inclusive
nach Vereinbarung		by agreement		Pauschalreise	nf	package holiday
Nachbar	nm	neighbour		pendeln	v	commute
Nachfrage	nf	demand		Pension	nf	board, boarding house
nachher		afterwards				
nachschauen	v	look, check		Personal	nn	staff
nächst	adj	next		Personalleiter	nm	personnel manager
Nachteil	nm	disadvantage				
Nachtisch	nm	dessert		persönlich	adj	personal
Nahrung	nf	food, nourishment		Pfeffer	nm	pepper
				Pflege	nf	care
Nahrungsmittel	npl	food		Physik	nf	physics
Name	nm	name		Pille	nf	pill
natürlich		naturally, of course		planmäßig	adj	scheduled
				Platz	nm	place, seat
Neapel	nn	Naples		Pommes	npl	chips, fries
neben		next		Pommes Frites	npl	chips, fries
nehmen	v	take		Post	nf	post, post office
nein		no		Praktikant	nm	trainee, someone on placement
Nektarine	nf	nectarine				
nett	adj	nice				
neu	adj	new		Preis	nm	price

prima		excellent, great
pro		per
Problem	nn	problem
Prospekt	nm	brochure, prospectus
prüfen	v	test, examine
Prüfung	nf	test, exam
Pullover	nm	pullover
pünktlich	adj	punctual
Putensteak	nn	turkey steak
putzen	v	clean
Radio	nn	radio
rasieren	vr	shave
Rathaus	nn	town hall
Raucher	nm	smoker
reagieren	v	react
rechnen	v	calculate
Rechnung	nf	bill
rechts		right
reden	v	speak, talk
regelmäßig	adj	regular
Regelmäßigkeit	nf	regularity
Regenschirm	nm	umbrella
rein	adj	pure
Reise	nf	trip, journey
reisen	v	travel, go
Reisepass	nm	passport
Reisescheck	nm	travellers' cheque
Reisetasche	nf	holdall, travel bag
rennen	v	run
Rente	nf	pension
Rentner	nm	pensioner
reparieren	v	repair
reservieren	v	reserve
Restaurant	nn	restaurant
richten	v	direct, send
richtig	adj	right, correct
Riese	nm	giant
Rindfleisch	nn	beef
Risiko	nn	risk
Rom	nn	Rome
Roman	nm	novel
rot	adj	red
Rückfahrkarte	nf	return ticket
Ruf	nm	reputation
rufen	v	call
rund		around
Sachsen	nn	Saxony
sagen	v	say, tell
Sahne	nf	cream
Salat	nm	salad
Salz	nn	salt
sammeln	v	collect
Samstag	nm	Saturday
Sattel	nm	saddle
saugen	v	suck
schaden	v	damage, harm
schädlich	adj	harmful
Schalter	nm	counter
Schalterbeamte/r	nm	counter assistant
Scheck	nm	cheque
scheinen	v	shine
Schirm	nm	umbrella
schlafen	v	sleep
Schlafzimmer	nn	bedroom
schlank	adj	slim
schlapp	adj	weak, limp
schlecht	adj	bad
schließen	v	close
schlimm	adj	bad
Schlüssel	nm	key
Schmerzen	npl	pains
Schokolade	nf	chocolate
schon		already
schön	adj	beautiful
schreiben	v	write
schüchtern	adj	shy
Schulabschluß	nm	school leaving certificate
Schule	nf	school
Schüler	nm	pupil (male)
Schülerin	nf	pupil (female)
schwarz	adj	black
Schweinefleisch	nn	pork
Schweiz	nf	Switzerland
schweizerisch	adj	Swiss
schwer	adj	heavy, difficult
Schwester	nf	sister
schwierig	adj	difficult
schwimmen	v	swim
sechs		six
sechzehn		sixteen
sechzig		sixty
See	nf	sea
See	nm	lake
Seele	nf	soul
sehen	v	see
sehr		very
sein	v	be
seit	prep	since
Sekt	nm	sparkling wine
Sekunde	nf	second
Senf	nm	mustard
September	nm	September
sie	pron	she, they

Sie	pron	you		Stunde	nf	hour
sieben		seven		Südafrika	nn	South Africa
siebzehn		seventeen		Süden	nn	South
siebzig		seventy		süss	adj	sweet
Silvester	nm or nn	New Year's Eve		suchen	v	seek, look for
singen	v	sing		Supermarkt	nm	supermarket
sitzen	v	sit		surfen	v	surf
Sommer	nm	summer				
Sonderpreis	nm	special price		Tablett	nn	tray
Sonne	nf	sun		Tablette	nf	tablet, pill
Sonnenschirm	nm	parasol		Tag	nm	day
sonnig	adj	sunny		täglich	adj	daily
Sonntag	nm	Sunday		Tankstelle	nf	petrol station
sonst		otherwise		Tante	nf	aunt
Sorge	nf	care, worry		Tanz	nm	dance
sorgen	v	care (for)		tanzen	v	dance
Sorte	nf	sort, type		Tasche	nf	pocket, bag
Soße	nf	sauce		tausend		thousand
soviel		so much		Taxi	nn	taxi
sowieso		in any case		Tee	nm	tea
Spanien	nn	Spain		Teelöffel	nm	teaspoon
spanisch	adj	Spanish		teilen	v	share
sparen	v	save		Teilzeitjob	nm	part-time job
Sparkonto	nn	savings account		Telefon	nn	phone
spät	adj	late		telefonieren	v	phone
Spitze	nf	peak, point		Tennis	nn	tennis
Spitzengehalt	nn	top salary		Termin	nm	appointment
Sport	nm	sport		Terrasse	nf	terrace
Sprache	nf	language		teuer	adj	dear, expensive
sprechen	v	speak		Textverarbeitung	nf	word processing
Spritze	nf	injection		Theater	nn	theatre
Spur	nf	trace		tief	adj	deep
Stadt	nf	city		Tiefgarage	nf	car park
Stadtmitte	nf	city centre				(underground)
Stammpublikum	nn	regulars		Tip	nm	tip
ständig	adj	constant		tippen	v	type
stecken	v	put, place		Tisch	nm	table
steigen	v	climb		Tochter	nf	daughter
steigern	v	increase		Tomate	nf	tomato
Stelle	nf	place, position,		Tor	nn	gate, goal
		job		Torwart	nm	goalkeeper
stellen	v	put, place		trainieren	v	train
sterben	v	die		treffen	v	meet
Steuer	nf	tax		treiben	v	drive, do (sport)
Steuer	nn	steering wheel		trinken	v	drink
Steuererklärung	nf	tax declaration		tschüs		bye!
Stil	nm	style		Tür	nf	door
Strand	nm	beach		Türkei	nf	Turkey
Straße	nf	street		türkisch	adj	Turkish
Straßenbahn	nf	tram		Tuch	nn	cloth
streichen	v	delete		tun	v	do
Student	nm	student				
Studentenwerk	nn	students' union		übel	adj	bad, evil
Studiengang	nm	course of study		übermorgen		day after
Stuhl	nm	chair				tomorrow

übernachten	v	stay overnight
überweisen	v	transfer
überzogen	adj	overdrawn (account)
Übung	nf	exercise
Uhr	nf	clock
umfangreich	adj	wide-ranging, extensive
umsteigen	v	change (trains, etc.)
umziehen	v	move house
umziehen	vr	change clothes
Umzug	nm	removal (house)
und		and
unglaublich	adj	incredible
Universität	nf	university
unmöglich	adj	impossible
Unreinheiten	npl	impurities
unser		our
Unterkunft	nf	accommodation
Unterlagen	npl	documents
Unternehmen	nn	firm, company
unterschiedlich		varying, different
unterschreiben	v	sign
Unterschrift	nf	signature
untersuchen	v	examine
unterwegs		under way, on the way
Urlaub	nm	holiday, leave
Urlaubsvertretung	nf	holiday cover
Ursache	nf	cause
ursprünglich		originally
verantwortlich	adj	responsible
Verantwortung	nf	responsibility
verbinden	v	connect
Verbindung	nf	connection
verbrauchen	v	consume, use
Verbraucher	nm	consumer
verdienen	v	earn
vergangen	adj	past
vergessen	v	forget
Vergnügen	nn	pleasure
Verhältnisse	npl	conditions, relationships
verheiratet	adj	married
verhindern	v	prevent
Verkauf	nm	sales
verkaufen	v	sell
Verkäufer/in	nm/nf	sales assistant
Verkaufsleiter/in	nm/nf	sales manager
verlangen	v	want, desire, wish
verlängern	v	extend

verlieren	v	lose
verpassen	v	miss (bus, train)
verrühren	v	mix up
verschieden	adj	various
verschlafen	v	oversleep
verschlechtern	vr	worsen
verschreiben	v	prescribe
Verspätung	nf	delay
verstecken	v	hide, conceal
verstehen	v	understand
Verwandte	npl	relatives
verzichten (auf)	v	give up, do without
Vetter	nm	cousin
viel		much
vielleicht		perhaps
vier		four
vierzehn		fourteen
vierzig		forty
voll	adj	full
von	prep	from
vor	prep	before, in front of
voraussichtlich		probably, likely
vorbei		past
vorbeikommen	v	call in
vorgestern		day before yesterday
Vorhang	nm	curtain
vorher		previously
vorig	adj	previous
Vorlesung	nf	lecture
Vorsicht	nf	caution
Vorspeise	nf	starter, hors d'oeuvre
vorstellen	v	introduce (someone)
Vorstellungsgespräch	nn	interview (for job)
Vorteil	nm	advantage
Vortrag	nm	lecture
wachsen	v	grow
Wagen	nm	car, carriage
Wahl	nf	choice, election
wählen	v	choose
während	conj	during
Warenhaus	nn	dept. store
warm	adj	warm
Warschau	nn	Warsaw
warten	v	wait
waschen	v	wash
Wasser	nn	neuter
Wechselkurs	nm	exchange rate
wechseln	v	exchange

Wechselstube	nf	bureau de change	Wunder	nn	wonder, miracle
wehtun	v	harm, hurt	wunderschön	adj	wonderful
Weihnachten	npl	Christmas	Wunsch	nm	wish
Wein	nm	wine	wünschen	v	wish
weiß	adj	white	Würfel	nm	cube, dice
weit		far	Wurst	nf	sausage
wenig		little	Wurstbrot	nn	sausage sandwich
werden	v	become			
Wetter	nn	weather	zahlen	v	pay
wichtig	adj	important	Zahnarzt	nm	dentist
wie		how	zehn		ten
wieder	adv	again	Zeit	nf	time
wiederholen	v	repeat	Zeitschrift	nf	magazine
Wiederhören		goodbye (telephone)	Zeitung	nf	newspaper
			Zentrale	nf	head office
Wiederschauen		goodbye	Zentrum	nn	centre
Wiedersehen		goodbye	Zettel	nm	sheet, slip
Wien	nn	Vienna	Zeugnis	nn	certificate
wieviel		how much	Ziel	nn	goal, aim
willkommen		welcome	ziemlich		rather
Winter	nm	winter	Zimmer	nn	room
wir	pron	we	zu	prep	to
wissen	v	know	zu Hause		at home
wo		where	Zubereitung	nf	preparation
Woche	nf	week	Zug	nm	train
Wochenende	nn	weekend	zulassen	v	admit
wöchentlich	adj	weekly	zum Beispiel		for example
woher		where from?	Zunahme	nf	increase
wohin		where to?	zurück		back
wohnen	v	live	zusammen		together
Wohnung	nf	flat	zwanzig		twenty
Wohnzimmer	nn	living room	zwei		two
Wolle	nf	wool	Zwiebel	nf	onion
Wort	nn	word	zwischen	prep	between
Wörterbuch	nn	dictionary	zwölf		twelve

English–German Vocabulary

a	ein	
A level equivalent	Abitur	nn
accommodation	Unterkunft	nf
account	Konto	nn
achievement, performance	Leistung	nf
acquaintances	Bekannte	npl
additionally	dazu	
admit	zulassen	v
advantage	Vorteil	nm
advice, consultancy	Beratung	nf
adviser, consultant	Berater	nm
after	nach	prep
afterwards	nachher	
again	wieder	adv
agency	Agentur	nf
air-conditioning unit	Klimaanlage	nf
al dente	bissfest	adj
all	all	
allergic	allergisch	adj
allergy	Allergie	nf
alone	allein	
along	entlang	prep
also	auch	
ambitious	ehrgeizig	adj
America	Amerika	nn
and	und	
announcement	Durchsage	nf
annual	jährlich	adj
ant	Ameise	nf
apparatus, machine	Apparat	nm
apple	Apfel	nm
applicant	Bewerber	nm
application	Antrag	nm
application form	Antragsvordruck	nm
apply	bewerben	vr
appointment	Termin	nm
appropriate	angemessen	adj
approximately	etwa	
area	Bereich	nm
arm	Arm	nm
around	rund	
arrival	Ankunft	nf
arrive	ankommen	v
article	Artikel	nm
as	als	
at home	zu Hause	
at last	endlich	
attention, caution	Achtung	nf
August	August	nm
aunt	Tante	nf
Australia	Australien	nn
Australian	australisch	adj
autumn	Herbst	nm
average	Durschnitt	nm
average, on average	durchschnittlich	adj
back	zurück	
bad	schlecht, schlimm	adj
bad, evil	übel	adj
bake	backen	v
baker	Bäcker	nm
baker's shop	Bäckerei	nf
ballpoint pen	Kugelschreiber	nm
Baltic	Ostsee	nf
banana	Banane	nf
bank	Bank	nf
basic course	Grundkurs	nm
basic knowledge	Grundkenntnisse	npl
bath	Bad	nn
bathroom	Badezimmer	nn
Bavaria	Bayern	nn
be	sein	v
beach	Strand	nm
beautiful	schön	adj
become	werden	v
bed	Bett	nn
bed and breakfast	garni	adj
bedroom	Schlafzimmer	nn
bee	Biene	nf
beef	Rindfleisch	nn
beehive	Bienenstock	nm
beer	Bier	nn
before, in front of	vor	prep
Belgian	belgisch	adj
Belgium	Belgien	nn
believe	glauben	v
belt (conveyor)	Band	nn
best	best	adj
better	besser	adj
between	zwischen	
big	groß	adj
bill	Rechnung	nf
birth	Geburt	nf
birthday	Geburtstag	nm
black	schwarz	adj
black ice	Glatteis	nn
blood	Blut	nn
blood pressure	Blutdruck	nm
blouse	Bluse	nf
blue	blau	adj
board	Brett	nn
board, boarding house	Pension	nf
boarding card	Bordkarte	nf
body	Körper	nm

boiler	Heizkessel	nm
book	Buch	nn
book, reserve	buchen	v
booked up	ausgebucht	adj
booking	Buchung	nf
bookkeeping	Buchhaltung	nf
boring	langweilig	adj
born, be born	geboren werden	v
both	beide	adj
branch (company)	Filiale	nf
brave	mutig	adj
bread	Brot	nn
bread roll	Brötchen	nn
breakfast	Frühstück	nn
breathe in	einatmen	v
broad, wide-ranging	umfangreich	adj
brochure, prospectus	Prospekt	nm
Brussels	Brüssel	nn
build	bauen	v
building site	Baustelle	nf
burden	belasten	v
bureau de change	Wechselstube	nf
bus	Bus	nm
business trip	Geschäftsreise	nf
but	aber	prep
butter	Butter	nf
buy	kaufen	v
by agreement	nach Vereinbarung	
bye!	tschüss	
calculate	rechnen	v
call	rufen	v
call in	vorbeikommen	v
called, be called	heißen	v
can, be able to	können	v
Cape Town	Kapstadt	nn
capital city	Hauptstadt	nf
car	Auto	nn
car park	Parkplatz	nm
car park (underground)	Tiefgarage	nf
car, carriage	Wagen	nm
card	Karte	nf
care	Pflege	nf
care (for)	sorgen	v
care, worry	Sorge	nf
career prospects	Berufsaussichten	npl
cash (cheques)	einlösen	v
cash desk, payment point	Kasse	nf
cash machine	Geldautomat	nm
cat	Katze	nf
cause	Ursache	nf
caution	Vorsicht	nf

ceiling	Decke	nf
celebration, festival	Fest	nn
centre	Zentrum	nn
certificate	Zeugnis	nn
chair	Stuhl	nm
Champagne (sparkling wine)	Champagner (Sekt)	nm
change (trains, etc.)	umsteigen	v
change clothes	umziehen	vr
cheap	billig	adj
cheque	Scheck	nm
child	Kind	nn
chips (fries)	Pommes (Frites)	npl
chocolate	Schokolade	nf
choice, election	Wahl	nf
choose	wählen	v
chop, cutlet	Kotelett	nn
Christmas	Weihnachten	npl
church	Kirche	nf
cinema	Kino	nn
city	Stadt	nf
city centre	Stadtmitte	nf
class	Klasse	nf
clean	putzen	v
clerk	Angestellte/r	nf/m
climate	Klima	nn
climb	steigen	v
clock	Uhr	nf
close	schließen	v
cloth	Tuch	nn
cloudy, dull	bedeckt	adj
club	Klub	nm
coast	Küste	nf
coffee	Kaffee	nm
coin	Münze	nf
cold	kalt	adj
cold, having a cold	erkältet	adj
colleague	Kollege/in	nm/nf
colleague, co-worker	Mitarbeiter	nm
collect	sammeln	v
Cologne	Köln	nn
combat, fight	bekämpfen	v
come	kommen	v
commute	pendeln	v
computer	Computer	nm
conditions, relationships	Verhältnisse	npl
connect	verbinden	v
connection	Verbindung, Anschluss	nf, nm
constant	ständig	adj
construction company	Hochbauunternehmen	nn
consultancy	Beratung	nf

consume, use	verbrauchen	v
consumer	Verbraucher	nm
contain	enthalten	v
content	Inhalt	nm
contribution	Beitrag	nm
cook	kochen	v
cool	kühl	adj
cool off	auskühlen	v
corner	Ecke	nf
cost	kosten	v
cosy, comfortable	gemütlich	adj
cotton	Baumwolle	nf
cough	Husten	nm
cough	husten	v
counter	Schalter	nm
counter assistant	Schalterbeamte/r	nm
courage	Mut	nm
course, rate of exchange	Kurs	nm
course of study	Studiengang	nm
cousin	Vetter	nm
cover	bedecken	v
cream	Sahne	nf
credit card	Kreditkarte	nf
crisis	Krise	nf
crowd, amount	Menge	nf
cube, dice	Würfel	nm
current	jetzig	adj
current account	Girokonto	nn
curriculum vitae	Lebenslauf	nm
curtain	Vorhang	nm
customer	Kunde/in	nm/nf
daily	täglich	adj
damage, harm	schaden	v
dance	Tanz	nm
dance	tanzen	v
danger	Gefahr	nf
dangerous	gefährlich	adj
dark	dunkel	adj
daughter	Tochter	nf
day	Tag	nm
day after tomorrow	übermorgen	
day before yesterday	vorgestern	
dealer	Händler	nm
dear, expensive	teuer	adj
December	Dezember	n
deep	tief	adj
definite	bestimmt	adj
degree	Grad	nm
delay	Verspätung	nf
delete	streichen	v
demand	Nachfrage	nf
dentist	Zahnarzt	nm
depart	abfahren	v

department (University)	Fachbereich	nm
department store	Kaufhaus, Warenhaus	nn
departure	Abfahrt, Abreise	nf
desire, wish	Lust	nf
dessert	Nachtisch	nm
diagnosis	Diagnose	nf
dictionary	Wörterbuch	nn
die	sterben	v
difficult	schwierig	adj
dinner	Abendessen	nn
direct, send	richten	v
disadvantage	Nachteil	nm
discuss	besprechen	v
diskette, floppy	Diskette	nf
do	tun, machen	v
do, carry out	erledigen	v
doctor	Arzt	nm
doctor (female)	Ärztin	nf
documents	Unterlagen	npl
dog	Hund	nm
door	Tür	nf
double room	Doppelzimmer	nn
drink	trinken	v
driving school	Fahrschule	nf
Dunkirk	Dünkirchen	nn
during	während	conj
each	jede/r	
ear	Ohr	nn
earn	verdienen	v
east	Osten	nn
easy	leicht	adj
eat	essen	v
egg	Ei	nn
eight	acht	
eighteen	achtzehn	
eighty	achtzig	
eleven	elf	
empty	leer	adj
end	Ende	nn
engineering	Maschinenbau	nm
English	englisch	adj
enjoy	genießen	v
enquiry, poll	Befragung	nf
enthusiastic	begeistert	adj
entrance (for vehicles)	Einfahrt	nf
entrance (pedestrian)	Eingang	nm
entry restriction (university)	Numerus clausus	nm
equipped	eingerichtet, ausgestattet	adj
especially	besonders	

establish, ascertain	feststellen	v
eternal	ewig	adj
eternity	Ewigkeit	nf
Euro	Euro	nm
evening	Abend	nm
exact, precise	genau	adj
exam	Examen, Prüfung	nn, nf
examine	untersuchen, prüfen	v
example	Beispiel	nn
excellent, great	prima	
except	außer	prep
exchange	wechseln	v
exchange rate	Wechselkurs	nm
excluding	ausschließlich	prep
excuse	entschuldigen	v
excuse, excuse me	Entschuldigung	nf
exercise	Übung	nf
exhibition	Ausstellung	nf
exit (for vehicles)	Ausfahrt	nf
exit (pedestrian)	Ausgang	nm
expect	erwarten	v
experience	Erfahrung	nf
experienced	erfahren	
extend	verlängern	v
far	weit	
fat	Fett	nn
favourable	günstig	adj
fetch, get	holen	v
fever	Fieber	nn
few	einige	
fill out (form)	ausfüllen	v
firm (company)	Firma, Unternehmen	nf, nn
firm (solid)	fest	adj
fish	Fisch	nm
flat	Wohnung	nf
floor	Fussboden	nm
floor (storey)	Etage	nf
flower	Blume	nf
fluent	fließend	adj
food	Nahrungsmittel	npl
food, nourishment	Nahrung	nf
foot	Fuss	nm
for	für	prep
for example	zum Beispiel	
foreign	ausländisch	adj
forget	vergessen	v
formation	Bildung	nf
forty	vierzig	
four	vier	
fourteen	vierzehn	
free	kostenlos, frei	adj
freeze	frieren	v
frequency	Häufigkeit	nf
frequent	häufig	adj
fridge	Kühlschrank	nm
from	von	prep
fruit	Obst	nn
full	voll	adj
funny	komisch	adj
furnished	möbliert	adj
furniture	Möbel	npl
garden	Garten	nm
garlic	Knoblauch	nm
gas	Gas	nn
gate, goal	Tor	nn
gentleman, Mr	Herr	nm
genuine	echt	adj
German	deutsch	adj
German language and culture	Germanistik	nf
get up	aufstehen	v
get (acquire)	bekommen, besorgen	v
giant	Riese	nm
give up (do without)	verzichten (auf)	v
give up (register)	aufgeben	v
glass	Glas	nn
go	gehen	v
go out	ausgehen	v
goal, aim	Ziel	nn
goalkeeper	Torwart	nm
God	Gott	nm
good	gut	adj
goodbye	auf Wiedersehen auf Wiederschauen	
goodbye (telephone)	auf Wiederhören	
gourmet	Feinschmecker	nm
gradual	allmählich	adj
graduate	Hochschulabsolvent	nm
grandfather	Großvater	nm
grandmother	Großmutter	nf
grant (student)	Bafög	nn
Greece	Griechenland	nn
Greek	griechisch	adj
green	grün	adj
greeting	Gruß	nm
grey	grau	adj
ground	Boden	nm
grow	wachsen	v
hair	Haar	nn
hairbrush	Haarbürste	nf
half board	Halbpension	nf
happy	froh	adj
harm, hurt	wehtun	v
harmful	schädlich	adj
have	haben	v
hay fever	Heuschnupfen	nm
he	er	pron

head office	Zentrale	nf
headache	Kopfweh	nn
health	Gesundheit	nf
health insurance company	Krankenkasse	nf
healthy	gesund	adj
heart	Herz	nn
hearty	herzlich	adv
heated	beheizt	adj
heating	Heizung	nf
heavy, difficult	schwer	adj
hello!	grüß Gott!	
help	Hilfe	nf
help	helfen	v
here	hier	adv
hide, conceal	verstecken	v
high	hoch	adj
history	Geschichte	nf
hobby	Hobby	nn
hole	Loch	nn
holiday cover	Urlaubsvertretung	nf
holiday, leave	Urlaub	nm
home (to home)	nach Hause	
homeless	obdachlos	adj
honey	Honig	nm
hospital	Krankenhaus	nn
hot	heiß	adj
hotel	Hotel	nn
hour	Stunde	nf
house	Haus	nn
how	wie	
how much	wieviel	
hundred	hundert	
husband	Mann	nm
I	ich	pron
ice cream	Eis	nn
ice cream parlour	Eiscafe	nn
identity card	Ausweis	nm
ill	krank	adj
immediately	gleich	adv
important	wichtig	adj
impossible	unmöglich	adj
impurities	Unreinheiten	npl
in all, all together	insgesamt	
in any case	sowieso	
including	einschließlich	
inclusive	pauschal	adj
income	Einkommen	nn
increase	Erhöhung, Zunahme	nf
increase	steigern	v
incredible	unglaublich	adj
inflammation	Entzündung	nf
inform	mitteilen	v
ingredients	Inhaltsstoffe	npl

injection	Spritze	nf
interesting	interessant	adj
interview (for job)	Vorstellungsgespräch	nn
introduce	einführen	v
introduce (somone)	vorstellen	v
it	es	pron
jacket	Jacke	nf
January	Januar	nm
Japan	Japan	nn
Japanese	japanisch	adj
jelly bear	Gummibär	nm
job	Job	nm
July	Juli	nm
June	Juni	nm
key	Schlüssel	nm
kilo	Kilo	nn
kilometre	Kilometer	nn or nm
kitchen (fitted)	Einbauküche	nf
kitchen, cooking	Küche	nf
know (be acquainted with)	kennen	v
know (fact)	wissen	v
knowledge	Kenntnisse	npl
lady	Dame	nf
lake	See	nm
lamb	Lammfleisch	nn
lamp	Lampe	nf
language	Sprache	nf
late	spät	adj
laugh	lachen	v
lawyer	Anwalt	nm
lay, put	legen	v
lazy	faul	adj
lead (guide)	führen	v
lead (manage)	leiten	v
leadership	Führung	nf
leading job	Führungsposition	nf
lean, low fat	mager	adj
leather	Leder	nn
lecture	Vorlesung, Vortrag	nf, nm
lecturer	Dozent	nm
left	links	adj
left, to the left	nach links	
leg	Bein	nn
let, allow	lassen	v
letter	Brief	nm
lie (be lying down)	liegen	v
lie (tell lies)	lügen	v
lie in	ausschlafen	v
Liège	Lüttich	nn
life	Leben	nn
life style	Lebensstil	nm

lift	Aufzug	nm		money	Geld	nn
light	hell	adj		month	Monat	nm
light blue	hellblau	adj		monthly	monatlich	adj
like to	mögen	v		Moscow	Moskau	nn
limited company	GmbH			mostly	meistens	
little	wenig			mother	Mutter	nf
live	leben	v		mountain	Berg	nm
live	wohnen	v		mouse	Maus	nf
living room	Wohnzimmer	nn		mouth	Mund	nm
loft, Attic	Dachboden	nm		move house	umziehen	v
look forward to	freuen (auf)	vr		move in	einziehen	v
look, check	nachschauen	v		move out	ausziehen	v
lose	verlieren	v		movement	Bewegung	nf
love	Liebe	nf		much	viel	
love	lieben	v		Munich	München	nn
low	niedrig	adj		must, have to	müssen	v
lunch	Mittagessen	nn		mustard	Senf	nm
lunch break	Mittagspause	nf		mutton	Hammelfleisch	nn
luxury	Luxus	nm		my	mein	
magazine	Zeitschrift	nf		name	Name	nm
magazine	Magazin	nn		Naples	Neapel	nn
maintenance of account	Kontoführung	nf		naturally, of course	natürlich	
make	machen	v		neck	Hals	nm
man	Mann	nm		nectarine	Nektarine	nf
manage	leiten	v		need	Bedarf	nm
manager	Leiter, Manager	nm		need	brauchen	v
manageress	Leiterin	nf		need (distress)	Not	nf
manufacture	herstellen	v		need (require)	brauchen, benötigen	v
manufacturer	Hersteller	nm		neighbour	Nachbar	nm
market	Markt	nm		new	neu	adj
married	verheiratet	adj		New Year's Eve	Silvester	nn or nm
May	Mai	nm		newspaper	Zeitung	nf
may (be allowed to)	dürfen	v		next	nächst	adj
meal	Mahlzeit, Essen	nf, nn		next to	neben	prep
measure	messen	v		nice	nett	adj
meat	Fleisch	nn		Nice	Nizza	nn
mechanic	Mechaniker	nm		nine	neun	
Mediterranean	Mittelmeer	nn		nineteen	neunzehn	
medium dry (wine)	halbtrocken	adj		ninety	neunzig	
medium sized	mittelgroß	adj		no	nein	
meet	treffen	v		noise	Lärm	nm
midday	Mittag	nm		none	kein	
middle	Mitte	nf		non-smoker	Nichtraucher	nm
midnight	Mitternacht	nf		not	nicht	
milk	Milch	nf		nothing	nichts	
million	Million	nf		novel	Roman	nm
minimum salary	Mindestgehalt	nn		November	November	nm
minute	Minute	nf		now	jetzt	
miss (bus, train)	verpassen	v		now and then	ab und zu	
mix up	verrühren	v				
mixed	gemischt	adj		occasionally	gelegentlich	adv
mobile phone	Handy	nn		occupied	besetzt	adj
moment	Moment	nm		October	Oktober	nn

of course	allerdings	conj
offer	Angebot	nn
offer	anbieten	v
office	Büro	nn
office staff, assistant	Bürokraft	nf
often	oft	adj
old	alt	adj
on	auf	prep
once	einmal	
one (number)	eins	
one ('you')	man	
one and a half	anderthalb	
onion	Zwiebel	nf
open	öffnen	v
open (account)	eröffnen	v
opening times	Öffnungszeiten	npl
opening up	Erschließung	nf
order	bestellen	v
originally	ursprünglich	
other	ander	adj
otherwise	sonst	
our	unser	
out	aus	prep
out, out of	aus	prep
outside of	außerhalb	prep
outstanding	hervorragend	adj
overdrawn (account)	überzogen	adj
oversleep	verschlafen	v
own	eigen	adj
pack	einpacken	v
package holiday	Pauschalreise	nf
pains	Schmerzen	npl
paint	Anstrich	nm
parasol	Sonnenschirm	nm
parents	Eltern	npl
park	Park	nm
part-time job	Teilzeitjob	nm
passenger	Passagier	nm
passport	Reisepass	nm
past	vergangen	adj
past	vorbei	
pastry chef	Konditor	nm
patisserie	Konditorei	nf
pay	zahlen, bezahlen	v
pay in	einzahlen	v
payment	Bezahlung	nf
pencil	Bleistift	nm
pension	Rente	nf
pensioner	Rentner	nm
people	Leute	npl
pepper	Pfeffer	nm
per	pro	
perhaps	vielleicht	
personal	persönlich	adj

personnel manager	Personalleiter	nm
petrol station	Tankstelle	nf
phone	Telefon	nn
phone	telefonieren, anrufen	v
physics	Physik	nf
piano	Klavier	nn
pill	Pille	nf
place (position, job)	Stelle	nf
place (seat)	Platz	nm
platform	Bahnsteig	nm
please	bitte	
please (be pleased)	sich freuen über	vr
please, don't mention it	bitte schön	
pleasure	Vergnügen	nn
pocket, bag	Tasche	nf
poison	Giftstoff	nm
poor	arm	adj
population	Bevölkerung	nf
pork	Schweinefleisch	nn
position	Lage	nf
positioned, located	befinden	vr
possess	besitzen	v
possession, ownership	Besitz	nm
possibility	Möglichkeit	nf
possible	möglich	adj
post, post office	Post	nf
potato	Kartoffel	nf
preparation	Zubereitung	nf
prepare	bereiten	v
prescribe	verschreiben	v
present	Geschenk	nn
pretty	hübsch	adj
prevent	verhindern	v
previous	vorig	adj
previously	vorher	
price	Preis	nm
probably, likely	wahrscheinlich, voraussichtlich	
problem	Problem	nn
profession, occupation	Beruf	nm
promotion	Beförderung	nf
pub, inn	Lokal	nn
pullover	Pullover	nm
punctual	pünktlich	adj
pupil (female)	Schülerin	nf
pupil (male)	Schüler	nm
purchases	Einkäufe	npl
pure	rein	adj
put, place	stecken, stellen	v
quick	schnell	adj

radio	Radio	nn	
railway	Bahn	nf	
rather	ziemlich		
reach	erreichen	v	
react	reagieren	v	
read	lesen	v	
ready	bereit	adj	
reason	Grund	nm	
recliner, bed	Liege	nf	
red	rot	adj	
reduction	Ermäßigung	nf	
register	einschreiben	vr	
regular	regelmäßig	adj	
regularity	Regelmäßigkeit	nf	
regulars (customers)	Stammpublikum	nn	
relatives	Verwandte	npl	
relieve, make easy	erleichtern	v	
removal (house)	Umzug	nm	
remove	entfernen	v	
rent	mieten	v	
rent	Miete	nf	
repair	reparieren	v	
repeat	wiederholen	v	
replace	ersetzen	v	
reputation	Ruf	nm	
request, ask	bitten	v	
reserve	reservieren	v	
responsibility	Verantwortung	nf	
responsible	verantwortlich	adj	
restaurant	Restaurant	nn	
return ticket	Rückfahrkarte	nf	
right	rechts		
right, correct	richtig	adj	
right (to the right)	nach rechts		
risk	Risiko	nn	
Rome	Rom	nn	
roof	Dach	nn	
roof cover	Dacheindeckung	nf	
room	Zimmer	nn	
run	laufen, rennen	v	
saddle	Sattel	nm	
salad	Salat	nm	
salary	Gehalt	nn	
salary increase	Gehaltserhöhung	nf	
sales	Verkauf	nm	
sales assistant	Verkäufer/in	nm/nf	
sales manager	Verkaufsleiter/in	nm/nf	
salt	Salz	nn	
Saturday	Samstag	nm	
sauce	Soße	nf	
sausage	Wurst	nf	
sausage sandwich	Wurstbrot	nn	
save	sparen	v	

savings account	Sparkonto	nn	
Saxony	Sachsen	nn	
say, tell	sagen	v	
scheduled	planmäßig	adj	
school	Schule	nf	
school leaving certificate	Schulabschluß	nm	
screen, monitor	Bildschirm	nm	
sea	See, Meer	nf, nn	
second	Sekunde	nf	
see	sehen	v	
seek, look for	suchen	v	
selection	Auswahl	nf	
sell	verkaufen	v	
sensitive	empfindlich	adj	
September	September	nm	
serious (problem)	gravierend	adj	
service	Bedienung	nf	
set down	abstellen	v	
set up, establish	einrichten	v	
seven	sieben		
seventeen	siebzehn		
seventy	siebzig		
share	teilen	v	
shave	rasieren	vr	
she	sie	pron	
sheet, slip	Zettel	nm	
shine	scheinen	v	
shop	einkaufen	v	
shop, business	Geschäft	nn	
shop, go shopping	einkaufen	v	
shower	Dusche	nf	
shy	schüchtern	adj	
sign	unterschreiben	v	
signature	Unterschrift	nf	
similar	ähnlich	adj	
simple	einfach	adj	
since	seit	prep	
sing	singen	v	
single (not married)	ledig	adj	
single (ticket)	einfach	adj	
single room	Einzelzimmer	nn	
sister	Schwester	nf	
sit	sitzen	v	
six	sechs		
sixteen	sechzehn		
sixty	sechzig		
skilled workers	Fachkräfte	npl	
sleep	schlafen	v	
slim	schlank	adj	
slow	langsam	adj	
smoker	Raucher	nm	
snack	Imbiss	nm	
so much	soviel		
soak up	aufsaugen	v	

someone	jemand	
something	etwas	
sometimes	manchmal	
soon	bald	adv
sort, type	Sorte	nf
soul	Seele	nf
South	Süden	nm
South Africa	Südafrika	nn
space	All	nn
spacious	geräumig	adj
Spain	Spanien	nn
Spanish	spanisch	adj
speak	sprechen, reden	v
special price	Sonderpreis	nm
splendid	herrlich	adj
spoon	Löffel	nm
sport	Sport	nm
spring	Frühling	nm
staff	Personal	nn
starter (hors d'oeuvre)	Vorspeise	nf
station	Bahnhof	nm
stay	bleiben	v
stay overnight	übernachten	v
steering wheel	Steuer	nn
stew, goulash	Gulasch	nn
still	noch	
stock exchange	Börse	nf
stomach	Magen	nm
stop (bus, tram)	Haltestelle	nf
stop, hold	halten	v
street	Straße	nf
strenuous	anstrengend	adj
student	Student	nm
students' union	Studentenwerk	nn
style	Stil	nm
subject	Fach	nn
suck	saugen	v
suitable	geeignet	adj
suitcase	Koffer	nm
summer	Sommer	nm
sun	Sonne	nf
Sunday	Sonntag	nm
sunny	sonnig	adj
supermarket	Supermarkt	nm
surf	surfen	v
sweet	süss	adj
swim	schwimmen	v
swimming pool (indoor)	Hallenbad	nn
swimming pool (open air)	Freibad	nn
Swiss	schweizerisch	adj
switch off	abschalten	v
switch on	anschalten	v
Switzerland	Schweiz	nf
table	Tisch	nm
tablet (pill)	Tablette	nf
take	nehmen	v
task	Aufgabe	nf
taste	Geschmack	nm
tasteful	geschmackvoll	adj
tax	Steuer	nf
tax declaration	Steuererklärung	nf
taxi	Taxi	nn
tea	Tee	nm
teacher	Lehrer	nm
teacher (female)	Lehrerin	nf
team	Mannschaft	nf
teaspoon	Teelöffel	nm
telephone call	Anruf	nm
telephone, call	anrufen	v
ten	zehn	
tennis	Tennis	nn
terrace	Terrasse	nf
test	Klausur, Prüfung	nf
test	prüfen	v
thank	danken	v
thank you	danke	
theatre	Theater	nn
then, next	anschließend	conj
there	dort	
there, since	da	
there, to there	hin	
therefore	deshalb	conj
they	sie	pron
thick	dick	adj
thin	dünn	adj
thing	Ding	nn
third	dritt	adj
thirteen	dreizehn	
thirty	dreißig	
this	diese/r	pron
thousand	tausend	
three	drei	
Thursday	Donnerstag	nm
time	Zeit	nf
tip	Tip	nm
tired	müde	adj
tiring	ermüdend	adj
to	zu	prep
today	heute	adv
together	zusammen	
tomato	Tomate	nf
tomorrow	morgen	
top salary	Spitzengehalt	nn
towards	entgegen	prep
town hall	Rathaus	nn
trace	Spur	nf

track, platform	Gleis	nn
trade fair	Messe	nf
trade	Handel	nm
trade press	Handelspresse	nf
trade, do business	handeln	v
train	Zug	nm
train	trainieren	v
trainee, apprentice	Auszubildende/r	nm/f
training	Ausbildung	nf
tram	Straßenbahn	nf
transfer	überweisen	v
travel bag, holdall	Reisetasche	nf
travel, go	reisen	v
travellers' cheque	Reisescheck	nm
tray	Tablett	nn
treat	behandeln	v
treatment	Behandlung	nf
tree	Baum	nm
trigger	anregen	v
trip, journey	Reise	nf
trousers	Hose	nf
Tuesday	Dienstag	nm
Turkey	Türkei	nf
Turkish	türkisch	adj
twelve	zwölf	
twenty	zwanzig	
two	zwei	
type	Sorte	nf
type	tippen	v
ugly	hässlich	adj
umbrella	Regenschirm	nm
uncle	Onkel	nm
under way, on the way	unterwegs	
unemployed	arbeitslos, erwerbslos	adj
unfortunately	leider	
university	Hochschule	nf
until	bis	prep
up to now	bisher	adv
urgent	dringend	adj
use	brauchen, nutzen	v
user	Nutzer	nm
useless (not working)	kaputt	adj
usually	gewöhnlich	conj
various	verschieden	adj
varying, different	unterschiedlich	
veal	Kalbfleisch	nn
very	sehr	
Vienna	Wien	nn
view, sight	Blick	nm
village	Dorf	nn
vinegar	Essig	nm
visit	besuchen	v
wage	Lohn	nm
wait	warten	v
waiter	Kellner, Ober	nm
waitress	Kellnerin	nf
wallet, case	Brieftasche	nf
want, desire, wish	verlangen	v
warm	warm	adj
Warsaw	Warschau	nn
wash	waschen	v
water	Wasser	nn
we	wir	pron
weak (limp)	schlapp	adj
weather	Wetter	nn
Wednesday	Mittwoch	nm
week	Woche	nf
weekend	Wochenende	nn
weekly	wöchentlich	adj
welcome	willkommen	
well, therefore	also	conj
where	wo	
where from?	woher	
where to?	wohin	
white	weiß	adj
wide-ranging, extensive	umfangreich	adj
wine	Wein	nm
winter	Winter	nm
wish	Wunsch	nm
wish	wünschen	v
with	bei, mit	prep
withdraw money	abheben	v
without	ohne	prep
wonder, miracle	Wunder	nn
wonderful	wunderschön	adj
wool	Wolle	nf
word	Wort	nn
word processing	Textverarbeitung	nf
work	Arbeit	nf
work	arbeiten	v
worker	Arbeiter	nm
worsen	verschlechtern	vr
wrist watch	Armbanduhr	nf
write	schreiben	v
year	Jahr	nn
yellow	gelb	adj
yesterday	gestern	adv
you	du	pron
you	Sie	pron
young people	Jugendliche	npl
your	dein	adj
your	euer	adj
your	Ihr	
your, their	ihr	

INDEX